The Age of
LOUIS
XIV

The Age of
LOUIS
XIV

The Rise of Modern Diplomacy

William James Roosen

Routledge
Taylor & Francis Group

LONDON AND NEW YORK

Originally published in 1976 by Schenkman Publishing Company.
Copyright © 1976 by Schenkman Publishing Company.

Published 2013 by Transaction Publishers

Published 2017 by Routledge
2 Park Square, Milton Park, Abingdon, Oxon OX14 4RN
711 Third Avenue, New York, NY 10017, USA

Routledge is an imprint of the Taylor & Francis Group, an informa business

Copyright © 2013 by Taylor & Francis.

Library of Congress Catalog Number: 2013018375

Library of Congress Cataloging-in-Publication Data

Roosen, William James.
   The age of Louis XIV : the rise of modern diplomacy / William James Roosen.
         pages cm
   Originally published: Cambridge, Massachusetts : Schenkman Publishing Company, 1976.
   1. Diplomatic and consular service--History. 2. France--Foreign relations--1643-1715. I. Title.
JZ1444.R66   2013
327.44009'032--dc23   2013018375

ISBN 13: 978-0-87073-581-3 (pbk)

To Suzanne, Andrew and Laura

Table of Contents

Introduction

In a long forgotten play, a fictitious envoy from Spain to a German court analyzed the benefits of diplomacy over war:

> For an intelligent man, is there anything more absurd than war? And by its very nature isn't war the born enemy of diplomacy? What objection can you make to a hundred thousand bayonettes and what argument can oppose a cannon shot? War is the misuse of power, the triumph of force; where the saber reigns thought is mute and civilization exists no longer. . . . But, when in the silence of an office, a man using only the influence of reason in happy and skillful combinations is able to put a limit on ambition, to maintain equilibrium and peace between the different powers, and to force men to be happy in spite of themselves without taking up arms and without spilling their blood, that!, that is something which cannot be admired too much; that is something beautiful, something sublime. It is the triumph and the work of genius! [1]

Although written a century and a half ago, these words make sense to us today. They would have made much less sense to people living a century and a half before they were written. In the seventeenth century many people did not assume that war was a scourge to be avoided if at all possible; rather, war was an ordinary part of life in which kings and nobles participated as a matter of course. Despite pious assertions to the contrary, diplomacy was not an activity whose main purpose was to maintain peaceful relations between rulers. Rather, diplomacy was becoming an ordinary activity in which states engaged as part of their normal operations just as they dispensed justice and collected taxes. In the mid-1600's diplomacy was not so much a substitute for warfare as it was simply the handmaiden which prepared the way for war's arrival, its course, and its departure. Perhaps by the Peace of Utrecht in 1713/14 which ended a quarter of a century of nearly continuous fighting diplomacy had become a substitute for war, but even this is not certain. We can only be sure that diplomacy had become a permanent function of every independent state.

The seventeenth century held other assumptions about war which were different from ours. Total war was not yet known. Thus normal relations like postal communications, visits, and even trade were sometimes maintained between the inhabitants of warring countries. [2] Instead of breaking off all contacts, governments usually maintained some kind of diplomatic relations with their opponents almost from the moment when cannons first began firing. Warfare still followed certain rules of gentlemanly behavior such as allowing defeated enemies to march out of captured fortresses under their colors or

1

negotiating agreements for the mutual exchange or ransom of prisoners. While seventeenth century warfare cannot be called a game, it certainly was more "civilized" than war has been in the twentieth century.

A number of attitudes about the character and nature of diplomacy were also somewhat different in the seventeenth century from today. For instance, most seventeenth century Europeans assumed that only a limited number of people had a right to know what was happening in foreign affairs. The actual number of elitists ranged from four or five in France to several thousand in the Dutch Netherlands. But no ruler would have accepted the idea that he was obligated to inform the public at large about "his" diplomacy. As a result, early modern diplomacy was much less subject to the problems which arise today from the conflict between the public's "right to know" about governmental activities and the necessity that negotiations be kept secret if they are to have much chance for success.[3] Among other different assumptions, we can note that in the seventeenth century the idea of making a life's career out of being a diplomat would have occurred to few people.[4] The concept of a "diplomatic corps" did exist but only in a very rudimentary form compared to the well-established principles and customs of today. Let us note one final example — whereas today most governments insist on having the exclusive loyalty of their agents abroad, it was not unheard of in the seventeenth century for a diplomat to serve two or even more masters abroad at the same time. In sum, the diplomatic world of the seventeenth century appears to be quite different from ours in the twentieth century.

Historians of early modern Europe who specialize in the study of any particular century, from the Renaissance to the Enlightenment, traditionally preface their work with some variation on the statement that their century somehow is the key period when the transition from medieval to modern times occurred. Such was not the case for the seventeenth century, at least so far as diplomatic institutions were concerned. The fundamental development of using permanent residents rather than temporary diplomats had become established practice a century or two earlier.[5] Other important changes were to come about after the turmoil of the French Revolutionary and Napoleonic Wars, but few occurred in the seventeenth century. Nevertheless, although it was not a period of great innovations, diplomacy in the Age of Louis XIV is worthy of study for the way it illustrates the workings of a system which was well suited to the gradually changing needs of its time. Even more importantly, the seventeenth century is far enough removed that people today seldom become emotionally involved with the issues, wars, etc., the way they often still do when the subject is World War Two, Korea, or the conflicts in Southeast Asia and the Middle East. By studying early modern diplomacy a person should be better able to understand the methods, techniques, and goals which often have not changed in the last three centuries. His emotional detachment should allow him to understand how and why the principles of statecraft are applied as they were and are. A twentieth century student may not be more willing to condone the secrecy, selfishness, and cruelty which are a part of international relations, but at least he should be able to put such current activities in a better perspective after studying the seventeenth century. Finally, anyone who aspires to play a role in diplomacy today should try to gain an understanding of seventeenth century diplomacy which at least one recent practicing diplomat has characterized as the best form of diplomacy ever developed.[6]

A study of diplomatic institutions and practices can also help increase our understanding of the early modern period in general. In recent years there has been widespread criticism of diplomatic history, much of it just. All too often scholars have considered their job simply to be the discovery and narration of every little detail of a negotiation on a certain treaty, of every proposal and counter-proposal, every twist and turn, until eventually the treaty under discussion is signed, sealed, and delivered. Studies of this kind are legion, and they are still being written as doctoral dissertations. But today diplomatic history must be approached in a different way.

> [It] must broaden its focus and turn its attention to the ideas, the interest groups, and the institutions that help to mold the policies that the diplomat in the field seeks to execute. . . . [The diplomatic historian today must] devote more thought than some of his predecessors have devoted to the difficult problem of determining the relationship between structures — whether ideological, socioeconomic or institutional — and personality in history.[7]

Discovering such relationships is one of the goals of this study.

It is also hoped that this book will show that, despite the obvious differences between the diplomacy of the seventeenth and twentieth centuries, there are also many similarities. Thus, studying early modern diplomatic personalities, institutions, and practices should increase our understanding of international relations today.

One might propose that there are already a number of studies of early modern diplomacy in existence which might serve to fill these goals. What need is there for another one? The answer is that there is no general study of Europe as a whole which is based on the actual diplomatic practices followed and institutions as they actually existed. Rather, the modern studies are primarily narratives of events or are largely based on books written by early modern authors about diplomacy (who in this book are usually grouped together under the rubric of ''theoreticians'').[8] These modern authors treat the theoreticians' books as if they were reality instead of simply descriptions of what the theoreticians thought practice should be.[9] A few modern studies have been based on practice rather than theory,[10] but they focus on one country rather than Europe as a whole. It should be noted that occasionally the present study has relied on the works of the theoreticians, but wherever possible their statements have been checked against actual practice and corrected if necessary.

It is particularly necessary to emphasize the importance of practice in the Age of Louis XIV because, as much then if not more than at other times, diplomatic procedures were based on practicality. In other words, the possible was as important as the desirable in determining what would be done. This is not to say that diplomatic practices and procedures were constantly changing. Quite the contrary! Continuing to do things in exactly the same way as they had been done before was often an effective way to carry out business. However, when it became necessary for the maintenance of effective communications or carrying out the other aspects of a diplomat's functions,[11] changes in diplomatic practices were made. A good example is the problem of diplomatic immunity. Even today police agencies and the general public frequently object to the immunity from prosecution granted to diplomats even for minor offenses like parking violations, and cries are frequently voiced that such immunities should be abolished. Such cries were even more common in the seventeenth century when the principle of diplomatic immunity was not so firmly established and the offenses were often more serious. But it was as obvious then as it still is today that such immunities were essential for diplomatic missions to be successful. Thus the early modern governments created the positive laws necessary to enforce the general principle.[12]

The basic reason governments were forced to establish and maintain reasonable procedures for dealing with diplomats is the same today as it was in the seventeenth century — the possibility of retaliation for any injuries done to a diplomat. Just as in recent years the expulsion of Russian diplomats from the United States has invariably led to the expulsion of an equal number of Americans of the same rank from the Soviet Union, so too did the principle of reciprocity operate in the seventeenth century. Let us take one example among many: in 1682 after a domestic servant of the French envoy in Vienna was arrested on charges of spying, the secretary of the emperor's representative in Paris was arrested and sent to the Bastille.[13] Every ruler knew that if he mistreated a diplomat accredited to him, it was likely that his own representative abroad would be treated the same way. Thus most rulers encouraged or least allowed the creation of procedures which helped rather than hindered diplomatic business. It is significant that most of the celebrated outrages against seventeenth century diplomats were committed by the sultans at Constantinople while one has to search hard for offenses in Europe itself. The sultans were only half-participants in diplomacy. They accepted European diplomats at their court, but they did not send any themselves until the late eighteenth century. Thus they had no representatives abroad who could suffer from reciprocal outrages. In general, Ogdon's statement about diplomatic immunity applied equally well to all aspects of diplomatic practice: "Necessity and the recognition of mutual advantage were among the forces which compelled the recognition of the diplomatic privilege." [14]

Diplomatic practices developed much the same way as early modern governments themselves had developed — haphazardly and in response to the need to solve certain immediate practical problems. Rulers and ministers were not consciously aware that the decisions they made and the institutions they established contributed greatly to the formation of the first big governments of modern times. Neither did they realize that they were establishing diplomatic practices and procedures which would still be followed centuries later.

Early modern governments were also creating the vocabulary which is still used in diplomacy — phrases like letters of credence and "chargé d'affaires." At the same time they used other words which are now archaic or which have changed their meanings significantly since the seventeenth century. Thus, it is appropriate to note a few of the more important differences and how the words are used in this book. Let us start with "international" as in "international affairs" or "international relations." In the early modern period, with the possible exception of Britain or the Netherlands, there simply were no "nations" in existence which could have relations. The relations which did exist between states were more in the nature of contacts between rulers than between nations (in the sense of a "people" taken as a whole under a unitary government). Yet, the use of "international" has become so widespread in modern times that it is almost an affectation not to use it to describe inter-state relations in the seventeenth century. [15]

Similarly there are difficulties today in describing the relationship between the diplomats and the rulers. It was quite common in the seventeenth century for an ambassador or an envoy to be referred to as, for example, the Danish ambassador or the Spanish envoy. This popular vocabulary was inaccurate. They were technically the ambassador or the envoy of the king of Denmark or the king of Spain. Yet, for convenience, it is often necessary to do as the seventeenth century did and refer to the diplomats as if they did represent the state as a whole. instead of just the ruler. In an attempt to maintain a certain amount of the flavor of the seventeenth century language, the words "prince" and "master" have frequently been used in their early modern senses. The word "prince" was widely used as a generic term (as in Machiavelli's *The Prince*) to refer to the kings, emperors, dukes, etc. who were sovereign rulers or at least those who were allowed to send diplomatic representatives to other rulers. In this general sense even the governing bodies of republics (like the States General of the Netherlands) were considered to be "princes." The word "master" is frequently employed the way seventeenth century diplomats themselves used it to refer to the "prince" whose agent they were.

Perhaps the greatest difficulty arises in the use of the word "diplomat." People living in the seventeenth century would not have understood its meaning. It did not come into use as a general word for ambassadors, envoys, etc. until the time of the French Revolution. Indeed, the French Academy did not officially consecrate its usage until 1835.[16] Instead, the seventeenth century generally used the word "minister" when referring both to the most important servants of a prince's home government (like secretaries of state and chancellors) and to the ambassadors, envoys, etc. abroad. Occasionally the seventeenth century used the term "public minister" to refer specifically to the latter group. In the interests of clarity in this book I have specifically limited the word "minister" to references to officials of the home government and have substituted the modern word "diplomat" for the ambassadors, envoys, etc.

Considerations of clarity and the desire that readers be able to understand the text easily have prompted another decision about the language of this book. It was a truism for early modern theoreticians that a diplomat should know a number of different languages. It is also a truism today that many English-speaking history students are unable to read easily in other languages. Thus this book has been written completely in English. Quotations and titles have been translated although occasionally the original is also given when it is obvious to an English reader.[17] However, since in later centuries French became the leading language of diplomacy and many important works on early modern diplomacy were written in that language, it is assumed that advanced students will be able to make use of that language. Thus, although the major emphasis in the notes and bibliography is on English language studies and sources, references are also made to French works. With a few exceptions materials in other languages have not been listed although specialists will recognize the author's debts to works in German, Spanish, and Italian. Similarly, illustrative examples are usually chosen and occasional citations made from English and French archives in order to give the flavor of the archival sources on which this study is partially based as well as to provide an abbreviated sample for advanced students who wish to undertake archival research themselves.

All too often readers skim over an author's recognition and thanks to those people who have helped in his work. Perhaps this is because it is only when a person actually writes a book himself that he becomes truly aware of how important these people actually have been. Thus it is a pleasure to record my thanks to former professors A. Lloyd Moote, Donald Queller, Ernest Hildner, and Joe Patterson Smith who influenced this work in a variety of ways. Northern Arizona University has been generous in providing time and grants to make the research and writing possible. My colleague Neil Kunze has undertaken the heavy task of reading the entire study and making astute and helpful comments. Like many scholars, I find that doing any work at all would have been next to impossible without the encouragement and help of my wife Suzanne. She has been involved in the preparation of this study from its inception through the revisions of the rough drafts (one of the world's most difficult tasks) to the final typing. Of course, responsibility for any errors of fact and interpretation remain my own.

FOOTNOTES

[1] E. Scribe. "Le Diplomate," Presented 23 October 1827, *Oeuvres complètes de Eugène Scribe*, 2nd ser., Vol. 16, Paris, 1881, p. 306. Unless otherwise indicated all translations are the author's.

[2] For the story of a Dutch merchant from Amsterdam who was tried and acquitted for trading with the enemy in wartime see J. Carswell. *The Descent on England. A Study of the English Revolution of 1688 and its European Background*, New York, 1969, p. 11.

[3] See below, Chap. II, pp.

[4] See below, Chap. III, pp.

[5] G. Mattingly. *Renaissance Diplomacy*, Boston, 1955, 323 pp. Several paperback editions of this important work are available.

[6] H. Nicolson. *The Evolution of Diplomatic Method*, London, 1954, pp. 48-71; H. Nicolson. *Diplomacy*, third edition, Oxford, 1963, *passim*.

[7] G. A. Craig. "Political History," *Daedalus*, Vol. 100, 1971, pp. 334-35.

[8] Among the important theoreticians were: A. van Wicquefort. *L'Ambassadeur et ses fonctions*, The Hague, 1681, 2 vols.; L. Rousseau de Chamoy. *L'Idée du parfait ambassadeur*, ed. by L. Delavaud, Paris, 1912 [written in 1697], 55 pp.; F. de Callières. *De la maniere de negocier avec les souverains*, Paris, 1716, 394 pp. — This is available in an English translation of questionable value as *On the Manner of Negotiating with Princes*, Trans. by A. F. Whyte, Notre Dame, Indiana, 1963, 146 pp. A new edition of another translation is in press, edited by H. M. A. Keens-Soper; A. Pecquet. *Discours sur l'art de negocier*, Paris, 1737, 168 pp.

[9] Modern scholars doing this include: H. Butterfield. "Diplomacy," in R. M. Hatton and M. S. Anderson, eds. *Studies in Diplomatic History*, London, 1970, p. 369; P. Amiguet. *L'Age d'or de la diplomatie*, Paris, 1963, pp. 301-28.

[10] For example, see P. S. Lachs. *The Diplomatic Corps under Charles II & James II*, New Brunswick, N. J., 1965, 269 pp; D. B. Horn. *The British Diplomatic Service, 1689-1789*, Oxford, 1961, 324 pp.; C.-G. Picavet. *La Diplomatie française au temps de Louis XIV (1661-1715): institutions, moeurs et coutumes*, Paris, 1930, 339 pp.

[11] See below, Chaps. VI and VII.

[12] M. Ogdon. *Juridical Bases of Diplomatic Immunity*, Washington, 1936, *passim* but especially pp. 3 & 60.

¹³ F. de Bojani. *Innocent XI, sa correspondance avec ses nonces*, Vol. III, Rome, 1912, p. 601.
¹⁴ Ogdon. *Juridical Bases of Diplomatic Immunity*, see note 12, p. 30
¹⁵ For example, two large scale studies of diplomacy from early times to the present use the word "international" in their titles: D. J. Hill. *A History of Diplomacy in the International Development of Europe*, New York, 1921-25, 3 vols.; P. Renouvin, ed. *Histoire des relations internationales*, Paris, 1953-58, 8 vols.
¹⁶ France, Ministère des Affaires Etrangères. *Diplomates écrivains*, Paris, 1962, pp. 3-4.
¹⁷ Throughout the book all translations are by the author unless otherwise noted. Quotations from seventeenth century English have been partially modernized in spelling, grammar, punctuation, and word choice.

CHAPTER I

The States of Europe,
Their Diplomacy and Wars

By the middle of the seventeenth century, a century and a half after Columbus
had discovered America, an awareness of the non-European parts of the world
had penetrated the European consciousness. A majority of Europeans believed
that the earth was round and that strange people with strange customs inhabited
the distant regions. By this time, acquisition of large hunks of world real estate
by European powers was well under way. Yet for most Europeans the Americas
and the Orient were so distant that they were not really a part of the "world."
European attitudes toward such distant places were comparable to current
attitudes toward the moon. We know it is there and that men have been there,
but there is so little likelihood that we individually will visit the moon that even
the possibility does not occur to us. Our real world is limited to the blue and
white sphere called Earth.

In the seventeenth century the "real" world, at least in terms of diplomacy,
was still limited to the tiny peninsula at the western end of the Eurasian land
mass called Europe. To be sure there was conflict over claims to non-European
trade and real estate which were dealt with in European treaties, and fighting in
the War of the League of Augsburg was sufficiently widespread that at least one
historian has called it "The First World War." [1] But for most rulers the
important events were those which happened in Europe itself. Events elsewhere
were peripheral to their interests. [2]

The Diplomatic Periphery of Europe

Even within continental Europe not all parts were equally important for
"international" affairs and for the development of diplomacy. The recent
practice of treating early modern European diplomatic history according to
geographic areas (western, northern, and southeastern) [3] is useful for helping
twentieth century undergraduates understand the main issues of each area. But
it is important to remember that seventeenth century statesmen could not and
did not separate the areas in their own plans and decisions. When dealing with
William III and Anne of England, Louis XIV had to be constantly concerned
with what Charles XII of Sweden and Leopold of Austria were doing or could
be expected to do. It has been argued that the concurrent fighting of the War of
the Spanish Succession and the Great Northern War in the early 1700's was

9

"the last time, as the German historian Treitschke points out, that two great wars could go on separately and simultaneously in Europe." [4] But the separateness was more apparent than real. Even though the major antagonists were not bound by formal alliances, every decision-maker had to be constantly aware of events in both wars, for the mixing of the two conflicts was a constant possibility. The intertwining of issues and conflicts between the so-called western and southeastern areas was so close during the decades of the 1680's and 1690's that separating the two makes both incomprehensible. For example, Emperor Leopold's relations with France were constantly thwarted and interrupted by the Turks, while the northern area was mingled with the southeastern when the Swedes called on the Turks to fight the common enemy — Russia. But, for the most part, diplomats and decision-makers tended to ignore Turkey and Russia as well as the Middle East and North Africa.

It is too strong to say that Russia (or Muscovy as it was usually still called) and the Ottoman Turks had no role at all in seventeenth century European diplomacy. Rather, they were outsiders who intervened intermittently rather than full fledged participants. For instance, the Sultan at Constantinople was willing to receive permanent embassies at his own court, but he himself maintained none abroad until the end of the eighteenth century. Furthermore, the fact that the Turks were Moslems, "the infamous infidels," helped to keep them from being part of the European system. Because of his cooperation with them, Louis XIV (whose courtesy title was "the Most Christian King") was frequently castigated in anti-French Protestant pamphlets as "The Most Christian Turk." Louis was sufficiently aware of the disadvantages of the situation that he usually did his best to conceal his connections with Constantinople. But despite their disclaimers, it is likely that the Protestants would have been willing to accept the Turks' aid if it had been offered. The theoretician Abraham van Wicquefort wrote to a friend at a time when the Nertherlands was gravely threatened by French forces saying that he had just heard that the Sultan was willing to help the Dutch against Louis XIV. Wicquefort added: "I am a good Christian and a good Protestant, thanks be to God, but I would not hesitate to make use of Turkish arms against the violence that Christians would like to do to me." [5] The occasion for the Dutch and other Protestant states to make use of Turkish aid did not arise, but the will to do so was there.

The insignificance of Russia is illustrated by the fact that a French ambassador writing home as late as 1697 apparently did not think that his use of the title Czar (spelled Kzaar) sufficiently identified the person he had in mind and that it was necessary to add the phrase, "the grand duke of Muscovy." [6] Furthermore, few western princes maintained any contact with Russia in the seventeenth century except for some low-ranking diplomats or consular officials. Peter the Great's visit to Western Europe in the late 1690's created almost as much excitement as visitors from outer space would today. The visit made westerners much more aware of Russia's existence, but it had little diplomatic effect. Although the Austrians signed a short-lived agreement with Peter to fight the Ottomans in 1697, the pact lasted barely a year. No other western power concluded an official military accord with Russia until 1726.[7] Important as Russia was to become in the eighteenth century and later, she simply was not a significant power in the seventeenth century. Claims that Russia had an important role in Western Europe are anachronistic.

The "Great Powers" of The Seventeenth Century

The powers which really did count in inter-state relations in the period from 1648-1715/21 can be named quite easily. Without defining the term exactly, there is a concensus that around 1648 certain states were "great powers" either in fact or in reputation: France, Spain, the Emperor, the Dutch Netherlands, Sweden, and England. A number of other states were sufficiently large and/or powerful that they could play an independent role at least most of the time: the kingdoms of Poland, Portugal, and Denmark; the German principalities of Bavaria, Brandenburg, and perhaps Saxony; and in Italy, the Duchy of Savoy, the Republic of Venice, and the papacy. There were a number of semi-independent states whose participation in international affairs was sporadic and often limited by the interference of a powerful neighbor. Most of the German principalities and cities, the small Italian states (like Genoa, Parma, and Modena), the Swiss cantons, and Lorraine fell into this category. A number of states which had played independent roles in previous centuries like Scotland, Hungary, and the Kingdom of the Two Sicilies had been absorbed and were no longer independent. They did of course contribute to the power of the ruler who now held them.

What determined how important the various countries were in the mid-seventeenth century? Obvious factors like area, location, size of population, natural resources, and ability of a government to utilize its wealth for diplomatic and military purposes were all important. Most historians would agree that the leader in almost all these factors was the kingdom of France. The problems threatening this government in the Wars of Religion during the late sixteenth century had been brought under control by Henry IV, Louis XIII, and Richelieu. Despite the temporary setback of the Fronde,[8] France at mid-century was at the point where it has generally been recognized as the epitome of absolutism. The old principle of "one faith, one king, one law" was as close to being a reality in France as in any other seventeenth century state. France's location at the crossroads of Western Europe made the kingdom seem almost predestined to take an interest in events everywhere in the western part of the continent — a situation which is still true today although French ability to influence these events has declined drastically.

Spain, which had been the great rival of France for the century and a half preceeding the Peace of Westphalia, was not even officially one state in the seventeenth century. The monarchs rarely used the word Spain to refer to the territories they ruled until the eighteenth century. Even then they only began to use the formula "Catholic King of the Spains, of the Two Sicilies, Jerusalem, the Indies, etc." because the idea of Spain was emerging as a popular notion within the peninsula and among foreigners who saw only the apparent unity rather than the autonomy of its various kingdoms. But in the mid-seventeenth century there were officially no kings of Spain: only kings of Castile, Aragon, Navarre, Sicily, counts of Flanders, Hainault, and Burgundy, dukes of Milan, Brabant, Luxemburg, etc., all united in the same person. In many ways the impression given by the multiplicity of titles is more accurate than the unity implied by the word Spain. The holdings of the Spanish Hapsburgs which earlier had threatened France with encirclement — the Netherlands (now Belgium), the Franche Comté (now eastern France), Milan, and the Iberian Peninsula — were by 1648 or 1659 like ripe fruit ready to be picked by Louis XIV. The government at Madrid was consistently on the verge of bankruptcy, unable to pay for defending itself, dependent on aid from friends and allies who were unwilling to see Louis do the gathering, and unable to enforce its orders to the governors of territories who acted more like sovereigns than agents of the king. Hampered by ineffective or incompetent kings and regencies, and haunted by visions of past greatness which it was unwilling to admit were past, Madrid tried to carry out a narrowly conceived diplomacy which was "unreliable, intransigent and haughty." [9] All in all, in the seventeenth century the Spanish crown played the role of "Sick Man of Europe" which the Turks were to play in the nineteenth.

Related to the Spanish rulers by blood and numerous dynastic marriages were the Austrian Hapsburgs. For generations they had been elected as rulers of what was nominally the foremost "state" of Christendom. The Holy Roman Empire of the German Nation, stretching from the North Sea to the Danube, from the Baltic Sea to the Rhineland, was, according to Voltaire, neither holy nor Roman nor an empire and, we might add, not even wholly German. The long pattern of declining authority of the emperor and rising authority of the princes had culminated in the treaties of Westphalia which recognized the right of the German states to be diplomatically independent:

> It shall be free perpetually to each of the States of the Empire to make alliances with strangers for their preservation and safety; provided, nevertheless, such Alliances be not against the Emperor, and the Empire, nor against the Public Peace, and without prejudice to the Oath by which every one is bound to the Emperor and the Empire.[10]

The restrictions on the diplomatic freedom of the German states were to prove virtually meaningless in the future. The Empire had become an association of sovereign princes, bishops, municipalities, and princelings more like the United Nations today than like a unitary state. The Empire's ineffectual Diet which met regularly at Regensburg, its constitutional law, and common language did not prevent the major principalities like Bavaria and Brandenburg and even a number of the minor ones from pursuing their own foreign policies. They were helped in doing this by the fact that a distinction was made between the Emperor and the Empire. The princes could defy the Emperor while still remaining at peace with the Empire.

After the Peace of Westphalia, Emperor Ferdinand III and his successor Leopold I appeared to be on the decline as much as their Spanish cousins. Ferdinand's heroic struggle to reverse the downward trend of the emperor's power and establish a truly monarchical state in Germany had been defeated by the resistence of the German princes and the intervention of outsiders, particularly the French and Swedes. Thus the emperor was thrown back to his hereditary territories which were made up of a congeries of titles which was even more confusing than those of the Spanish Hapsburgs. In addition to being emperor he was king of Bohemia, Archduke of Austria, Duke of Silesia, Styria, Carniola, Count of Tyrol, etc. There was almost no unity to these miscellaneous states except that imposed by the happenstance that they had a common ruler and were mostly located in the same general area inside and outside of the southeastern borders of the Holy Roman Empire.

To outsiders the government which the Austrian Hapburgs provided for their realms seemed to be the most inefficient in the world. One English statesman described how the court of Vienna had procrastinated on a vital matter, and thus "according to their usual custom of being behind hand, have this day made the first application for the Queen's interposition on that behalf, so that they must be always in debt to the foresight of their friends more than their own ease for their preservation."[11] Another English leader wrote: "That house of Austria has been the evil genius of Britain. I never think of the conduct of that family without recollecting the image of a man braiding a rope of hay wilst his ass bites it off at the other end."[12]

At the opposite end of Europe from the Austrian Hapsburgs were two states which are often referred to jointly as the Maritime Powers — the Dutch Netherlands and England. The use of that phrase is defensible in the eighteenth century, perhaps, but it is inaccurate in the seventeenth. It makes people assume that the two countries were essentially the same in organization and goals and, as in the eighteenth century, that England was definitely superior to the Netherlands. This was simply not the situation in the mid-seventeenth century. Emerging from the Peace of Westphalia in which mighty Spain had finally recognized the independence of her former provinces, the Dutch Netherlands was one of the richest countries in Europe. In an age when travel by water was generally safer, quicker, easier, and cheaper than land travel, the Dutch owned more ships than the rest of Europe put together. Their location at the mouth of the Rhine where the North Sea and the English Channel met allowed them to dominate two of Europe's three greatest waterways (the third is the Danube). These factors helped to make the Dutch a great power in the 1650's, but perhaps even more important in these years was the fact that none of their neighbors could challenge the Dutch position. Germany was still suffering the effects of the Thirty Years War; France was undergoing the struggles of the Fronde; Spain and France were still fighting their extension of the Thirty Years War; and England had just undergone its Civil War which culminated in the execution of Charles I in 1649. Obviously, the Dutch would scarcely have recognized English predominance nor the idea that the interests of the two states were closely linked, much less identical. The three Anglo-Dutch wars, the conflicts with France, and the threats to Dutch commercial prosperity (and thus its political position in the European states system) posed by the English Navigation Acts and French Colbertism, were all still in the future. These events plus their relatively small population, their exposed and easily invaded territory, and their dependence on free trade, all combined during the last half of the seventeenth century to tumble the United Provinces from their high position.

Italy, the homeland of modern diplomacy during the Renaissance, had become essentially a sideshow in international relations in the seventeenth century. With the exception of the period of the War of the Spanish Succession, when the Italian problem was central to European politics, the peninsula was usually ignored. Only the papacy, Venice, and Savoy played noticeable roles in European diplomatic affairs, and even these were quite limited. During the Renaissance the popes had acted like secular rulers in establishing diplomatic relations with secular states and had later sent nuncios throughout Europe.[14] But the Protestant Reformation had cut off all formal diplomatic relations between Protestant rulers and the popes. With a few exceptions like the ties established between Rome and Prussia in the 1700's, these diplomatic relations were not restored until the time of Napoleon. Unable to exert any diplomatic influence on the Protestant half of Europe, the popes became increasingly ineffective with Catholic states also after 1648. Innocent X's condemnation of the Peace of Westphalia was simply ignored, while his successors were treated quite harshly by many secular princes who pressured popes just like any other secular ruler. On the other hand, papal control of the territory of the States of the Church in central Italy was rarely threatened. From 1648 to 1789 it became increasingly common for secular governments simply to refuse to recognize the position or authority of a nuncio. Nevertheless, Rome continued to be an important diplomatic center simply because of the popes' power to grant the desires of Catholic rulers like cardinals' hats, dispensations of all kinds, and prestige. Furthermore, the papal capital was a city where many diplomats were accredited and where important news was to be discovered.

The venerable Republic of Saint Mark, a cluster of islands surrounded by lagoons, had once been quite important. Consequently, the reports of Venetian ambassadors have been oft-quoted sources for the history of many European states ever since the German historian Ranke began using them more than a century ago. But by the late seventeenth century Venice had settled into a refined decay recognizing that its greatness was past and would not come again. The Republic still maintained some of its possessions in the eastern Mediterranean and along the Dalmatian coast of the Adriatic, but no one expected it to do much more than hold on to what it had. Venice did join the Emperor in the war against the Turks but more as a last gasp than a major effort. Rather, Venetians and numerous visitors saw the Republic primarily as a place of pleasure and entertainment rather than as an important diplomatic power. There were occasions when important diplomatic decisions were still made in Venice by visiting rulers. The Duke of Savoy and the Duke of Bavaria discussed Savoy's desertion of France during a visit made with the excuse of attending the famous carnival of the city of canals. The Republic also continued to send ambassadors to most of the important states of Europe, but their role was usually that of observer rather than participant.

Of all the Italian states, only Savoy was a matter of concern to the major states because of its own importance. Straddling the maritime Alps between the kingdom of France and the Spanish duchy of Milan and the Spanish-dominated city-state of Genoa, Savoy was constantly forced to play a devious game of being a mouse where the cats were playing. Dukes Charles Emanuel II and Victor Amadeus II played their game very well although the contemporaries would more likely have described them as rats than mice. One ambassador described the latter as a "spiney creature who shows his thorns on all sides. He likes to see troubled waters in order to profit from the difficulties. . . ." [15] To a degree unusual even in the seventeenth century, Victor Amadeus continually negotiated with anyone who would talk, whether enemy or friend. Even in 1707 when he was ravaging southeastern France he did not cease to make propositions to Louis XIV or to respond to those sent by the Sun King. His underhanded dealings were notorious. Louis XIV had proposed peace conditions between France and Savoy which were very favorable to the latter in the hope of persuading the Duke to withdraw from the Allied side in the War of the League of Augsburg. The French thought that peace was virtually assured, but the Duke sent an abbot to Vienna to show the Allies the French offers and ask if they were not prepared to recompense him even better if he remained in the war. He suggested the marriage of his daughter to the King of the Romans. Leopold took a long time to decide and, playing his own underhanded game, even informed Louis XIV of the Savoyard propositions. Many decision-makers were hard-pressed to understand Victor Amadeus's position. A poor, relatively weak duke like him could not play by the same rules as the rich and powerful Sun King. One of the overwhelming realities in the second half of the seventeenth century was the preponderant position of France and Luois XIV.

Diplomacy And War:
The Sports of Kings from 1648 to 1715/21

One reason some scholars have discussed seventeenth century international relations in terms of three geographic regions[16] is that they wished to avoid the emphasis on Louis XIV and France which is characteristic of most studies of the topic. But for purposes of understanding diplomatic institutions and the course of events, this is one case where the traditional and majority opinion is still best. Louis XIV's France did play such a central role that any attempt (like this one) to narrate the events of the period in a relatively short space is still best organized according to the pattern imposed by French international relations. For most of the period from 1648 to 1715/21, the pattern consists of Louis XIV with one or two allies fighting or dealing with a number of opponents whose common opposition to France often did not provide enough adhesive to hold the coalitions together.

After the treaties of Westphalia were signed in 1648, much of Europe was too exhausted to do more than gratefully accept the cessation of hostilities. But Spain and France were unwilling to resolve their differences and continued their war. The French, and Cardinal Mazarin who directed French policy until his death in 1661, were unable to press the war because they were distracted by the troubles of the Fronde. The essential weakness of Philip IV's Spain, on the other hand, is shown by the fact that he was unable to gain any significant advantage from his opponent's internal conflict. After Mazarin and the Queen Mother overcame the threat of the Fronde, the Franco-Spanish war dragged on mostly with French successes and Spanish losses. Attempts to negotiate a settlement foundered on the problem of "Le Grand Condé," a rebellious French prince who had gone over to the Spanish after the failure of the Fronde. Both sides needed peace. France needed it because of financial difficulties, the desires of the populace, and Mazarin's hope to make a peace "treaty that would crown his career and firmly establish his reputation as a statesman." [17] Philip IV's financial difficulties and the desire of his people for peace were, if anything, even greater than those of the French. Perhaps even more important was the desire of him and his chief minister, Don Luis de Haro, to end the war with France. They wanted to devote all of the Catholic King's feeble energies to a last attempt to reconquer Portugal, which had been in "rebellion" since 1640. The device which actually forced Philip to begin serious negotiations involved the marriage of Louis XIV. Almost since their births two decades earlier, both the French and the Spanish courts had assumed that Louis would eventually marry Marie-Thérèse, daughter of Philip IV. A royal journey to southeastern France, ostensibly to probe the possibility of Louis's marriage with a daughter of the Duke of Savoy, brought a quick offer of peace negotiations from Philip.

Ths spring of 1659 saw a gathering of diplomats and royalty at the western end of the Pyrenees Mountains. On the Island of Pheasants in the middle of the river dividing the two kingdoms, a temporary structure was erected, half on "Spanish" and half on "French" soil. There Mazarin and de Haro worked out the details of the Peace of the Pyrenees and of the marriage contract between Louis and Marie-Thérèse. For the signing ceremonies, each king stayed within his own kingdom although they were in the same room. The difference was symbolized by the decorations of the two halves, red and yellow for the Spanish and blue and gold for the French. Surrounded by courtiers and relatives, the two monarchs took an oath to maintain the peace and signed the treaties. Louis agreed to stop aiding Portugal and to reinstate the rebel Prince of Condé to his positions and estates. Philip IV ceded a number of towns and territories and agreed to his daughter's marriage to Louis XIV. As part of the marriage agreement, Marie-Thérèse renounced her claims to her father's thrones, but the renunciation was clouded by the famous "moyennant" clause which stated that she made the renunciation in return for her dowry of 500,000 écus. The questionable validity of the renunciation, especially since the dowry was never paid, was to be a point of contention for the rest of the century. But for the moment the Treaty of the Pyrenees reestablished peace in Catholic Europe and was easily the crowning glory of Mazarin's career which he had desired.

Elsewhere in Europe the decade following the Peace of Westphalia was marked by the somewhat hesitant diplomacy of Cromwell in England, although he did launch the first of the Anglo-Dutch wars. This was a threat to the Dutch who ardently desired to maintain the favorable status-quo established in 1648. In Germany there were attempts to guarantee the Westphalian settlement including the League of the Rhine of 1658, whereas Scandinavia was racked by a series of "preventive" wars involving Sweden, Denmark, Prussia, and Poland.

The decade of the 1660's opened with a profound peace settled over Europe. The Treaties of the Pyrenees and of Oliva had ended the last important conflicts of the 1650's. The disappearance of a number of the old decision-makers and the appearance of new rulers gave opportunities to hope that the peace could continue. Charles II was restored to the English throne in 1660 without help from other sovereigns and thus did not feel bound by promises he had made while in exile. Louis XIV took over personal control of his government when Mazarin died in 1661 and felt that he had any number of different options from which to choose in international affairs. The warlike Charles X of Sweden died in 1660 and was succeeded by his infant son — a situation which made a regency inevitable; and regencies for child rulers were notoriously weak and often unable to carry out vigorous foreign policies. Leopold I had recently succeeded to the Austrian Hapsburg territories upon the death of his father in 1657 and had been elected Holy Roman Emperor the following year. In Spain the worn out Philip IV was soon to die in 1665 leaving his thrones to the sickly child Carlos II under the regency of his mother. The diplomatic status-quo could probably have been left relatively undisturbed had none of the rulers desired to change it. But, not surprisingly, major change and conflict were soon to arise again.

For a brief period, interstate politics remained relatively calm. Philip IV tried to regain control of Portugal, but the situation in that kingdom had been substantially altered from that which had existed in 1640 when the Portuguese first revolted. Then Philip might well have been able to recapture the rebellious kingdom, for the House of Braganza had not yet established its control over the country nor had foreign powers come to its aid. But by 1660 both Louis XIV and the newly restored Charles II (who was soon to marry a Portuguese princess) were carefully supporting Portuguese independence despite the former's promise in the Treaty of the Pyrenees to stop doing so. In the early 1660's the utterly exhausted Castilian forces were no match for the Portuguese. Philip was in an even worse position to challenge his French son-in-law in the conflict over precedence which broke out in London between the French and Spanish ambassadors.[18] The Spanish king was unable to do more than protest that Dunkirk still belonged to him when Charles II sold that city to Louis XIV in 1662. This agreement was but one aspect of Louis's diplomatic activities in which he was trying to maintain good relations with the English, Dutch, Portuguese, and even the emperor at the same time.

The Sun King was so successful in maintaining good relations that the first important conflict of the 1660's in Western Europe, namely the Second Anglo-Dutch War, did not even involve the French. The tension which had been rising between the States General and Charles II ever since the latter's restoration led to hostilities in 1664 when the English occupied several Dutch territories in Africa and captured New Amsterdam (which they renamed New York). The relative unimportance of colonial questions in the seventeenth century is illustrated by the fact that the Dutch reacted to these conquests by making complaints through diplomatic channels. Only after these were unsuccessful did they declare war in March of the following year. Louis XIV was bound to support his Dutch Allies, but he was really more interested in his own goals and in maintaining good relations with Charles. He eventually took advantage of the Anglo-Dutch War to seize some Spanish territory which he claimed belonged to his wife after the death of her father. Utilizing the rather feeble excuse that a law governing private inheritances in some provinces of the Spanish Netherlands also applied to the inheritance of sovereignties, he began his so-called War of Devolution against Spain. French armies were successful in the Netherlands and the Franche-Comté. But to the Sun King's astonishment, the English and Dutch almost immediately patched up a peace treaty at Breda; the Spanish regency government recognized Portugal's independence and made peace with the Braganza king; and then, the Dutch and English concluded a treaty in the unbelievably short time of five days which, with the addition of Sweden, was called the Triple Alliance of The Hague. Ostensibly designed to force peace on both Spain and France, the Alliance actually was directed against France. Louis moderated his demands and made peace with the regency government of Carlos II at Aix-La-Chapelle in 1668.

In retrospect, Aix-La-Chapelle can be seen as the first of many times when Louis XIV's goals were to be thwarted by an Anglo-Dutch combination. But at the time the gains he made in the treaty seemed very impressive. Louis's position was so strong that Emperor Leopold even concluded a treaty with him in the same year on a matter which had been under negotiation ever since the death of Philip IV. This was an agreement on how the territories of Carlos II were to be partitioned among the claimants to the inheritance when the sickly child monarch succumbed, an event expected momentarily. Since Carlos did not die, the treaty had no immediate significance, but it was to be crucially important three decades later in negotiations for a later treaty, mistakenly but traditionally called the First Partition Treaty. This treaty with the emperor marked the beginning of a policy which Louis embarked on almost immediately after the Peace of Aix-La-Chapelle: the dismemberment of the Triple Alliance and the diplomatic isolation of the Dutch. These policies were preludes to his war of revenge against the presumptuous republicans of the Netherlands who had prevented him from inflicting his will upon the Spanish Netherlands.

Louis did not make the decision to go to war immediately after the Peace of Aix-La-Chapelle was signed. Rather, the Sun King seems to have decided gradually as the months passed; he came to feel that the arrogance of the Dutch was insufferable, especially when conflicts over commercial matters and tariffs continued to plague the two countries. Louis started diplomatic and military preparations for a Dutch war in 1670. In January the English and the Swedes had renewed the Triple Alliance, which apparently reinsured Dutch security. Several months later, however, Louis XIV empowered his sister-in-law to meet with her brother Charles and settle the secret treaty of Dover. There the English king promised, among other things, to support Louis in a war against the Dutch. Concomitantly, the Swedes needed subsidies to maintain their armies so badly that they also secretly withdrew from the Triple Alliance and accepted French money. A secret treaty of neutrality with the emperor, an alliance with the Archbishop of Cologne who owned the territory which the French had to cross to attack the Dutch,[19] and an agreement with the Elector of Bavaria completed the French diplomatic preparations, although neither the Elector of Brandenburg nor the Spanish had agreed not to help the Dutch. Nevertheless, the diplomatic position of France and England seemed unassailable when they declared war against the Netherlands in the spring of 1672.

The astonishingly successful French military successes soon brought the Dutch to the point that they begged the Sun King to grant them peace on terms which would have had the effect of nearly destroying their independence. But Louis refused and continued the war. The breaking of their dikes which flooded the land between the French army and the Province of Holland (particularly Amsterdam), followed by an unusually mild winter in which the water did not freeze, gave the Dutch the precious commodity of time. Despite the efforts of French diplomats, Brandenburg, the emperor, Spain, and other powers came to the aid of the Dutch within the next few years while even the English and the Archbishop-Elector of Cologne withdrew from the French side. An unsuccessful attempt was made to assemble a peace conference at Cologne in 1673 with the king of Sweden as mediator. As was usual in the seventeenth century, negotiations continued among the belligerents, but serious negotiations did not take place for several years even though a new peace conference was assembled at Nijmegen in 1676. The failure to agree to a cease fire during the negotiations helped hold off settlements until 1678/9. The Peace of Nijmegen is often held up as the high point of Louis XIV's diplomatic and military success and in some ways it was. He acquired some important territories and was able to force his enemies to return almost all their conquests to Sweden, the one country which had remained faithful to its French alliance. But, in terms of the original goals of the war[20] and what could have been acquired in 1672/3, Nijmegen can be considered a distinct failure for the Sun King. Finally, the Dutch War had brought into existence the nucleus of an alliance of the emperor, the Netherlands, Spain, and (though not yet officially) England. This alliance would bedevil Louis for the rest of his reign.

Although most of the western European states had been involved in the peace settlements at Nijmegen or the related treaties, and though most of them remained nominally at peace with one another for the next decade, a number of conflicts did occur in the 1680's. Louis XIV began his "reunion" policy wherein special French courts adjudicated the question of exactly which territories were now French as a result of the recent treaties in which certain places "and their dependencies" were ceded to France. The courts decided, according to ancient documents and traditions, which places were ceded; and then, French armies "reunited" them to the kingdom despite the fact that many had belonged to other princes for generations. Not surprisingly the owners objected to such unilateral decisions and accused Louis of brigandage. One modern author has called the Sun King as exquisite a bandit as Billy the Kid.[21] Princes throughout Europe felt their security threatened by Louis's highhanded methods. Even Louis's one ally who had remained firm in the last war, Charles XI of Sweden, saw himself deprived of Zweibrücken. Numerous princes hastened to form alliances to protect themselves against the French aggression, and Spain even began armed conflict. Another large scale war against France might have broken out in the early 1680's except for the great peril which loomed up in eastern Europe: the advance of the Ottoman Turks on Vienna.

Emperor Leopold had signed a twenty years truce with the Turks in 1664 and, as its expiration drew near, he confidently sent a delegation to negotiate its renewal. To his astonishment and horror, the Turks refused. And in 1683, a year before the truce was supposed to expire, a giant Turkish army laid siege to Vienna. Thanks primarily to a Polish army under King John Sobieski, the siege was lifted and Leopold was given the opportunity to pursue the Turks down the Danube. In order to do this, Leopold, acting both for himself and for the king of Spain, signed the twenty years Truce of Regensburg which had been negotiated under the diplomatic sponsorship of the Dutch. According to the terms of the agreement, the Franco-Spanish fighting was to stop and Louis's acquisitions since the Peace of Nijmegen were to remain provisionally in his hands. During the next few years, while Leopold's armies were achieving magnificent successes against the Turks, Louis and his diplomats were busily trying to turn the truce into a permanent peace. There were numerous obstacles to that goal. For instance, the widespread distrust of France in Protestant countries was greatly increased by the masses of persecuted Huguenots who fled France as a result of the revocation of the Edict of Nantes in 1685. But the Catholic powers were equally unwilling to give permanence to the French aggressions. Louis had not joined the Holy League of the emperor, Poland and Venice, then under the presidency of the pope, to fight against the Turks. He was even widely thought to have cooperated with the infidels. Concurrently, his refusal to recognize the succession of the emperor's Catholic relatives, the house of Neuburg, to the title and lands of the Elector of the Palatinate engendered more anti-French feelings among Catholic rulers, especially in Germany.

One result of this anti-French feeling was the formation of the League of Augsburg at the instigation of William of Orange. The participants were the emperor, the king of Spain, the States General of the Netherlands, the king of Sweden, and a number of German princes. Louis, on the other hand, could not count on the support of a single significant ally. Even the Duke of Savoy was soon to cast his lot with the allies while James II of England, completely misunderstanding his situation, rejected the French king's advice and offers of help until it was too late to save his throne. Louis decided to break relations with the emperor and sent his troops into Germany in September, 1688. Meanwhile he expected the coming invasion of England by the Prince of Orange to lead to a civil war which would prevent either English or Dutch intervention in the French war against the emperor. But he was mistaken. Within a few months, William and Mary were established as the new British sovereigns and James was a refugee at Saint Germain, a chateau near Paris. Even then the French could hope that the war would be short. But it was not; it was to last nearly a decade and end only when the combatants, especially France, were exhausted.

The war of 1688-1697 goes by a number of names: the Nine Years War, the War of the League of Augsburg, King William's War, even the "First World War." The variety of names reflects the variety of partcipants and issues involved — including what had become the traditional conflict between the Dutch, English, and Spanish versus the French over colonies, trade, and the southern Netherlands. But the Glorious Revolution had added another issue which was illustrated by a placard Louis XIV had posted in all the towns, ports, and harbors of his kingdom in May, 1689. The placard announced that Louis had declared war against the "Usurper of England," (William of Orange).

Then it explained that the king would have declared war earlier except that he did not want to intermingle the adherents of the Usurper with the faithful subjects of His Britannic Majesty (James II). The French king had also hoped that the good people of England would overthrow the Prince of Orange and return to their duty. On learning that the Prince of Orange had declared war on him on May 17, Louis himself declared war and ordered all his subjects, vessels, etc. to cease communications with England and Scotland on pain of death.[22] But yet another issue also became involved when England and the Netherlands signed a secret treaty guaranteeing that the entire Spanish succession would go to one of the Austrian archdukes, sons of Leopold I. They did this despite William's definite preference for the candidacy of the Bavarians. He was willing to sacrifice everything to the need to create a coalition including the emperor against Louis XIV. William's task was made easier, especially in Germany, when Louis XIV ordered that the Palatinate in western Germany should be ravaged so that it could not serve as a base of operations for his enemies. The destruction of towns, villages, and fields brought on the Sun King the excoriation of pamphleteers who called him the new "Scourge of God" and the "French Attila." The Bavarian Wittelsbachs and other German princes quickly joined the coalition. The circle of enemies surrounding France was completed when Carlos of Spain and Victor Amadeus of Savoy joined the circle in 1690.

Despite its apparent advantages of numbers, wealth, force, and mutual promises of support, the anti-French coalition suffered from the fundamental problem of all coalitions — the members had their own goals and purposes which, throughout the war, would not be subordinated to the goals of the other members. Several of the allies, particularly Savoy and the Netherlands, scarcely slowed their negotiations with Louis XIV throughout the whole course of the war. Louis, of course, was anxious to split off any of the allies he could from the coalition — his first success was with Savoy.

The negotiations leading up to the Treaty of Turin of August, 1696, were carried out in classic cloak and dagger fashion. In January, 1696, the French general commanding in the area, the Count of Tessé, was ordered to resume the secret negotiations with Duke Victor Amadeus of Savoy which had been going on and off for four years. Tessé made use of a Jesuit priest who had contacts with the Duke's confessors, while a Savoyard official was sent to contact the French disguised as a peasant. The rough draft of the treaty was scarcely agreed upon when the Duke requested that Tessé's secretary be sent secretly to Turin. Arriving in the middle of "the most dark and dreary night there ever was," the secretary was received by the Savoyard official in charge of codes at two o'clock in the morning. The secretary of state interviewed him at five while the Duke himself appeared at eleven. All three pressed the poor secretary, trying to make him express some imprudent opinions or secret information, even plying him with wine to loosen his tongue. But the secretary continued to claim that he was just an insignificant nobody who knew nothing about the French king's decisions on the treaty.

Despite such tactics Louis was so anxious to make peace with the Duke that he signed the Treaty of Turin on June 30. Victor Amadeus was so pleased that when he was alone in his rooms with only his valets around, he jumped up and down for joy in front of his mirror congratulating himself. The Duke had good reason for his joy over the treaty! He obtained the fortress of Pignerol in the Alps which the French had held since 1648; his territories and forts which had been captured by the French were to be returned without demolition and with their stores intact; his daughter was to marry the heir to the French throne, Louis's grandson, without his having to pay a dowry; Louis promised to give him the title of Royal Highness and his ambassadors were to be treated in France in the same way as were the ambassadors of crowned heads. Of course, Louis XIV also received important benefits. One modern scholar states that Savoy's "defection was a disaster for the allies."[23] The war in Italy had pinned down French troops and was very expensive, and this was the key reason for the allied superiority in the north in earlier years. After the Duke of Savoy convinced the emperor to neutralize Italy and to withdraw his troops from the peninsula, the French were able to mass their troops in the north. This was a key factor in the decision of the Dutch and the English to meet with France for a peace congress at Ryswick.

William III's palace at Ryswick where the formal meetings took place was perfectly designed to fit the ceremonial needs which were so important a part of diplomacy in the seventeenth century.[24] The building was located about half-way between the town of Delft where the French plenipotentiaries were housed and The Hague, seat of the States General and residence of the allied diplomats. The symmetry of the palace was perfect. In the center, served by the main driveway and entrance, was a large hall which was used by the Swedish mediator. The two wings were exact duplicates, each with its own bridge, gate, avenue, and entrance. Since neither side could complain that the other was given better quarters than itself, quarrels over ceremony and precedence were limited to the allies themselves rather than involving the French. At the first formal meeting of the plenipotentiaries in May, 1697, the representatives from each side presented their credentials to the mediator and resolved that the Congress would meet every Wednesday morning and Saturday afternoon. But it soon became obvious to everyone that nothing significant was going to be negotiated at Ryswick itself, despite the desperate pressures on both sides to come to an agreement.

Louis wanted peace too badly and the Maritime Powers were too pleased with the concessions the Sun King had already made for either side to break off negotiations. Arrangements were made for William Bentinck (the Dutch-born favorite of William III who had been granted the English title of Earl of Portland) and the Duke de Boufflers (a French marshal) to talk informally in Flanders. Meeting in a variety of places, even in fields and orchards, the two men discussed the outstanding problems. As Matthew Prior, the English secretary to the delegation at Ryswick, noted in his private diary:

> Whilst the conferences between my Lord Portland and Monsieur de Bouf- flers went on with success in Flanders and the negotiation at Ryswick was at a standstill, Monsieur Harley remarked that the generals were making peace while the ambassadors were making war.[25]

With the exception of Louis's recognition of William as king of England, most of the important items like the Barrier Fortresses for the Dutch, tariff reductions, and the treatment of the exiled James II in France were left for private agreements rather than the public treaties which were signed in September in the palace at Ryswick. The emperor and the king of Spain at first refused to make peace, but the withdrawal of the Dutch and English fleets as well as their financial support soon forced these recalcitrants to come to terms with Louis XIV. The longest and most debilitating war Europe had seen since the Thirty Years War was finally brought to an end.

The fighting in Eastern Europe was also to end shortly thereafter when the Turks signed the Peace of Karlowitz in January, 1699, leaving the emperor in possession of all of Hungary and Transylvania. This treaty was especially significant as it marked the first time that the Turks actually acknowledged that they had been defeated by Europeans.

Unfortunately, the most important question facing Europe in 1697 had not been settled: the Spanish succession. If Carlos II had died before peace was made at Ryswick, there is no doubt but that the allies would have recognized Emperor Leopold's claims as they had promised to do in the secret treaty of 1689. The problem of the Spanish Empire's ownership would have merged with the War of the League of Augsburg. Despite all expectations to the contrary, Carlos continued to cling to life just as he had for thirty years. When the Treaty of Ryswick was signed, the Maritime Powers retracted their pledge on the grounds that the emperor had not kept his word to the Elector of Bavaria. William and the Dutch pretended that they would let Carlos make up his own mind about his successor. But the problem was still very real. Everyone knew that Carlos could not last much longer and that chances were nil that he would have an heir of his own body. Everyone also knew that unless some solution could be found, the conflicting dynastic claims of the French Bourbons, the Austrian Hapsburgs, the Bavarian Wittelsbachs, the duke of Savoy, the Braganzas of Portugal, and even several Spanish nobles would inevitably lead to a new war. The main problem, of course, was to find a solution which would be acceptable to the Bourbons, the Hapsburgs, and, if possible, the Spaniards themselves.

If the question were simply one of hereditary claims, there was no doubt but that the dauphin, the son of Louis XIV and Marie-Thérèse, should inherit the Spanish dominions. But the issue was clouded by renunciations, the testament of Philip IV, disagreement about which laws of inheritance applied, and the desires of Carlos II himself. However, all these technicalities were over-shadowed by the fact that after Ryswick nobody wanted to give up his "just claims" to the Spanish succession. The result was a most unusual diplomatic action. Three countries, two of which had no claims whatsoever, took it upon themselves to negotiate a treaty disposing of the territories of a crown with which they were all at peace without even consulting the current owner of that crown.

Louis XIV took the first steps. He recognized that the other states of Europe would not allow him to acquire the Spanish Empire for himself or his direct heirs because the combination of France and Spain under one ruler would make the Bourbons preponderant in Europe. Thus Louis decided to try to arrange a compromise whereby the Spanish territories would be partitioned among the most important claimants. Louis knew that the Emperor Leopold would not willingly negotiate a new partition treaty because Leopold expected that his younger son would soon inherit all the possessions. For want of a better opportunity, Louis broached the subject in a roundabout way to "Mylord" Portland, William III's ambassador to France, during Portland's first public audience in March, 1698. Because of William's close ties to the Netherlands, Louis was in effect also broaching the subject to the Dutch.

At first the Maritime Powers were hesitant even to agree to negotiate. Merely to participate in such negotiations was to give tacit recognition that the renunci-ation of the dauphin's mother was not legitimate or binding, for if he had a right to a part of the Spanish territories, he obviously had a right to the whole. Furthermore, the Dutch and the English would be taking positive action to contravene the treaty they had signed in 1689 recognizing the emperor's claims. The Sun King helped them overcome their scruples by showing them the treaty Leopold himself had made in 1668 agreeing to partition the Spanish Empire between Louis and himself. Finally, the disbanding of the English and Dutch armies at the insistance of Parliament and the States General made William and Heinsius, the most important Dutchman of the time, believe that they were in no position to stop the French from taking everything on the death of Carlos II. Thus they decided that the Maritime Powers might just as well negotiate to get as much as they could.

Portland turned out to be an unsatisfactory agent for carrying out the delicate negotiations so the scene was shifted to London where Louis XIV's newly arrived ambassador, the Count de Tallard, was to prove himself a much better diplomat than he was later to be a general. Despite innumerable difficulties, Tallard and Louis XIV persisted until the agreement which has come to be called the First Partition Treaty was signed between France, England, and the Netherlands in the autumn of 1698. The key point was the decision that the Electoral Prince of Bavaria, the Wittelsbach candidate, would inherit the bulk of the territories including Spain and the overseas empire. The French dauphin was to receive Naples and Sicily, while the Austrians would acquire Milan. A few other minor territories were included in both shares. Like his Spanish subjects, Carlos had no desire to see his territories partitioned. He therefore wrote a will making the Electoral Prince his universal heir. Either the treaty or the will might have been accepted by the powers but for an unexpected death. Instead of Carlos II it was the young Electoral Prince who succumbed in early February, 1699. This was disastrous as there was no other compromise candidate available whose claims were sufficiently strong to be accepted by the Austrians and/or the Bourbons.

The western powers went to work again. William and Heinsius tried to substitute the candidacy of the Elector of Bavaria for that of his son despite his lack of substantial hereditary claims but gave up when they realized that it was impossible. Another crisis arose when Portland decided to withdraw from the English court, but he returned when he was assured that his presence was essential for the negotiations with Tallard. Eventually the Second Partition Treaty was signed in March, 1700. It gave the Spanish crowns and the bulk of the territories to Emperor Leopold's younger son, while the dauphin's share remained the same except for the addition of Milan. Louis XIV's diplomats worked indefatigably throughout Europe trying to get other rulers, particularly the emperor, to accede to the treaty and guarantee its provisions. Their efforts were to be brought to naught by an astonishing development. Carlos II confounded the hopes and plans of everyone concerned by dying in November, 1700, and leaving a will which made Louis XIV's second grandson, Philip of Anjou, his universal heir.

The testament was cunningly written to put Louis XIV in a difficult position. If the Sun King refused to accept the entire inheritance for either his grandson Philip or Philip's younger brother, the Spanish ambassador was to go directly to Vienna and offer the crowns to the Archduke Charles, second son of Emperor Leopold. Louis's decision seemed inevitable, but the Spanish ambassador was astonished on his arrival at Versailles to have Louis respond to the tremendous offer with his customary remark: "We shall see." There were good arguments both in favor and against accepting the offer. Eventually Louis decided in favor and presented Philip to the ambassador with the remark that the Spaniard could salute his king. The ambassador's supposed reply that the Pyrenees mountains had ceased to exist and that France and Spain were now one reflected both the hopes and fears caused throughout Europe by Louis's acceptance of the will.

His decision immediately changed the pattern of diplomatic activity in Europe. Ever since negotiations for the First Partition Treaty had begun, the Maritime Powers and France had been trying to avert war through a division of the Spanish possessions rather than allowing them to be added to another crown. The device of giving them to Louis's second grandson created a third alternative since technically Philip was not in the direct line of succession to the French crown. But many decision-makers naturally feared that French interests would henceforth predominate at Madrid, and there was always the possibility that Philip would in fact succeed to the throne of France if his elder brother died without heirs.

When deciding whether or not to accept Spain for his grandson, Louis probably assumed that he would have to fight Leopold in either case. Now the question became one of whether the conflict of France and Spain against the emperor could be limited to them or whether other powers would become involved, thereby precipitating the general war nearly everyone wished to avoid. In the months after the partition treaties had been signed, French diplomats throughout Europe (somewhat weakly seconded by Dutch and English diplomats) had been trying to get other rulers to agree to the partition. After the acceptance, their job suddenly became one of convincing these same rulers that they should now accept the new situation and recognize Philip as legitimate ruler of the Spanish Empire. The French diplomats were remarkably successful at first. The pope, the Duke of Savoy, and a number of other sovereigns rapidly recognized Philip. Even William III, whom Louis had notified of his decision as soon as possible,[26] and the Dutch recognized the new king. These last two were the key powers in determining whether the war would become general. Unfortunately for the peace of Europe, they found themselves in positions where they did not think they could stay uninvolved.

Blame for the outbreak of the War of the Spanish Succession has often been placed directly on Louis XIV himself. He undoubtedly should bear some blame because he did commit several blunders. For example, he publicly affirmed that Philip would retain his rights to the French throne even after he became king of Spain. This rekindled fears of a potential Bourbon hegemony in Europe which in itself weakened the positions of the peace parties in Britain and the Netherlands. In addition, Louis's expelling the Dutch troops from their "Barrier" fortresses in the Spanish Netherlands and his accepting special benefits for French traders in Spain completed the rout of the Anglo-Dutch peace parties. However, a certain amount of blame must also be placed at the feet of Emperor Leopold. He had had a number of opportunities to accept the Partition Treaty which would have given the bulk of the Spanish inheritance to his son, but he had refused, insisting instead that his son should receive the whole. Even after Louis had recognized his grandson as king, there is evidence that the Sun King was still willing to compromise with Leopold.[27] But Leopold prepared for war, not for compromise, especially since he knew that the Turks were unlikely to break the recently concluded Peace of Karlowitz. In his conflict with the Austrians, Louis XIV would no longer enjoy the advantage of having a helpful belligerent at his enemy's rear. Furthermore, Leopold was right when he asserted that the Maritime Powers would be forced to join him against the Franco-Spanish combination. They did just that when the Grand Alliance was reestablished by a treaty signed at The Hague in September, 1701. The death of the exiled King James a few weeks later and Louis's recognition of his son as James III thus did not cause the outbreak of the war. But Louis's generous act did greatly strengthen William's position in England for the coming war despite French avowals that the recognition in no way changed their relationship with William. The English ambassador in France left without taking formal leave, and the French secretary in London was expelled.[28]

The Franco-Spanish diplomatic situation looked very good in 1700 and improved in the short run with the adhesion of the Duke of Savoy, Portugal, Bavaria, and Cologne to their cause during the months when William III and the States General had recognized Philip V. But the Bourbon position soon worsened as more and more princes joined the Grand Alliance of The Hague — including the Danes and several German states. The Elector of Brandenburg adhered to the emperor's cause in order to receive imperial recognition of his new dignity as King in Prussia. The outbreak of the Second ("Great") Northern War involving Sweden, Russia, Poland, and Saxony in the early weeks of 1700 lessened the possibility that the Sun King could get direct aid from the northeast. The war started badly for the French and Spanish. The Austrians fought effectively in Italy and soon forced the Elector of Cologne to declare his neutrality. The death of William III, after a fall from his horse, gave temporary hope that war could be halted. But William was replaced as a military-political leader by John Churchill, the Duke of Marlborough, whose wife Sarah was the constant companion of the new Queen Anne. Marlborough was to dominate the English government and carry out William's programs even more successfully than William himself was likely to have done.

Among the earliest diplomatic successes of the Allies was the detachment of the king of Portugal from his rather hesitant support of Philip and Louis. He openly sided with England and the Grand Alliance by signing the Methuen Treaties in May, 1703. Less than six months later, Victor Amadeus of Savoy was once again to betray his ally, this time Louis XIV, in a way which is reprehensible to people who believe that honesty and keeping one's pledged word is more important in diplomacy than duplicity and benefitting one's interest. The Allies simply were willing to give the Duke more than Louis and Philip would — specifically some Spanish territories in Italy. Victor Amadeus shifted from being supreme commander of the Franco-Spanish armies in Italy to being supreme commander of the Allied armies in Italy. The diplomatic isolation of the Franco-Spanish was almost complete. It only took the disastrous battle at Blenheim in 1704 to destroy the effectiveness of the last ally they had. The Elector of Bavaria withdrew from his devastated electorate into France to avoid being captured. There were now no potential French allies available. All the important states of Europe were already involved in one or the other war. Both sides in the western conflict hoped to bring Charles XII of Sweden over to their side, but the attempts came to naught. The few neutrals left, like Venice, were simply of no significant value.

As usual, negotiations were attempted during the course of the War of the Spanish Succession. Louis XIV discussed the Spanish Netherlands with the Dutch. He even corresponded with the man whom he considered a renegade, the Duke of Savoy, at a time when Savoyard armies were ravaging southeastern France. But no serious negotiations developed until 1709 when the French military position had become so disastrous that Louis decided he had to have peace at almost any cost. Discussions opened in the Netherlands. The Dutch and English were in such a strong position relative to France (although they were unsuccessful in Spain) that they kept upping their demands. At last Torcy, the French Secretary of State for Foreign Affairs, went north to the Hague to talk with the Allies himself. Louis had ordered him to find peace at almost any price. The Allies demanded that Louis give up much territory including Strasbourg and withdraw his support and troops from Philip V; they also insisted that Louis actually send French troops to expel his grandson from Spain. Louis replied that it was better to make war on his enemies than on his own family and, despite the disastrous French situation, prepared to try to continue the struggle.

It turned out that 1709 was truly the darkness before dawn for the French, while the Allies were to find their position eroded significantly. Just as Louis would have been wise to accept the highly beneficial terms offered him years before by the Dutch in 1672,[29] so the Allies were soon to rue their decision not to accept Louis's terms in 1709. In 1710 Louis again tried unsuccessfuly to make a peace by giving up much French territory and withdrawing his support of his grandson. Thereafter a weakening of the Allied military situation, the death of Emperor Joseph I which made his brother "Charles III of Spain" the new emperor, and a change in the English government were shortly to lead the English to negotiate the peace preliminaries known as "Matt's Peace." [30] Despite their dissatisfaction with the situation, the Dutch were forced to invite all the belligerents to send representatives to a peace conference at the Dutch town of Utrecht in the early months of 1712. Despite delays typical of early modern conferences, the English were able to pressure most of their allies into signing peace treaties at Utrecht in 1713. The Empire and the emperor held out until the next year when they eventually signed after another pair of conferences were held at Rastatt and Baden.

These settlements, known collectively as the Peace of Utrecht, and the Treaty of Nystad which ended the Great Northern War in 1721 marked the end of the great wars of the seventeenth century. They set the conditions of the "international" stage which were to last until the great wars of the French Revolutionary period began three quarters of a century later. Utrecht was not the unqualified success the Allies had hoped for and could probably have had in 1709. Philip retained the Spanish throne although he lost his Italian possessions to the Austrian Hapsburgs and had to give trading concessions to the Dutch and the English. The French kingdom came out relatively intact but with no substantial benefits from her extraordinary efforts. At least Utrecht did accurately reflect the true power relationships of eighteenth century states. Thus it may be that the quarter of a century of relative peace which followed the settlement of 1713/14 was primarily the result of the fact that it was a negotiated rather than an imposed peace settlement.

FOOTNOTES

[1] J. Wolf. *Louis XIV*, New York, 1968, pp. 446-88.

[2] Even the Spanish Council of State and the Spanish Crown, which had more overseas interest than almost any other early modern country, considered Europe to be more important than the American scene. G. Bensusan. Early draft of "The Spanish Struggle against Foreign Encroachment in the Caribbean, 1675-1697," Ph.D. dissertation, UCLA, 1970, Chap. 10.

[3] See, for example, A. L. Moote. *The Seventeenth Century*, Lexington, Mass., 1970, pp. 235-36.

[4] R. B. Mowat. *A History of European Diplomacy, 1451-1789*, N.P., 1928 [reprinted 1971], p. 189. See below, Chap. II.

[5] F. Krämer, ed. *Lettres de Pierre de Groot*, The Hague, 1894, p. 233, 20 November 1673.

[6] Archives des Affaires Etrangères. Paris. Correspondance Politique, Danemark, Vol. 57, Bonrepaus to Louis XIV, 25 June 1697.

[7] K. A. Roider, Jr. *The Reluctant Ally: Austria's Policy in the Austro-Turkish War, 1737-1739*, Baton Rouge, 1972, pp. 32-36.

[8] The Fronde was the revolt against the French royal government and Cardinal Mazarin from 1648 to 1652. Disturbances and conflict were widespread in the kingdom but have traditionally been called the parlementary Fronde and then the Fronde of the princes. The best study of the Fronde available in English is A. L. Moote. *The Revolt of the Judges*, Princeton, 1971, 407 pp.

[9] G. L. Belcher. "Anglo-Spanish Diplomatic Relations, 1660-1667," Ph.D. dissertation, University of North Carolina at Chapel Hill, 1971, p. v. See also A. D. Ortiz. *The Golden Age of Spain, 1516-1659*, Trans. from Spanish by J. Casey, New York, 1971, pp. 1-2.

[10] This or a very similar statement was included in most of the different treaties signed at Munster or Osnabruck which are jointly called the Peace of Westphalia. The texts of sample treaties have been widely published in many different editions. Today they are most easily available in C. Parry, ed. *The Consolidated Treaty Series*, Dobbs Ferry, New York, 1969-   ; F. L. Israel, ed. *Major Peace Treaties of Modern History, 1648-1967*, Commentaries by E. Chill, New York, 1967, 4 vols; and F. G. Davenport, ed. *European Treaties bearing on the History of the United States and its Dependencies*, Gloucester, Mass., 1917-1937 [reprinted 1967], 4 vols.

[11] J. F. Chance, ed. *British Diplomatic Instructions 1689-1789; Sweden, 1689-1727*, London, 1922, p. 35, Robert Harley to Dr. John Robinson, 3/14 June 1707.

[12] Bolingbroke as quoted in D. B. Horn. *The British Diplomatic Service, 1689-1789*, Oxford, 1961, pp. 22-23.

[13] F. P. Dalerac. *Anecdotes de Pologne*, Vol. I, Paris, 1699, pp. 8-11.

[14] See below, Chap. III, pp.   All students of early modern diplomacy are indebted to G. Mattingly. *Renaissance Diplomacy*, Boston, 1955, 323 pp., now available in several paperback editions.

[15] Rambuteau, ed. Lettres du maréchal de Tessé, Paris, 1888, p. xiv.

[16] See above, Chap. I, p

[17] Wolf. *Louis XIV*, see note 1, p. 116.

[18] See below, Chap. VII, pp.

[19] See map in G. Zeller. "Les Temps modernes, II, de Louis XIV à 1789," Vol. III of *Histoire des relations internationales*, Paris, 1955, p. 39. See also H. H. Rowen. *The Ambassador Prepares for War*, The Hague, 1957, 210 pp.

[20] P. Sonnino. "Louis XIV's *Mémoires pour l'histoire de la guerre de Hollande*," French *Historical Studies*, Vol. VIII, 1973, pp. 29-50.

[21] J. L. White. *The Origins of Modern Europe*, New York, 1964, p. 90.

[22] Issued 25 June 1689. Biliothèque Nationale. Paris. Manuscripts. Fonds français, NA 7487, fol. 16.

[23] S. B. Baxter. *William III and the Defense of European Liberty, 1650-1702*, New York, 1966, p. 341. See also P. Canestrier. "Comment M. de Tessé prépara, en 1696, le traité de paix entre Louis XIV et Victor-Amédée II de Savoie," *Revue d'histoire diplomatique*, Vol. 48, 1934, pp. 370-92.

[24] See below, Chap. VII, p.

[25] British Museum. London. Loan 29/335, Matthew Prior's private journal, 17/27 May 1697. See below, Chap. IV, pp. for biographical sketch of Prior.

[26] See below, Appendix, pp.   for a translation of the letter Louis XIV sent to William III on 7 December 1700.

[27] Wolf. *Louis XIV*, see note 1, pp. 506-10.

[28] See below, Chap. IV, p.

[29] See above, Chap. I, p

[30] See below, Chap. IV, pp

CHAPTER II

Kings and Ministers: The Central Administration of Diplomacy and Creation of Foreign Policies

When dealing with diplomatic affairs, governments are like the old Roman god Janus. They must look two ways at the same time: inward when dealing with diplomats residing in their own capital and outward when dealing with their own diplomats abroad. By the seventeenth century most governments had developed some kind of "foreign office" with its own personnel to facilitate the playing of these dual roles. Most "foreign offices" were headed by a "secretary of state for foreign affairs" (or someone with a similar title) who maintained contact with diplomats at his own court and corresponded with his master's representatives abroad. Depending on the form of government, there was often yet a third direction which the "foreign office" had to face — dealing with the prince in whose name the actions were taken.

Political scientists have coined the phrase "decision-makers" to refer to those individuals who are in a position to participate in the process of formulating and adopting policies. The phrase is helpful and will be used here in just that sense. Just as is the case today, the titles and positions of the decision-makers varied from country to country in the seventeenth century. Indeed, there was more variety in central administration than in any other aspect of diplomacy. This was because the central diplomatic organization primarily reflected the type of government the state had rather than the common diplomatic heritage of Europe.

It is impossible to deal with all or even most of the different administrative forms without turning this chapter into a history of political institutions. But brief descriptions of some of the most important states and a few unimportant ones will show the variety possible. The roles of individuals will be examined as they fit into the discussions of the various governments. In some cases individual functions were circumscribed by the traditions of well-established offices like the English secretaries of state. In other cases the office primarily seems to have been a reflection of the person who held it like Louis XIV's being his own first minister. The middle part of the chapter will examine the so-called secretariats or chancelleries which churned out the paperwork and performed other practical functions. The chapter will end with an examination of some of the assumptions and presuppositions which underlay the decisions that decision-makers made. Included here will also be an examination of the underlying motivation of the decision-makers as they chose the goals for which they strove.

Central Administrations

Historians rarely agree on the answer to any question. But there is a consensus on two points involving Louis XIV: first, that the Sun King and France dominated international relations in the last half of the seventeenth century, and, second, that the king personally directed French foreign policy throughout his personal reign from 1661 to 1715. This second point is not surprising to us today, but Louis's contemporaries were astonished at his announcement after Mazarin's death that he intended to govern as well as reign. France itself had been governed by a succession of royal favorites for half a century, while young rulers in all countries traditionally spent their time enjoying the pleasures of life rather than enduring the routine of everyday government. Thus the Sun King's ambassadors were surprised to receive letters from him which began: "I have decided to reply myself to all the letters which I have ordered my ambassadors to write me in care of Monsieur de Lionne. . . ." Even after receiving their first direct letters, ambassadors often remained convinced that the young king would lose interest after a while. In this they committed the same error as Fouquet whom Louis eventually had arrested and jailed, some think as the original of the "Man in the Iron Mask." But Louis did indeed take steps to insure that he would in fact control the correspondence with ambassadors. At first he allowed the ambassadors to write just on important topics to himself and on less significant or personal topics to the secretary of state for foreign affairs, Lionne. Later he tried to insist that his diplomats write everything to him, but they were unwilling to send personal requests or frivolous details directly to the king. Thus the tradition established at the beginning of Louis's personal government was continued even after he tried to change it. But the king maintained his control of the diplomatic correspondence by insisting whenever he chose that the secretaries read him the "personal" letters as well as the formal ones.[1]

Less is known about how the Sun King maintained his control of outgoing letters other than that their contents reflected the decision making process used for other aspects of French government in addition to diplomacy. Decisions were made after oral discussions between the king and his ministers and/or secretaries. Since records were not generally kept of these discussions, we are dependent on scraps of notations, memoirs, chance remarks, etc. to understand how the decisions were made and who participated in making them. But we do know that, whatever arguments went on in meetings, Louis insisted that after he made a decision all his subordinates were obligated to stop arguing and accept it. This had the effect in diplomacy of strengthening the position of French diplomats, since French policy was unitary and not fragmented by conflict at home as happened in a number of other seventeenth century states.

Of course, the king did not actually write the thousands of letters sent to his diplomats. Even the many formal letters of congratulation, condolence, and ceremony sent to other sovereigns and described as "written by his own hand" were actually penned by one of the clerks who surrounded him and wrote in his sprawling style. Secretary Lionne wrote one ambassador a sort of key explaining which letters Louis himself had actually signed: "His Majesty has . . . ordered me to tell you that when you find my initials under his signature, you will thereby know that he signed the letter himself, but that when the letter is countersigned by me, he will not have bothered to do so. Nevertheless, whichever method is used, his will is expressed there."[2] The last sentence is the key and accurately describes the situation under the Sun King.

Although Louis XIV generally had as tight or tighter control of foreign policy than any other seventeenth century ruler, one must be careful not to emphasize it so much that it appears that he knew everything which went on and that everything happened just as he wished. All chief executives are to some degree prisoners of their own assistants, and Louis XIV was no exception. The devices which his underlings and ambassadors used are not well documented for obvious reasons, but occasional glimpses are available. For instance, it is known that Louis rarely actually read the documents sent him. Rather the ministers and/or secretaries of state read him excerpts which, with his consent, skipped what the reader thought was not important — a tremendous opportunity to influence the king, especially in minor and/or personnel questions. But diplomats abroad had much better opportunities to influence the king's decision for the simple reason that they were not working under his direct supervision. Since there were few alternative sources of information which the king could use, diplomats could overemphasize or play down aspects of policy as they wished. It was always possible for subordinates to subvert the intent of an order even while appearing to obey it — a perennial problem for all governments.[3]

Louis XIV also had difficulty making his secretary of state for foreign affairs completely and singularly responsible for communications with French diplomats abroad and with foreign representatives in France. In earlier centuries French secretaries of state were simple clerks who received direct orders from the king to write and send out letters, orders, and patents. It was only gradually that they had become involved in administration and then decision making. Before the early seventeenth century, responsibility for foreign affairs had been divided among the four secretaries of state according to geography;[4] one dealt with England, Scotland, and Ireland; another with Spain, Piedmont, Italy, and Switzerland; the third with the Low Countries, Germany, and the Emperor; and the last with ordinary and extraordinary affairs of war. It was only in 1626 that Richelieu had persuaded Louis XIII to unify all foreign affairs in one department under the direction of a single secretary of state. But exclusive specialization in one area of affairs was not characteristic of early modern governments. Although specialization had increased by 1661, it was far from complete. For example, it was not until 1669 that responsibility for the navy and commerce was removed from the secretary of state for foreign affairs. Throughout Louis XIV's reign, the foreign secretary continued to be responsible for the administration of various provinces like Brittany, Champagne, and the Lyonnais.[5]

As the French government became more effectively organized, it became common for the same man to hold both the titles of secretary and minister at the same time. Supposedly a minister was involved in the decision making part of government and attended meetings of the king's councils, while the secretary handled the clerical duties; but the distinction was not clear under Louis XIV. The awkwardness of two different men holding the positions had, however, been made very clear at the beginning of Louis's personal control of government. The position of secretary was venal and belonged to Henri-Louis de Loménie de Brienne, but Louis did not like Brienne and wanted to work with Hugues de Lionne on foreign affairs. It would have been logical for Louis to force Brienne to sell his position, but the king did not wish to use force against such devoted servants as Brienne and his father, even though he did not like them. Thus Brienne was told to act in concert with Lionne and write what, when, and to whom the minister ordered. At the same time, diplomats abroad were supposed to continue to send the official despatches to Brienne and to accompany them with secret material intended for Lionne. The result was that the important political correspondence intended for the king was sent to the minister without the secretary of state (in title) being informed. Brienne continued to receive and respond to the unimportant despatches. Brienne eventually tired of this game and sold Lionne his position. Thus after 1668, Lionne was both minister and secretary and officially controlled all the correspondence. Another dual situation arose late in the reign when Pomponne and Torcy shared responsibility for foreign affairs, but the two worked together amicably.

Even holding both titles did not assure the secretary-minister complete control over foreign affairs. The other French secretaries and ministers often became involved in discussion and/or decision making with the king or by their own belief that they were obligated to deal with ambassadors in order to carry out their own responsibilities. On several occasions during his reign, Louis issued edicts ordering that any of the other ministers who wished to correspond with ambassadors should do so through the secretary for foreign affairs. But in fact, especially in the early years of Louis's reign, all the ministers continued to discuss affairs with foreign diplomats in France and to write to French representatives abroad. The minister of war and the controller general of the finances were particularly noted for their intervention. The conflict caused some difficulties for ambassadors who were told by one minister to write only to him about a specific matter only to have another minister specifically countermand the order. One French diplomat in Germany solved the problem by writing to the minister of war but also sending a copy of what he sent and received to the secretary for foreign affairs. At the very end of Louis's reign, Secretary Torcy was made aware of the problem by Dutch complaints during the negotiations leading to the Peace of Utrecht that there were a number of French agents of "uncertain status" active in the Netherlands. These agents worked on behalf of several different ministers, especially the minister of war.[6] Unfortunately, they were more effective in confusing the situation than in helping to make peace.

On the other hand, not all the French ministers tried to expand their authority in the area of foreign affairs. The famous Jean-Baptiste Colbert refused to correspond about the marriage of the Duke of York with his brother who was French ambassador in England on the grounds that the topic was the responsibility of the secretary of state for foreign affairs and that he (Colbert) had not been informed on the matter by the king. Colbert had even withdrawn himself so much from dealing with diplomats in France that an English diplomat complained about not even being able to have an audience with him on a matter which lay within Colbert's area of responsibility. Colbert, the Englishman lamented, had "wholly disengaged himself from all manner of correspondence with strangers." This was quite appropriate because maintaining contact with foreign diplomats in France was one of the key responsibilities of the minister-secretaries for foreign affairs.

Diplomats, of course, would have preferred to deal directly with the king. Although they were allowed to mingle with the other courtiers without hindrance, they were required to request a special formal audience in order to discuss anything officially. The Sun King granted these audiences sparingly and insisted that requests be made through the minister-secretary for foreign affairs. Access to the ministers was easier, at least in the early part of Louis XIV's reign. According to one observer, it was the appointment of Colbert de Croissy as secretary for foreign affairs in 1679 which moved his brother Jean-Baptiste Colbert to refuse to meet with foreign diplomats any more. This move to strengthen his brother's position worked since the secretary for war, Louvois, had to go along.[7] Thereafter the minister-secretary for foreign affairs regularly received envoys, nuncios, ambassadors, and other diplomats on Tuesdays. The French diplomatic archives contain many volumes of the short notes made by Colbert de Croissy and his son Torcy on which were jotted the date, the title of the diplomat, and a brief description of what was discussed at the audience. Apparently the diplomats gathered in the secretary's anteroom and were allowed to enter on a first come, first served basis. Attempts to deal with the other ministers informally at parties or receptions were likely to meet with a snub, a point which was valuable from the French government's point of view, for it helped keep knowledge about foreign affairs in a limited circle and thus more secret.

The appointment of Colbert de Croissy as secretary-minister was significant in a number of other ways. It seems to mark the point where the small, almost personal and familiar style of French central diplomatic administration which had been practiced under Louis XIV's first two secretaries, Lionne and Pomponne, was replaced by a bureaucratic machine. To be sure such changes do not really occur overnight. The shift from the situation where the whole personnel of the "foreign office" would fit into one carriage under Lionne to the large scale operation run by Torcy obviously occurred gradually. But the replacement of the easy-going Pomponne by the hardbitten Colbert de Croissy seems to symbolize the change. Croissy has been described as "an efficient and unscrupulous legalist, brutal in words and narrow in outlook." [8] His treatment in 1685 of the English envoy extraordinary Sir William Trumbull, certainly bears out the description. Trumbull gave Croissy a letter about some English traders and received a rather undiplomatic response: "Monsieur de Croissy having begun to read my letter threw it away in great passion saying that the thing was false, that there was no such occasion of complaint, [and] that there was no treaty to exempt the English from being subject to soldiers. . . ." [9] Fortunately for the reputation and effectiveness of French diplomacy, Croissy's manner was not continued by his son Torcy who maintained good personal relations with the Englishman Matthew Prior.[10] Overall, as one scholar put it, after Croissy's takeover the "foreign office" was characterized by being "much less of the man and much more of the machine." [11]

When Louis XIV died in 1715, he ended the longest reign that Europe has ever seen. This sheer longevity of the monarch contributed significantly to the relative stability of the organization and operation of the central administration of French diplomacy. In no other seventeenth century state did a monarch have such absolute, unbroken control over foreign affairs. But there were countries in which monarchical control was significant though tempered by other factions of government. Sweden is the best example.

During the reign of Queen Christina the Chancellor Oxenstierna maintained his influential role in foreign affairs,[12] but after her abdication, her successor Charles X was able to keep the direction of foreign affairs in his own hands. As was traditional in Sweden, the senate was also given certain powers to act on unimportant or routine matters while the king was out of the country. The death of Charles X in 1660 and the succession of Charles XI (1660-1697) as a child

Kings and Ministers   39

led to the diffusion of governmental power typical of regencies. During the king's minority power was formally vested in a special government consisting of the queen mother, five high dignitaries of the kingdom, and the whole Swedish senate. Governmental power was in fact in the hands of the senators residing in Sweden, although the estates of the diet intervened as much as possible.

A new statute of the chancellery promulgated in September 1661 made the chancellor of the kingdom of Sweden a sort of minister-secretary for foreign affairs. He was more important than the minister-secretaries in France and comparable to the secretaries of state in England. He himself had responsibility for appointing and directing Swedish diplomats abroad, for receiving and negotiating with diplomats accredited to Stockholm, and making sure that all written records of negotiations were kept in good order. However, as was usual in early modern Europe, edicts did not describe reality. The functions of the chancellor were actually split up among several different men rather than united in one chancellor as the statute had assumed.

Control of foreign affairs became somewhat confused during the 1670's when Sweden was the only ally of France during Louis XIV's Dutch War. Only after the Peace of Nijmegen (from which Sweden only came out well because of strong French support) was Charles XI able to make his rule absolute. The ability of the estates of the Swedish diet to participate in foreign affairs disappeared completely. There was a decline in the importance of the senate which had traditionally served as an intermediary between the estates and the king. Charles was able to reestablish the principle that the king made decisions about all governmental questions, including foreign affairs, "according to his good pleasure." After his absolutism was firmly established, Charles XI occasionally allowed the senate to discuss certain aspects of foreign affairs, but these sessions were more like briefings about events than ruling or even advisory sessions. Although evidence is insufficient to be positive, it appears that the role of the college of the chancellery also became quite restricted as well, no longer having much contact with either diplomats accredited to Sweden or with Swedish representatives abroad. There is a certain similarity between the control of foreign affairs by Charles XI and by Louis XIV in that both did allow advisors to discuss foreign affairs before making their decisions and both were able to maintain their control until their deaths. But Louis XIV's control was not challenged because his absolutism had been established on a firm traditional, institutional, and practical basis, which enabled him to maintain it even during the disastrous wars of the last half of his reign. Charles XI's control was undoubtedly aided by his keeping his country at peace for the last two decades of his reign.

At the accession of Charles XII in 1697 as a lad of fifteen, certain important Swedes hoped that they would be able to seize control of foreign affairs, while the enemies of Sweden thought the Swedish Baltic empire would be ripe for dismemberment. Both were proved mistaken, at least in the short run. Charles XII threw off the ephemeral regency government, seized control of the Swedish government and administration including foreign affairs, and went to war. In a sense one can say that during much of Charles XII's reign there was almost no central administration of foreign affairs. Charles did establish rules whereby the college of the chancellery in Sweden was supposed to concern itself with foreign affairs, deal with diplomats accredited to Sweden, and direct Swedish diplomats abroad. But, since the king actually kept control of foreign affairs himself and left the chancellery no real authority, foreign ambassadors were unwilling to remain in Stockholm while the king was on campaign. Since, with few exceptions like his months at Altranstadt,[13] Charles refused to allow diplomats in his camp, there was something of an impasse in Swedish foreign relations. The situation was particularly awkward during the years Charles was a guest-prisoner in Turkey and had very tenuous communications with Stockholm. After his death the great Swedish nobles were able to change the constitution and once again prevent the king from dominating foreign affairs without limitation, a period sometimes referred to as the "Age of Liberty."

In seventeenth century England control of foreign affairs lay somewhere between the absolutism of France and Sweden on the one hand and the decentralized Netherlands and "anarchic" Poland on the other.[14] During the confused constitutional situation after the restoration of Charles II in 1660, it was not certain whether authority for internal affairs rested with the monarch or with Parliament. But Charles appeared to have charge of foreign affairs. In matters of importance, "this renowned enemy of virginity and chastity" acted as his own foreign minister.

The awkward way in which responsibility for foreign affairs was divided between the English secretaries of state helped Charles and his successor monarchs to maintain their power. Like France and other countries the authority of English secretaries had in earlier centuries been divided along geographical lines. Unlike France the English system had not been reorganized to put all foreign affairs under one secretary. The Northern Department continued throughout our period to deal with the Netherlands, the Scandinavian monarchies, the Hanse Towns and other constituent parts of the Holy Roman Empire, Poland, and Russia. The Southern Department was responsible for relations with France, Spain, Portugal, Switzerland, the Italian states, and Turkey. The separation of the two departments as late as the reign of William III was illustrated when a secretary of the Northern Department commented: "I have nothing to do with what relates to the southern provinces." [15] Not until 1782 was the English system modernized with foreign affairs given to the Northern Department and home affairs to the Southern. Since the monarchs were able to take an overview of foreign affairs, they were able to exert a certain amount of authority over all.

But events were to prove that, despite the apparent superiority of the monarchs in foreign affairs, they were not truly supreme after 1660. Their policies were carried out when the nation's will as expressed by Parliament agreed with them. When Parliament did not or would not agree, the monarch was forced to dissimulate or to abandon his policy. Such was the case when Charles II was forced to withdraw from the war against the Dutch on the side of Louis XIV. And when Parliament dismissed the English troops after the Peace of Ryswick, William III had to make the compromise Partition Treaties because he was no longer able to act from a position of strength. But it should be noted that Parliament's ability to intervene in foreign affairs was in the area of policy, not in the diplomatic service itself. The monarch could change the number or status of his diplomats abroad whenever he chose to do so. Only the English kings' perennial lack of money restricted them in this. They either limited expenditures on diplomatic ventures or ran into debt.

It is generally recognized that of all the English monarchs from Charles II to George I, William III was the most interested in foreign affairs. With the possible exception of Charles II, William was also the most effective in controlling them. Reputedly, he did this primarily by keeping affairs secret from his English subjects while entrusting them to his Dutch and refugee French protestant friends. But a recent biographer has shown that William really did not trust anyone completely. He kept secrets from the Earl of Portland, his Dutch favorite for a quarter of a century, just as he did from everyone else. Secrecy and a very limited and specific delegation of authority were William's way of preventing "any single one of his servants from achieving too powerful a position." [16] Of course William tried to control all aspects of English government in these ways, not just foreign affairs. His subjects in turn tried to expand their authority or, in some cases, just to stop the erosion of duties which were traditionally part of their office's responsibility. This erosion is illustrated in an interesting letter in the Public Record Office. Henry Sydney, who had recently been appointed as a principle secretary of state with Sweden under his jurisdiction, wrote an almost apologetic letter expressing a desire to receive information from the English envoy in Sweden:

Whitehall, 3rd February 1690
I have received your [letter]s. . . . I have only to acknowledge the receipt of

them, and to let you know that though during the King's stay at The Hague
you will correspond with my Lord Nottingham attending His Majesty there,
and will upon all occasions receive His Majesty's commands from his
Lordship during that time, yet seeing your department is within my province,
I shall be glad to be well informed of everything which may in any way relate
to it.[17]

It is not surprising that William III hesitated to trust anybody too much. After
half a century of revolution in England, he could not be certain of any man's
loyalty to him. Yet throughout his reign, he was generally well served by his
English diplomats.

The accession of Queen Anne on William's death significantly changed the
role of the monarch in English diplomatic administration. The English were
already committed to the Grand Alliance and participation in the War of the
Spanish Succession, and decisions were basically determined by this fact. Real
control of foreign policy lay in the hands of an inner group of advisors; the Duke
of Marlborough; Godolphin, the Lord High Treasurer; and Robert Harley,
Speaker of the House of Commons and later secretary of state.[18] Both policy
and personnel were still occasionally influenced by the queen. For instance, she
was a limiting factor in the career of Matthew Prior[19] because she did not
believe that important diplomatic appointments should be given to men of low
birth like him. But on the whole, English diplomats were recruited by her
ministers. Anne's major effect on policy occurred when she decided to end her
reliance on the Duchess of Marlborough, dismissed the Duke and Godolphin,
and thus enabled Harley and Saint John to make the Peace of Utrecht with Louis
XIV. After Anne's death, with the exception of George III, English monarchs
seldom intervened in the making of foreign policy or the administration of the
diplomatic service.

Venice and the Netherlands exemplify still other ways in which the central
administration of diplomacy was organized in the seventeenth century. The
Venetian Doge was a figurehead rather than truly in control of government. He
invited all the ambassadors in Venice to a large reception in the ducal palace
four times a year, where they were joined by some Venetian patricians and
senators for a splendid entertainment. Otherwise the Doge was invisible to
diplomats except for private audiences. According to Venetian law, ambassadors could only be received by the Council of Ministers called the Collegio or
Serenissima Signoria presided over by the Doge. For very secret or very
important communications, the three chiefs of the Council of Ten were added.
At each audience a secretary took notes (as accurately as possible in those days
before the invention of shorthand) of everything said by both sides. Later the
notes were transcribed onto parchment, many of which are still to be found in

Venetian archives. Informal contacts between diplomats and Venetian citizens were generally discouraged. A Venetian who dealt with a diplomat in a way which the government considered treasonable was likely to be found dead some morning hanging upside down by one leg in the Piazza.

The situation was somewhat different in the Netherlands since people there often talked very freely about all aspects of government. Appointment as ambassador to "Their High Mightinesses the States General" must have been appalling to the appointee when he considered the difficulties of his position. The States General were not sovereign; true sovereignty lay with the Provincial States in each of the seven units which made up the United Netherlands. As a result diplomats went through the motions of being received by the President of the States General or by their "Greffier" who was a sort of secretary. But diplomats knew that in reality, in order to carry on negotiations or influence the Republic's government, they had to contact many of the estimated two thousand regents who could potentially influence decisions of the States General. Thus, diplomats had to keep in touch not only with the States General at The Hague but with Dutchmen in the Provincial States and even in the towns of the various provinces. Amsterdam was especially important as it dominated the Province of Holland which in turn dominated the Republic as a whole. It was obvious to everyone that such a government could not possibly work. Yet it did function and govern the country through a century when the Netherlands acted and was treated as if it were a great power.

The government worked because, despite the apparent stability of governmental institutions, the actual patterns and personnel of authority shifted within the Republic according to changing realities of power. Thus, during the "First Stadtholderless Period" from the death of William II of Orange until Louis XIV's attack in 1672, the States General delegated their authority to certain functionaries and committees. Since there were no rules specifically stating their various functions and duties, the relative importance of each shifted according to what individuals held which positions. The Pensionary of Holland, John de Witt, played such a substantial role in Dutch diplomacy that many statesmen abroad and diplomats in the Netherlands thought of him as the minister for foreign affairs and head of government. But the regents who controlled the various Provincial States and the cities like Amsterdam certainly considered de Witt to be their agent and not their superior. Nevertheless, because of his position it was de Witt who usually received the most secret correspondence of Dutch diplomats abroad and was the most important figure in the formulation and execution of Dutch diplomacy.

After the cruel murder of John de Witt and his brother in which their bodies were cut up and the pieces sold for souvenirs, the Dutch gave power to the one

man who seemed likely to be able to repel the French invasion of 1672 —
William III of Orange, the future king of England. Nothing was formally
changed in the constitution. But the fact that William was now an adult
combined with the pro-Orange traditions of many Dutchmen to enable him to
acquire membership in the State Council and supreme command of the army
and navy, and to have one of his supporters appointed Grand Pensionary of
Holland. As a result William had unprecedented authority in Dutch foreign
affairs. Nevertheless, even during the war against Louis XIV his power was not
total. He was opposed by the city of Amsterdam and others who were eventually able to force him to accept the Peace of Nijmegen. William continued to
hold his Dutch offices after the Glorious Revolution put him on the English
throne, and he was usually able, with the help of his friend Antonie Heinsius
(the Grand Pensionary of Holland), to have the Dutch carry out his wishes.
After William III's death in 1702, the "Second Stadtholderless Period" began.
William's heir was only elected stadtholder in two provinces and, after his
death by drowning in 1711, his posthumous son was essentially ignored.
Heinsius was able to continue his role in Dutch diplomatic administration, but
in general the pattern which had existed under de Witt once more came into
existence in the Netherlands, except that no one really believed that the Dutch
were still a great power.[20]

Secretariats and Chancelleries

It would be possible to go on discussing the different kinds of central
administration of foreign affairs and diplomacy, but since examples of the most
important types have been discussed, it is appropriate now to move on to those
aspects of central administration which were common to all or almost all
seventeenth century governments. There were a number of these including such
things as secretariats (or chancelleries), the clerks who actually wrote the letters
(and performed other less official but equally or more important functions),
archives, and other related topics.

Every seventeenth century government was small in comparison to the giant
organizations which are now the norm. The number of men in the foreign office
of even a small state like Switzerland or Portugal today would dwarf the office
of the French secretary of state for foreign affairs at the end of Louis XIV's
reign which at the time was one of the largest, if not the largest, in Europe. As a
result, individuals who today would be merely a tiny cog in the diplomatic
machine — the clerk-typists, filers, runners, etc. — often played a significant
role in the central administration of seventeenth century diplomacy. One reason
for their importance was that they were usually not specialists who performed a
single job. As the seventeenth century wore on and the secretariats [21] became

larger and took more functions upon themselves, the man in charge was less and less able to oversee all the more routine activities. Responsibility for routine matters thus passed to the clerks just as the secretaries themselves had acquired more authority in earlier centuries.

The number of men a secretariat employed depended upon the wealth of the government in question (in other words, how many people it could afford) and the extent of its involvement in foreign affairs. At one end of the scale were the small German principalities and city states whose personnel consisted of but a clerk or two who handled all the public business, both foreign and internal. Near the other extreme was the Swedish chancellery. According to the Swedish statute promulgated in 1661 there were to be two secretaries of state, one for interior affairs and the other for exterior although, according to an ancient tradition, the former also dealt with Danish affairs. The "foreign secretary" was to have at his command two clerks and a copyist, two of whom had to know Latin, French, and German. Certain kinds of foreign affairs were sometimes confided to two "despatch secretaries" who did not have the rank of secretaries of state. At the same time, the post of "secretary with commission" was created. These secretaries were used abroad as diplomats, but when they were in Sweden their function was to maintain contact with other Swedish diplomats abroad.[22] Of course, it was unusual for the full complement of personnel allowed by the statute actually to be working at any one time. The two English secretaries of state, both of whom dealt with foreign affairs, each had an undersecretary and also a small staff of clerks.

Throughout Louis XIV's personal reign, the French secretary of state for foreign affairs was usually assisted only by two or three "chief clerks." However, there had been a substantial increase in the number of support personnel. It is impossible to be certain about the names and/or numbers of these men as they were then considered to be too low on the social and/or occupational scale to be worthy of notice. Furthermore, a new class of employees whose legal status was very poorly defined had arisen between the secretary of state and the chief clerks, both offices which had well established legal existence. These men were simply called "secretaries" and were similar to what today might be called a personal secretary. At the end of Louis XIV's reign, Torcy had two such secretaries whose functions were very important. The first took Torcy's dictation, delivered passports, kept the duplicates of ciphers, and handled the minister's secret correspondence. The second secretary served as a replacement when the first was sick or absent and made extracts of the negotiations which had been carried on since the Peace of Ryswick. The chief clerks had once again been reduced to two in number in 1714. Each had three sub-clerks and, interestingly, had reverted to the old practice of arranging their responsibilities according to geography. One wrote the letters for Spain, Portugal, England, Holland, Switzerland, and Italy. The other wrote to the rest of the world — Germany, the Low Countries, Lorraine, the Scandinavian kingdoms, Turkey, Asia, and Africa. In many countries the lower level clerks were connected in some personal way with the secretaries of state and, when he left office, his employees usually departed with him. In France this practice had no particular effect on the secretary of state for foreign affair's office since there were only four different officeholders between 1663 and 1715. Two died in their position, one was still in office at the death of Louis XIV, and only one was dismissed. Thus, their subordinates were often kept on until the subordinates themselves died. As a result the French secretariat was somewhat more efficient than those of other countries like England where the secretaries of state and their helpers were changed quite frequently.[23]

Like all other parts of the central administration of diplomacy, the secretariat dealt with both foreign diplomats at home and its own diplomats abroad. Not surprisingly, the latter function was more important. Although there were variations resulting from the form of government and the personalities involved, the daily procedure followed by the papal secretariat was typical, especially in the way it handled correspondence. As each "ordinary" mail service or courier arrived with mail from nuncios abroad, the undersecretary divided it into two parts. The miscellaneous pieces like newspapers, copies of edicts, and placards which most diplomats sent along with their despatches, were put aside for possible later use. The despatches themselves, memoirs, requests and other documents which required an answer or a solution were first deciphered if necessary and then forwarded to the appropriate office. Important despatches were extracted or summarized for presentation to the cardinal secretary of state or the pope. Early each morning the cardinal secretary met with the pope, gave him the summaries and extracts, and discussed what responses should be made. In many but not all secular states a council was involved at this point. Then the cardinal secretary met with the undersecretary to give him brief outlines of what responses should be made to each missive. A rough draft was usually written of each letter to be sent out. This was then corrected by the cardinal secretary of state and/or the pope before being recopied in its final form. The rough draft might be kept for the records or yet another file copy in a letterbook might be made. Finally, if necessary, the letter or parts of it was enciphered before being sent on its way.[24] These relatively simple procedures were time-consuming enough to require the efforts of several clerks for a court which was even moderately involved in diplomacy. But the personnel of the secretariats performed a number of other functions as well.

The secretariats, for instance, were responsible for producing the large number of documents, both formal and informal, which played such an important role in early modern diplomacy: instructions, copies of previous instructions, treaties, relevant negotiations, and the other materials diplomats were given as they started their mission.[25] The secretariats also produced formal documents like letters of credence, letters of ceremony, condolences on deaths, and congratulations on births and marriages. Even at the beginning of the period, most governments had formulary books of some kind which gave in detail the forms which were used. One sample among many is a "Formulary for the letters which the King sends to the Powers of Italy and the way in which they write to His Majesty" found in the Foreign Affairs Archives in Paris. The six folio pages consist of parallel columns describing the practice followed for each of thirteen Italian governments including the Pope, the College of Cardinals, Venice, Florence, Parma, and Malta. Such things are noted as the quality and size of paper used in letters, the form of address used (for example, "Most Holy Father" for the pope), the title used in the body of the letter, the formal ending sentence, signature, and whether to leave space for other signatures.[26] How carefully such forms were observed and their consistency can almost serve as measurements of the effectiveness of early modern governments. The government of Poland was undoubtedly one of the least effective in the seventeenth century and its secretariat showed it. The Polish chancellery had no settled formulary nor even any records of the ceremonies practiced in Poland toward other princes. The Polish secretariat was so inefficient that in 1686, an envoy extraordinary's letter of credence was addressed to the deceased Duke of Savoy. The current Duke would have been justified in sending the envoy to his father's tomb to declare the purpose of his mission. Fortunately, the envoy noticed the error and had the name changed.[27] Considering the importance at this time of such items as the form of address used, the signature, etc., whereby disagreement could hold up important negotiations, it is inconceivable that a government would not create and keep formularies, first, to know what to write and, second, to back up its usage.

Closely related to the maintenance of such formulary books was the creation of diplomatic archives. Twentieth century undergraduates are often astonished to discover that in the early modern period many statesmen treated papers which they wrote and received while in official positions as if the papers were their own private possessions. They took the papers with them when they retired or the papers became the property of their heirs at their death. As a result, some governments did not even have copies to use for official business. There were cases in the seventeenth century where a new secretary of state had to write to all the diplomats abroad asking for copies of their instructions. But despite the obvious need to keep originals or at least copies of diplomatic documents, many governments ignored the problem.

Not surprisingly, the Italians had been the earliest to establish systems for keeping important documents. The Venetian records are especially well known, but the House of Savoy's accomplishments equaled if not surpassed those of Venice. The archives at Turin were protected and expanded with perfect regularity from 1179 to 1861 when the House of Savoy became the royal house of a newly united Italy. This was a truly remarkable achievement considering the tremendous number of wars and other disasters which constantly threatened the Savoyards. Perhaps the key reason for the early creation and continued existence of the Savoyard archives was that their dukes were relatively weak and always threatened by external enemies. They recognized the strength which keeping regular records gave to their diplomacy. Part of their success was due to the requirement that Savoyard diplomats swear an oath to give up all their records at the end of their mission:

> I swear to preserve registers of the letters which I will write to the court, the original letters which I receive from the court as well as all the other writings which will be delivered or sent to me by the court, and to return the said registers of letters and writings to the first secretary of state within a month after my return without keeping any copy.

The first secretary was then to give the papers to the superintendent of the archives who in turn was to have a brief relation (summary) compiled by officials who were specifically appointed to do this work.[28]

Archives in most other states were neither established so early nor administered so well. The papal archives were started well before the period, but some records were lost during the early seventeenth century when the cardinal-nephews of the popes kept parts of the papal diplomatic correspondence. After the reign of Clement X (1670-1676), the cardinal-secretaries of state faithfully retained the documents, having them bound in volumes according to the year in which they were written. In the eighteenth century the papal archives were organized in the form which they maintained until the twentieth century. The English diplomatic archives were created in the early seventeenth century during the reign of James I.[29] The French were even farther behind than the English. Mazarin left his papers to the king on his death in 1661, and at the death of Secretary-Minister Lionne in 1671, his official papers were sealed and the government took possession of them. This could possibly be considered the beginning of the French Foreign Affairs Archives. Diplomatic papers were henceforth not considered private property. There were even scattered attempts to organize them and make relevant extracts for the use of statesmen. But it was not until the end of Louis XIV's reign that Secretary Torcy received permission to acquire Richelieu's papers and permission to establish a permanent diplomatic archive in the Louvre. In connection with an attempt to establish the Political Academy, the materials were organized and summaries of French negotiations in the last half of the seventeenth century were prepared. The archives of certain other governments were either so poor as to be of little value or were non-existent. As late as the eighteenth century, the Holy Roman Emperor's chancellery was not keeping copies of the instructions given to his diplomats. The Swiss cantons did not even have a common administration until 1798, and their diplomacy was maintained on an irregular basis by the principal cantons of Bern, Zurich, and Lucerne. Thus, their diplomatic documents were scattered with many kept in private hands where they still remain today. In any case, maintaining archives was a valuable practical aid to those secretariats which did so and a hindrance to those which did not.[30]

The lower level employees in the secretariats often played a role which was of great importance to the diplomats abroad. Since the letters written by most princes were relatively short and were mostly filled with directives, diplomats had to have an alternative source of information from home. One diplomat explained why when writing to his secretary of state, asking for

some news about events and affairs which can be passed around. This is necessary so that people do not think that I am being crafty and so that I can do my part at court by furnishing some news for the trade here. You know that in [diplomacy] as in other ordinary transactions it is necessary to give in order to receive.[31]

If the diplomat were important and well connected, he might receive such information directly from the sovereign or the secretaries of state. Others had to depend on correspondence from friends or relatives, but they were often unsatisfactory sources because they were slow to write or were unable to acquire significant information. Here the clerks in the secretariat could be quite helpful since they were well placed to know what was happening both at their own court and at foreign posts. For example, in addition to their other duties, French clerks occasionally wrote ambassadors giving information, gave advice which enabled ambassadors to avoid blunders, commented on their despatches, and also transmitted the diplomats' personal requests to the minister-secretaries.

Other governments formalized the procedure of keeping their diplomats informed. The Swedish statute of the chancellery promulgated in 1661[32] had created the position of "secretary with commission"; its primary duty was to serve as an intermediary between the royal goverment at home and Swedish diplomats abroad. But the purpose was not well served. In 1693 the college of the chancellery discussed the possibility of maintaining communication by means of a newsletter which would be circulated every week or two. The thought was to establish a printed sheet similar to that the Dutch goverment sent to its diplomats, but the Swedes decided that this procedure would be too dangerous for the security of information and it came to naught.

Other than the Durth, the most advanced government was the English. From time immemorial ambassadors and other English diplomats abroad were sent handwritten newsletters compiled in the office of the secretary of state. A report, written by a chief clerk to the Keeper of the Office of His Majesty's Papers and Records in 1674, described how the newsletters were prepared and to whom they were sent. There were fourteen "correspondents — foreign — Monday" who were not charged for their weekly copy and a number of other "interior" correspondents who were charged. The four clerks in the office divided the work "according to the fastness of their writing", while the chief clerk helped write when he had time to spare from collecting the copy and looking after the business. On Mondays, Wednesdays, and Fridays two of the clerks went to "the Rolls" office to collect information, while the others remained in the office to "do the business and attend the extracts of the foreign packet." On Tuesdays, Thursdays, and Saturdays they all wrote letters, either "long", containing a whole week's collection of news, or "short", containing only two days' news. The year's profit amounted to 174 pounds, of which 120 were paid to the four young men and the rest kept by the chief clerk for his "pains and maintenance" and to pay certain minor expenses like candles, candlesticks, snuffers, cleaning of the room, and other "such little things." [33] Other states, including France, were more backward in such business. There are examples of "nouvelles" (news) dated from Paris which were sent regularly to individuals in France and abroad, but this does not seem to have been done in an organized way. In the later years of Louis XIV's reign, extracts of correspondence from other French diplomats abroad were sent directly to the French ambassador in London, but how widespread this practice was is not known. In any case, it was not uncommon for French ambassadors to be reduced to the point of almost having to beg the French secretary of state for foreign affairs to send him news from home. Diplomats from all too many other countries faced the same problem.

Assumptions, Motives and Goals

It is widely recognized that diplomacy was in the process of becoming a normal activity of states during the early modern period and that the institutions necessary to maintain diplomatic contact were just in the process of "becoming" as well. The foregoing discussion has shown some of the ways in which the institution of secretariats of chancelleries was already "modern" or still "pre-modern." Yet, it must never be forgotten that the purpose of the institutions was fundamentally to carry out the goals and purposes of the sovereigns (or decision-makers as they have been called here) in whose name diplomats spoke and acted. Thus it seems appropriate to examine, however briefly, the motivations of these decision makers. The study of pyschohistory has not yet reached the stage where we can point with certainty to any specific "factor" or "factors" as being "the motivation" of seventeenth century sovereigns. Furthermore. the evidence suggests that in most cases a specific choice was the result of the unique circumstances surrounding the decision. There are enough similarities and differences among seventeenth century sovereigns themselves, however, to make it appropriate to discuss some of the attitudes and assumptions which underlay foreign policy decisions. We may also try to discover some generalizations about the goals or at least types of goals which were sought.

The major obstacle which twentieth century undergraduates face in trying to understand the assumptions of seventeenth century decision makers is their tendency to transfer their preconceived notions about what motivates decision makers today to the early modern period. The search for power, economic reasons, and nationalism (in one order or another) are today seen as such overwhelmingly important determinants that students are often unwilling to accept the idea that these were not necessarily the basic goals of seventeenth century sovereigns. Today the student may look for the "real" reason when told differently or simply assume that he is being misled or misinformed. The fact remains that many of the assumptions and goals of the 1600's were simply different from those of today. To understand how and why things happened as they did, we must get inside the minds of the men who lived then.

In retrospect, it is quite obvious that the Peace of Westphalia in 1648 marked both the definite end of the medieval view of Christendom as a unified whole and the existence of a Europe which consisted of independent or "sovereign" states. But this does not mean that the sovereign princes themselves saw this so clearly. True, they generally recognized, indeed vigorously maintained, their independence. At the same time, they tended to view relations between the units of the system not as international (between nations) but as interpersonal (between princes) while making due allowance for the existence of those anomalies, the republics. Furthermore, the relationships between rulers were similar to relationships within states in that both were hierarchical. One's place within the hierarchy was important, for it was determined as much by "superficial" forms as by "true" power. Only when we realize this do the tremendous efforts of early modern decision-makers to maintain or acquire the forms and trappings of place make sense. A good illustration is the desire of Frederick, the Elector of Prussia, to become King of Prussia. His near cousin William III had been raised to the British throne and his closest neighbor, the Elector of Saxony, had been elected King of Poland. Frederick had no intention of letting himself be left behind in the matter of titles and thereby find himself lower in the "international" hierarcy. Of course, seventeenth century decision-makers realized, just as their modern counterparts do, that having a higher or more impressive title or reputation gave one an immediate advantage in diplomatic relations.

Titles were also important because of the connection between the ruler and the state. It can be said either that the state was the personification of the ruler or that the ruler embodied the state. Such was the case particularly in the middle of the seventeenth century when rulers like Louis XIV referred to a diplomat's taking an action for "my service" or that another country should desire "my alliance." Toward the end of the seventeenth and beginning of the eighteenth centuries, Louis and other rulers began to refer to "the state" in an attempt to depersonalize it. But the situation was still far from that which prevails today where

> The personality of the State [not the ruler personifying the state] is accepted . . . as a fact of international practice. The State is . . . regarded as the personified legal order which, being autonomous, prevails over given territory, ruled by an effective and independent government. The State, being an artificial person, must act through agents. . . . The acts of these agents are imputed to the State.[34]

Throughout the seventeenth century the acts of agents were imputed to the prince who had sent them. The imputation was correct because it was the individual decision-makers who fundamentally decided what would be important issues in diplomacy and what potentially important issues would be ignored or resolved rapidly into insignificance. Recognition of this fact is necessary to understand the diplomacy of any period for, as one modern scholar has pointed out, "If one begins by thinking of diplomacy as an attempt to solve problems by mere reasoning, mere discussion — all based on the assumption that the better argument will prevail — one is liable to be led seriously astray." Rather,

diplomacy is used in a situation where both or all the decision-maker participants might understand the arguments and viewpoint of the other(s), yet still be
unwilling to resolve the issue according to the "merits of the case." This occurs
because the problems are not questions of right and justice but are the result of
conflicts of interest; "there is a conflict of wills." [35] This, of course, means that
it is more important than ever to understand the assumptions as well as the goals
of early modern (and modern) decision-makers in order to understand their
diplomatic maneuvers.

To begin, we must recognize that only the first of the "big three" motivating
factors of the twentieth century — the search for power, economics, and
nationalism — was significant for most seventeenth century decision-makers.
And even power was thought to be something different then than it is now when
power is primarily defined in military and economic terms. Then, power was
seen more in terms of prestige and, that concomitant of military power, a
satisfactory financial position.[36] With the exception of the Netherlands and
Britain, few decision-makers were overly concerned with economic goals as
ends in themselves. After 1648 the promotion of trade interests became the
principal aim of the States General's foreign policy, and gaining the Asiento
was one of England's main goals in the negotiations leading to the Peace of
Utrecht. It is inconceivable that Louis XIV, Leopold II, or Charles XII would
ever have defined their principal diplomatic goals in such terms. The same is
true of the third factor. Nationalism in the modern sense simply did not exist in
the seventeenth century with the possible exception again of England or the
republics (especially the Netherlands). To be sure, as the end of our period
neared, there were expressions which may indicate that some of the rulers were
becoming "nationalistic." For example, Louis XIV referred in an edict given
in 1705 to the "attachment which native born subjects owe to the sovereign and
to their fatherland *(patrie).*" But it is still difficult to believe that he could ever
have understood the modern meaning of the term "the French nation."

If one could ask seventeenth century decision-makers what kinds of goals
they had, they would probably respond in terms like *gloire,* religion, and
dynasticism. *Gloire* (usually simply translated as glory) is one of the most
widely repeated yet least understood words used to describe the goals of that
most important ruler, Louis XIV. Contrary to popular opinion, when the Sun
King said that something should be done for the benefit of his *gloire,* he did not
mean for satisfying his vanity; rather, he meant what would today be called his
reputation. Concern for his reputation was not mere vanity either; it was his
feeling that he had to live up to the high standards of behavior which were
required by his position. Louis XIV believed that he had to perform his "métier
du roi" (the job of being a king) as well as he could. Other rulers were equally

concerned for their "reputation", even if they did not use the word *gloire* to refer to it.

In textbooks of the history of Western Civilization, reference is frequently made to the Thirty Years, War as the last war in which religion was an important factor. Thus it may seem curious that religion is listed as one of the important general factors motivating late seventeenth century rulers. There are several reasons for this assertion. First, it is sometimes easier to change the substance of something than to change its vocabulary. Such was the case with religion in early modern diplomatic relations. It was often easy to use the old vocabulary of religion to cloak or express somewhat more secular purposes. Second, religion could serve as propaganda. For instance, William III used the call to defend Protestantism as a rallying cry to get allies against Louis XIV. The claim that the call of religion was more propaganda than real is strengthened by the fact that the "Protestants" fighting against the Sun King usually included the Emperor, His Most Catholic Majesty the King of Spain, and other staunch Catholics. One also suspects that religion was probably not really an important factor in the decisions of the German princes to join William III since many of them became Roman Catholics when it was to their political advantage to do so. The conversion of the Elector of Saxony for the sake of acquiring the Polish Crown is merely the best known of dozens of changes of religion in both directions. However, one should not pass off all references to religion by decision-makers as having no validity. Their common Protestantism was undoubtedly a factor in the cooperation between England and the Netherlands in the decades after the 1670's. Queen Anne continually attempted to persuade Catholic princes such as the Emperor Leopold to be tolerant of their Protestant subjects, even when such interventions threatened political cooperation. That religion was important to Leopold too is illustrated by the English envoy's report in 1693 that it would have been difficult to overcome his religious scruples against allying himself with "heretics" (Protestants) if it had not been for one of his minister's ability to mix religious argument with political expediency.[37] Religion remained a nebulous but potentially important factor in diplomatic decision making throughout the seventeenth century, and the modern student who ignores it is in danger of fundamentally misunderstanding the period.

Like religion, dynasticism[38] provided a vocabulary which could be used to cover up a variety of other kinds of goals. Yet there can be no doubt but that rulers who believed in the Divine Right of Kings were also likely to truly believe in the dynastic aspects of God's will. God's will was shown by the genealogical relationships which were much more important in giving the right to rule certain territories than were "nationalistic" factors like language, ethnography, or geography. Nevertheless, dynasticism as a force was dying out in the period. This seems to be the best explanation of Louis XIV's giving up large parts of his son's Spanish inheritance in the Partition Treaties. Yet Louis's eventual acceptance of the testament of Carlos II, giving the whole of the Spanish empire to his second grandson, led to the Duke of Savoy's making a statement which shows very well the difference between the meaning of dynastic and "national" interests. The Duke wrote that Louis was a good father (i.e. he acted according to dynastic principles), for in placing his grandson on the throne of Spain he "deprived France of Lorraine and several other states in Italy;" the Duke added that if he were in Louis XIV's place, he would have made a different decision (i.e. he would have acted according to "nationalistic" principles) because he was convinced that the young king "would in a short time be as good a Spaniard as the kings who had possessed this crown before him." [39] Usually it is impossible to say exactly whether a decision-maker were really basing his decision on dynastic considerations or whether he were merely using dynastic rhetoric to cover up or dignify some other purpose. Intermarriages, claims to territories of deceased rulers, testaments, and the like were usually so complicated and subject to such conflicting interpretations that it was possible for a major prince to discover a dynastic pretext to meddle in almost any affair or to justify almost any actions he wished to take.

It is impossible to delve into the specific goals of all the various rulers in the period; but it is necessary to try once again to put to death an old fable that has been killed innumerable times and still appears again and again in textbooks, examination papers, and even scholarly studies dealing with the seventeenth century. This is the claim that Louis XIV's diplomacy was motivated by "the historical French policy of trying to put the eastern frontier of France on the 'natural' line of the Alps and the Rhine." [40] The idea of "natural" frontiers of states like France and Germany[41] was very popular with ninetennth century nationalists. Thus they picked up the references to "natural frontiers" of France made by seventeenth century "publicists" (or propagandizers as we might call them today) and attributed the goal to Louis XIV and other French decision makers despite the fact that the statesmen themselves did not use the term or even express the concept. Indeed, especially in the early part of his reign, when Louis XIV conceived of the Kingdom of France primarily as being the ensemble of territories he ruled and not an entity in its own right, he could not even conceive of such a thing as "natural frontiers" ! The "state" did not even have its own existence apart from him, his predecessors, and his successors. More than a third of a century ago, in 1938, at a time when Germany and France were more likely to want items which would justify conflict between them rather than decrease it, a Franco-German committee of historians laid the whole idea of Louis XIV's so-called interest in "natural frontiers" to rest in terms which should have prevented it from ever being more than a simple curiosity to those interested in the history of the nineteenth and early twentieth centuries.[42] Let us hope that it finally will be put in the special wastebasket reserved for those popular historical myths which simply have no basis in fact. And let us further hope that when students examine the motivations of seventeenth century decision makers, they will remember that the rulers were only human beings who, like other people, usually had a tendency to react to the specific situations in which they found themselves at different times. In general, they did not have great plans nor did they necessarily even have specific long term goals for their foreign policies. Such plans are more often the invention of their biographers than of the rulers themselves.

FOOTNOTES

[1] J. J. Jusserand, ed. *Recueil des instructions données aux ambassadeurs et ministres de France . . . Angleterre,* Vol. I, Paris, 1929, p. xxvii; J. de Boislisle, ed. *Mémoriaux du conseil de 1661,* Vol. I, Part 2, Paris, 1905, p. 276; J. A. Wijnne, ed. *Négociations de . . . le comte d'Avaux . . . Suède,* Vol. I, Utrecht, 1882, p. 141.

[2] Jusserand, *Recueil,* see note 1, p. xxvii.

[3] For an example see J. O. Kemble, ed. *State Papers and Correspondence, Illustrative of the Social and Political State of Europe [1686-1707],* London, 1857, pp. 2-3.

[4] Somewhat the same procedure was followed by the English throughout the seventeenth century. See below, Chap. II, p.

[5] The Archives des Affaires Etrangères in Paris has a volume entitled "Organisation et Règlements du Ministère, 1547-1806" which gives much information on this topic.

[6] C.-G. Picavet. *La Diplomatie française au temps de Louis XIV,* Paris, 1930, pp. 42-47; H. M. A. Keens-Soper. "The French Political Academy, 1714," *European Studies Review,* Vol. II, 1972, p. 332.

[7] E. Spanheim. *Relation de la cour de France en 1690,* new edition, ed. by E. Bourgeois, Lyon, 1900, pp. 350-53.

[8] A. Lossky. "Dutch Diplomacy and the Franco-Russian Trade Negotiations in 1681," in R. Hatton and M.S. Anderson, eds. *Studies in Diplomatic History,* London, 1970, p. 41.

[9] R. Clark. *Sir William Trumbull in Paris, 1685-1686,* Cambridge, 1938, p. 58.

[10] See below, Chap. IV, p.

[11] Jusserand, *Recueil,* see note 1, Vol. II, p. 273.

[12] Much of the following discussion is based on A. Munthe. "L'Administration des affaires étrangères de 1648 à 1720," in S. Tunberg, et al. *Histoire de l'administration des affaires étrangères de Suède,* Trans. from Swedish by A. Mohn, Uppsala, 1940, *passim.*

[13] See below, Chap.   , pp.

[14] Since the large number of works English historians have done on their country's history in the seventeenth century are easily available, only a very brief sketch of the central organization of diplomacy will be given here. See especially P. S. Lachs. *The Diplomatic Corps under Charles II & James II,* New Brunswick, 1965, 269 pp. and D. B. Horn. *The British Diplomatic Service 1689-1789,* Oxford, 1961, pp. 324

[15] M. Lane. "The Diplomatic Service under William III," *Transactions of the Royal Historical Society,* 4th ser., Vol. X, 1927, pp. 87-88.

[16] S. B. Baxter. *William III and the Defense of European Liberty, 1650-1702,* New York, 1966, pp. 274-75.

[17] Public Record Office. London. SP 104/153, Foreign Entry Book, fol. 142v, Sydney to Duncomb.

[18] H. L. Snyder. "Formulation of Foreign and Domestic Policy in the Reign of Queen Anne," *Historical Journal,* Vol. XI, 1968, p. 144.

[19] See below, Chap. IV, p

[20] Much of the preceeding discussion is based on M. A. M. Franken. *Coenraad van Beuningen's Politieke,* Groningen, 1966, 289 pp. and R. Hatton. *Diplomatic Relations between Great Britain and the Dutch Republic, 1714-1721,* London, 1950, 283 pp.

[21] A general name of the body of men performing the duties of the embryonic "foreign offices" — usually under the direction of an individual bearing a title of secretary of state or chancellor.

[22] Munthe, "L'Administration des affaires étrangères," see note 12, pp. 133 and 182. Also see below, Chap. IV, p

[23] C. Piccioni. *Les Premiers commis des affaires étrangères au XVII et au XVIII siècles,* Paris, 1928, pp. 269-70; many of the relevant portionso f J.-P. Samoyault, *Les Bureaux du secrétariat d'état des affaires étrangères sous Louis XV,* Parris, 1971, *passim,* are simply direct quotations from the "Organisation" volume cited above, note t.

[24] P. Richard. "Origines et développement de la secrétairerie d'état apostolique, 1417-1823," *Revue d'histoire ecclésiastique* (Louvain), Vol. XI, 1910, pp. 743-45.

[25] See sample documents in the appendix.

[26] Archives des Affaires Etrangères. Paris. Mémoires et documents, France, Vol. 307, 1705-1709, fols. 158-63.

[27] F. P. Dalerac. *Anecdotes de Pologne,* Vol. II, Paris, 1699, pp. 78-80.

[28] J.-J. Armingaud. *La Maison de Savoie et les archives de Turin,* Paris, 1877, pp. 10-11; J.-J. Armingaud. "Documents relatifs á l'histoire de France recueilles dans les archives de Turin," *Revue des sociétés savantes des départements,* 6th ser., Vol. V, 1877, 126-27.

[29] C. H. Carter. *The Western European Powers, 1500-1700,* Ithaca, 1971, p. 127; Richard, "Origines . . . de la secrétairerie d'état apostolique," see note 24, p. 746.

[30] J. Flammermont. "Rapport . . sur les correspondances des agents diplomatiques étrangers en France avant la Révolution conservées dans les archives de Berlin, Dresde, Genève, Turin, [etc.]," *Nouvelles archives des missions scientifiques et littéraires,* Vol. VIII, 1896, p. 283; Derek McKay. "Diplomatic Relations between George I and the Emperor Charles VI, 1714-19," Ph.D. dessertation, University of London, 1971, p. 370; Keens-Soper, "French Political Academy," see note 6, pp. 332-33.

[31] Jusserand, *Recueil,* see note 1, Vol. II, p. 156.

[32] See above, Chap. II, p.

[33] W. D. Christie, ed. *Letters Addressed from London to Sir Joseph Williamson,* Vol. II, Westminster, 1874, pp. 161-65.

[34] J. M. Jones. *Full Powers and Ratification,* Cambridge, 1949, p. xiii.

[35] H. Butterfield. "Diplomacy," in R. Hatton and M. S. Anderson, eds. *Studies in Diplomatic History,* London, 1970, pp. 360-61.

[36] J. Viner. "Power Versus Plenty as Objectives of Foreign Policy in the Seventeenth and Eighteenth Centuries," *World Politics,* Vol. I, 1948, p. 6, sees power primarily as the ability to conquer and attack and the prestige and influence gained thereby as well as the ability to "maintain national security against external attack."

[37] Great Britain. Historical Manuscripts Commission. *Calendar of the Manuscripts of the Marquis of Bath Preserved at Longleat.* Vol. III, London, 1908, p. 9.

[38] The interests of a ruling family.

[39] Archives des Affaires Etrangères. Paris. Mémoires et documents, Fonds Divers, Sardaigne, Vol. 6.

[40] V. S. Mamatey. *Rise of the Habsburg Empire, 1526-1815*, New York, 1971, p. 67; Other examples are: J. Mollo. *Military Fashion*, New York, 1972, p. 27; R. B. Mowat. *History of European Diplomacy, 1451-1789*, N. P., 1928 [reprinted 1971], Chap. XIX.

[41] The same idea had a different name in the United States where it was called "Manifest Destiny."

[42] G. Zeller. "La Politique extérieure de l'Acien Régime," *L'Information historique*, Vol. I, 1938, p. 15.

CHAPTER III

Ambassadors

Ambassadors in ordinary, plenipotentiaries, extraordinary envoys, nuncios, secretaries of embassy, ambassadors extraordinary, residents! The variety of titles borne by seventeenth century diplomats seems almost endless, especially when two or more titles were given to the same person. One result of this has been that modern students are frequently and justifiably confused about what the various titles signified and how they were related to each other. Unfortunately, any attempt to organize the material results in an appearance of more rationality than was characteristic of early modern reality. Nevertheless, it is necessary to try to bring order out of chaos in this chapter. An appropriate way to start is to examine the meanings of the different diplomatic ranks. Then we can examine the backgrounds of the highest ranking diplomats — the ambassadors. There is, of course, no such person as a "typical" early modern ambassador, but an examination of the career of Jean-Antoine d'Avaux, a Frenchman who served in Venice, the Netherlands, and Sweden will illustrate certain aspects of ambassadors' backgrounds not readily apparent in a general overview. The chapter will end with an examination of the ways ambassadors were chosen and prepared for their positions, what their personalities were like, and how effectively they carried out their duties.

Ranks and Titles

Several problems arise when one reads works like Abraham Van Wicquefort's *The Ambassador and His Functions* published in the mid-seventeenth century and Rousseau de Chamoy's *The Idea of the Perfect Ambassador* written in 1697. Some theoreticians used the word "ambassador" in the same general sense as "diplomat" is used today to refer to all diplomatic representatives, no matter what their title. Others used the word only to refer to those men officially called ambassadors. This confusion in the use of words impairs the usefulness of seventeenth century theoreticians in understanding the meaning of differences in rank. Rousseau de Chamoy, however, does show at least one possible distinction between individuals who held the title of ambassador and those who did not. He defines the "ambassador" "as a public minister chosen by a prince (or a sovereign state) to go in his name to another prince or sovereign state, to negotiate the affairs which the prince commits to his care, and to represent the person of the prince abroad in virtue of the letters of credence, the full powers, and the instructions which the prince has given him." But, the author continues, except for the fact that the "ambassador" actually represents the person of the sovereign, the definition applies equally well to all other ranks of diplomats.[1]

The other problem is that the theoreticians' discussions are concerned more with the differences between "ordinary ambassadors" and "extraordinary ambassadors" than with the relationships between ambassadors and other diplomatic ranks. Unfortunately, there is not even unity in this matter. Wicquefort does not draw any distinction between the two kinds of ambassadors on the grounds that there were no essential differences between them and he says "nothing about one which does not apply equally as well to the other."[2] One could suppose that Wicquefort was simply showing that a distinction which had once been real was no longer valid, but another author whose work was published as late as 1731 argues that there really were distinctions still in existence. La Sarraz du Franquesnay says that princes sent "ordinary ambassadors" to courts where the prince customarily had ambassadors or because the men were destined to stay there several years. Extraordinary ambassdors, he continues, are so called "because the prince who sends them is thereby departing from his ordinary practice, because the object of the mission is only to give some kind of greeting or some uncommon negotiation, or because the sojourn abroad will be short."[3] Obviously, we must look elsewhere for an understanding of the meaning of the different titles given to diplomats in the seventeenth century.

Unfortunately, turning to modern scholars does not help much. Their disagreement reflects the confusion of the early modern age. Some scholars argue that there were but two grades labeled conveniently as "first" or "full" rank and "second" rank. Others refer to three, four or more main grades: 1. ambassadors, 2. envoys, 3. residents, and 4. agents. When there is so much disagreement, the best recourse is to try to discover what the practice actually was in the seventeenth century. It rapidly becomes apparent when reading contemporary correspondence that early modern statesmen in fact divided diplomats into two main groups which the English simply called ministers of the first or second order. The practice was so well established that an English secretary of state was astonished in 1699 when the Portuguese ambassador and the Swedish resident felt it necessary to ask the English government to agree that, when ambassadors met ministers of the second order, the former should have precedence. The secretary noted that the English, of course, concurred but that it really was not necessary to sign an agreement about the matter, the thing in its own nature not requiring it."[4] In this the English were in line with the practice of most seventeenth century courts including Rome, Poland, and

Copenhagen. They all recognized ambassadors as a class apart and lumped the other ranks together. Paris and Vienna, two of the most active courts diplomatically, were beginning to make a distinction between the title of resident and envoy in the last half of the seventeenth century.[5] Since there was universal agreement that ambassadors were indeed a class apart from other diplomats, it seems appropriate to devote the rest of this chapter to them and leave further discussion of lower ranking diplomats to the next chapter.

Even accepting the traditional distinction still leaves several issues of rank which should be resolved. In particular, was there any real distinction in practice between the "ordinary" and the "extraordinary" ambassadors? The weight of modern scholarship seems to accept Wicquefort's judgment that there were no significant differences between the two.[6] In fact, whether there was or not depended primarily on the wishes of the princes who sent and received the ambassadors. The reason so many modern scholars have accepted Wicquefort's claim seems to be that they put special emphasis on Louis XIV's refusal to recognize any difference, and they have assumed that the other states in Europe simply followed his example. In some cases, the assumption of French influence appears accurate as in 1668 when Charles II of England refused to give the newly arrived Venetian ambassador the usual three days' entertainment. The excuse given for this change was that Charles had resolved that in the future he would pay for the entertainment of extraordinary ambassadors but not ordinary ones, since the same custom was observed in France. The objection must immediately be raised that this disproves the assumption that Louis XIV treated ordinary and extraordinary ambassadors the same. The answer is, of course, that Louis did generally treat them the same, but exception could always be made in specific cases.

It also appears that at least some rulers continued well into the last half of the seventeenth century to draw a distinction between the purposes for which they appointed the two kinds of ambassadors. The Dutch, for instance, continued to send extraordinary ambassadors for ceremonial tasks, for important political negotiations, and for missions of much shorter duration that those of ordinary ambassadors, almost exactly the conditions expounded by La Sarraz de Franquesnay.[7] Wicquefort should have been aware of the fact that the Dutch made such a distinction since one of his friends who was an ordinary ambassador wrote him a letter stating that he (the Dutch ordinary ambassador) was negotiating nothing of importance "since important affairs are only confided to extraordinary ambassadors, not ordinary ones."[8] The Swedes made similar distinctions in their use of the word "extraordinary." They believed that sending ordinary ambassadors was generally a sign of friendly relations, and treaties of alliance that they made often contained agreements for reciprocity of such missions. But Sweden's diplomatic contacts were not necessarily or even usually through permanent residents of one kind or another. Unlike most other states which had long before adopted the practice of maintaining permanent diplomatic representation at other courts, Sweden tended to maintain contact through a series of successive extraordinary emissaries and to have resident diplomats stationed at posts abroad only for short periods.[9] Finally, it should be recognized that in many European courts, a distinction was made between ordinary and extraordinary ambassadors in the area of ceremonial, especially in matters of precedence.[10]

The topic of ceremonial leads naturally into the question of the difference between permanent and ceremonial (temporary) missions of ambassadors. Scholars usually treat the two as being quite different even though the title of ambassador was given the diplomat in both types of missions. The point is often made that ceremonial embassies were sent to give congratulations or condolences on births, marriages, or deaths of reigning monarchs or their relatives. Since most of the time abroad was spent in what the twentieth century tends to consider meaningless formalities and ceremonies, scholars have generally ignored them.

Though understandable, this neglect of ceremonial embassies is not always appropriate. There were numerous occasions when a supposedly simple ceremonial mission actually covered a number of serious activities. For instance, the Marquis de Ruvigny's embassy escorting the French fiancée of the king of Portugal to Lisbon in 1666 hid the more serious end of having a sagacious and experienced man observe the situation there. Ruvigny's actual goal was to discover how solidly the king held his throne and to make an estimate about the future of the Braganza dynasty. William III sent a man to Dresden in 1693 obstensibly to present the insignia of the Order of the Garter to the new elector of Saxony. But the true purpose of the mission was to try to persuade the elector to join the Allies in the war against France or, at least, to prevent the creation of a league of neutrals in central Europe.[11] Even the choice of the person who was sent on a ceremonial embassy could be used as a device for getting across a serious message. After the Peace of Ryswick, William III sent the Duke of Saint-Albans to compliment Louis XIV on the marriage of his grandson. The choice showed how secure William was on his throne since Saint-Albans was a nephew of King James II whom William had run out of England.

Ceremonial embassies were considered so important by seventeenth century rulers that even as haughty a monarch as Louis XIV was forced to swallow his pride in order to get the right man to accept the position. In 1688 the Sun King needed a man to congratulate James II on the birth of his son; the man also had to be well acquainted with England so that he would be able to report on the military and political preparations James was making to counter the threat of William of Orange. Philibert de Gramont had married into an English noble family and knew the island kingdom well. He was also known to Louis XIV as a flippant individual who would not even humble himself before the king in person. For instance, one day while Louis was explaining to his entourage the changes that he had made in the park of his chateau, he turned and said: "Do you remember, Monsieur de Gramont, having seen a windmill here yesterday in this spot?" Gramont's response was not very diplomatic: "Certainly, Sire; the mill has disappeared, but the wind is still here." Despite Gramont's rather unsatisfactory attitude, Louis was forced to send him to England on the ceremonial mission simply because he lacked a more suitable candidate.[12] Obviously, anyone who wishes to understand either the political or institutional workings of early modern diplomacy should not overlook the supposedly unimportant ceremonial missions.

The title born by a diplomat was sometimes significant for more than just ceremonial reasons even when it was for a standard permanent mission. But its significance is not always apparent at first glance. For instance, governments which were anxious to improve their status were often quite anxious to receive a high ranking diplomat from an important state. The prestige of the receiving state was increased by such an appointment. For example, in 1670 the secretary of the English mission in Venice wrote: "This state is most ambitiously desirous of having an ambassador here, especially since the loss of Candia [to the Turks] so as to make up in show what they have lost in substance."[13] Of course, the opposite situation was also true. Not all states or princes had the right to give their appointees the exalted title of ambassador. Tradition played an important role in determining who could do so if they wished, but states which were becoming important might acquire the right to use the title. The determining factor was the attitude of the important courts. If the emperor, the kings of Spain, France, Sweden, etc. were willing to accept ambassadors from a prince who had previously not sent them, that was a sign of the prince's growing importance in the international system. On the other hand, declining powers like Venice and Poland were usually able to maintain their right to send ambassadors despite their loss of power.

The pope did not send ambassadors but this was not because he was unimportant or did not have the right to do so. The reason was simply that his diplomats bore a different title and performed religious duties in addition to diplomatic ones. During the Middle Ages, secular rulers had used the Latin term *nuncius* for some of their agents, but by the seventeenth century the term had come to be used exclusively to designate the highest ranking diplomatic representatives of the Roman pontiff. Nuncios were not, of course, accredited to Protestant rulers, but in Catholic courts they were generally recognized as diplomats of the first order, the equivalent (or even superior) of men bearing the title of extraordinary ambassador.[14] But a distinction was made between first and second class nunciatures, the capitals where nuncios served. Rulers whose courts were first class nunciatures could be sure that a nuncio accredited to them would be named a cardinal at the end of his tour of duty. Furthermore, the ruler had the right of approving in advance the man to be selected as nuncio. This right of approval led to arguments between the popes and Vienna, Paris, and Madrid. The distinction between first and second class nunciatures had the same sort of symbolic importance to the receiver as did the reception of an ambassador or lower ranking secular diplomat. King John V of Portugal engaged in a long and ultimately successful struggle to have Lisbon recognized as a first class nunciature. Whether this actually increased his status is questionable, but King John undoubtedly thought it was worth investing years of effort to attain the desired result. Some modern scholars have ignored papal diplomatic practice in the early modern period on the grounds that it was too unconnected with secular diplomacy. But in terms of functions, traditions, and even institutions, nuncios played a full and important role in seventeenth century diplomacy.

"National," Social, and Occupational Backgrounds of Ambassadors

While nationality in the twentieth century sense did not exist in the seventeenth and early eighteenth centuries, the idea does seem to have developed that a monarch's own subjects or citizens of a republic were better suited to serve as diplomats than were foreigners. Nevertheless, cases where governments used foreigners can be found in many seventeenth century states. In some most unusual cases, the diplomat represented his foreign master to his own true master. However, this was rare because the foreign prince would be especially hesitant to charge him with significant responsibilities. More importantly, few rulers were willing to accept their own subjects as diplomats accredited to themselves. Rather, they tended to appoint non-subjects to third countries. Examples abound. One Frenchman moved to Denmark, entered the service of King Christian V as his private secretary, became secretary of the Danish legation in London, and later served Denmark at Hamburg and The Hague. Another Frenchman represented the elector of Prussia in Sweden and later in a mediation for the king of Denmark. These two examples were chosen deliberately to emphasize the fact that the French and, to a slightly lesser extent the Swiss, were the "nationalities" most frequently utilized by foreign princes for their diplomatic services. This was at least partially the result of the revocation of the Edict of Nantes which sent French Protestants fleeing abroad while the Swiss were plagued by the perennial poverty of their homeland. But Louis XIV also used foreigners such as a German in Sweden and Hamburg and an Italian at Florence. Two points should be noted about this use of foreigners: 1. these men usually served as lower ranking diplomats rather than as ambassadors, and 2. they were often naturalized in their new country before taking up diplomatic duties.[15]

Under some speical circumstances, non-subjects served in the highest diplomatic positions. This was the case when the state they served was non-national itself such as the papacy whose nuncios were seldom Romans (although usually Italians) or the Holy Roman Empire. For instance, Franz Paul von Lisola entered the emperor's service when he was twenty-five years old and, during the next thirty-five years, held diplomatic posts in Prussia, Poland, Spain, Portugal, the Netherlands, and England. His "nationality" was uncertain to say the least. Italian by name, he was a Spanish subject born in the Franche-Comté which meant that he was French in education and language although his career was Austrian.[16] Emperor Leopold also used Spanish subjects as diplomats after the death of Carlos II, when Leopold claimed that his own son was the true king of Spain.

Perhaps the best example of how special circumstances could lead to the use of foreigners as diplomats is England. Under Charles II and James II most English diplomats were native Englishmen. After the Glorious Revolution, William III often chose Dutchmen, refugee French Huguenots, and Swiss Protestants. For the most important diplomatic mission of his reign, the embassy to France in 1697, William chose a Dutchman, William Bentinck, who had been given the English title of Earl of Portland. It has been argued that William hesitated to use Englishmen because he could not trust them and also because he is supposed to have believed "that no Englishman could keep a secret." Gradually, as William came to know his English subjects better, he seems to have chosen more native-born English servants. He was pushed in this direction by the increasing jealousy in England of foreigners who received diplomatic appointments from a king who was himself regarded as a foreigner and was even called "Dutch William." In 1700 William was forced to cancel the appointment of a Dutchman as English envoy to Brandenburg because of murmurs in England. In 1701 a Parliamentary Inquiry into the diplomatic service accused the government of extravagance and of employing foreigners. The government claimed that the English-born Dr. Aglionby was the English envoy at Madrid when that post was really held by a Dutchman. After the accession of Anne, the decision to use only Englishmen as diplomats and not to give English credentials to foreigners was widely applauded in England.[17]

The "nationalistic" pressures on William III to use Englishmen were similar to those found in many other European states, although how much the pressures were truly nationalistic and how much they were the result of natives' wanting positions for themselves cannot be determined. In any case, the same sort of pressures were found in other European states. In Sweden, for example, foreigners were still widely used in the mid-seventeenth century, but during the reigns of Charles XI and Charles XII such practice became the exception. In 1720 an ordinance explicitly stated the principle that diplomatic posts were henceforth to be restricted to Swedes.[18]

As a curiosity, it can be noted that there were regional preferences in the selection of diplomats in some states. The province of Holland dominated the Netherlands in the seventeenth century, and most Dutch diplomats came from there. Although the predominance of Castile in the Spanish Empire had been weakened, there was a predominance of Castilians in the Spanish diplomatic service, although other "nationalities" were not excluded. Scots were actually prevented from holding any kind of office under the English Crown in the late seventeenth century. However, after the Act of the Union was passed in 1706, a number of Scots became diplomats. They were a very important element of British diplomacy in the eighteenth century.[19] Other seventeenth century states such as France were sufficiently homogeneous that regional divisions did not play a significant role in the selections of diplomats.

In thinking about the backgrounds of early modern ambassadors, several other questions come to mind such as what was their social position, were they professionals, and what other kinds of jobs if any did they hold? The problem of social standing is complicated by the fact that there is no generally accepted terminology for describing early modern society. Words like middle class and bourgeoisie just do not fit the seventeenth century very well. Thus we are forced to use early modern terms rather than modern concepts like "class" which seem so important today. The problem is further complicated by the fact that, with the exception of France and England, very little work has been done on the social standing of ambassadors. Thus we are forced to depend on scattered references which may well merely indicate impressions rather than reality. But the scattered references are enough to indicate that there were some substantial differences in the ambassadors from various countries. Perhaps the one common denominator was that, whenever possible, ambassadors were chosen from the ranks of the nobility. One theoretician gave a good explanation of why this was so: the receiving prince would feel slighted or scorned if he were sent an ambassador of low standing. Furthermore, since it was the function of an ambassador to represent the person of his sovereign and thus his grandeur, it was simply assumed that a noble could do this while a commoner could not.[20]

There were exceptions of course. Dutch ambassadors were usually chosen from the non-noble regents. With few exceptions papal nuncios were bishops or archbishops, although they might hold nothing more than the title of a see which was actually controlled by the Turks. While many nuncios were heredi-tary nobles, others were not. Most other countries used nobles almost exclu-sively. Spain depended largely on the Castilian nobility, while the English monarchs, even the somewhat democratic William III, usually used nobles. Under Queen Anne English diplomats were largely drawn from the relations and dependents of the ministers. But Matthew Prior, who was definitely a client of several important ministers and who was well qualified to serve as an ambassador to France, was never seriously considered for the position because of his lack of pedigree. All French ambassadors under Louis XIV were nobles.[21]

Within the nobility, several groups traditionally served as ambassadors. In France these were the high clergy, judicial and administrative officers (the nobility of the robe), and military officers (the nobility of the sword). Some ministers argued that secular rulers should not appoint ecclesiastics as dip-lomats because their loyalties would be divided. For instance, a Catholic priest's first loyalty might be to the pope. Nevertheless, Louis XIV made use of the clergy for ambassadorial missions to Catholic countries although never to the papacy. They played a substantial though minor role throughout his reign. A large proportion of Louis XIV's ambassadors were appointed from the ranks of the nobility of the robe in the 1670s and 1680s. As the reign wore on, the proportion of military men grew even larger until two thirds of the appoint-ments in the last five years of the reign were men of the sword. Supposedly, this change occurred because the Sun King came to think that men of the sword were "properer" ambassadors than the robe and that the sword served him better.[22] The increasing use of military men as diplomats by the French was paralleled by a similar change in England to the point that after 1709 every major English diplomatic post was held by a military officer. It may be that the anti-robe feeling found in the correspondence of military men serving as diplomats[23] was shared by some monarchs and that this led to the change, but there is no evidence on the matter. Nor is it even known if the shift to using military men occurred in countries other than England and France.

The fact that ambassadors were drawn from other occupations raises the question of whether diplomacy was seen as a career in the seventeenth century. In general the answer seems to be no, at least for individuals who served as ambassadors. There were any number of lower ranking individuals who re-mained at a diplomatic post for decades or who held a number of different positions over a long period of years.[24] But a large majority of the ambassadors seem to have taken just one or two diplomatic missions and then returned to their old career at home. Furthermore, if the example of France applies to other countries, ambassadors generally did not try to find diplomatic positions for their sons but instead tried to place them in military, judicial, or administrative careers. As a result, at least in France, there were seldom the constellations of members of the same family found in diplomacy which were so common in other areas of early modern French government. One of the major reasons for this relative lack of career interest in diplomacy was its instability. Unlike the administration and army where offices were often venal, ambassadorial positions were not purchased and were subject to instant disappearance. This was particularly true of England where by the latter years of Anne's reign the tradition was established that a change in secretaries of state or of ministries should lead to the dropping of earlier diplomatic appointees and replacing them by friends of the new Government.[25] Ambassadorial positions were equally uncertain in other courts.

The inevitable exceptions of the early modern period should also be pointed out. For instance, members of the Venetian diplomatic service tended to be career diplomats who spent long years on missions abroad. Within the major European diplomatic services, there were a number of men who can only be referred to as "career diplomats." Franz Paul von Lisola, a career diplomat for Emperor Leopold, has already been mentioned,[26] but there were others like the Spaniard Pedro Ronquillo who served in Poland and England or the French Count d'Avaux.

Jean-Antoine d'Avaux, A French Ambassador

Jean-Antoine de Mesmes, Count d'Avaux, or "Figuriborum"[27] as some of his friends affectionately referred to him, was a member of an important French "robe" family. Like many other such families in the late seventeenth century, the nobility of the de Mesmes was of "recent" origin. They could only trace their genealogy back two centuries with some degree of accuracy, although, again like other families, they "discovered" that their ancestors had been noble at the time of King Philip-Augustus in the twelfth century. The more recent de Mesmes had acquired important positions in the Parlement of Paris. Jean-Antoine's uncle, who also bore the title of Count d'Avaux, held numerous important French diplomatic posts during the Thirty Years War including service as a French representative at Münster for the Peace of Westphalia. Jean-Antoine was born in 1640. He became a counselor to the Parlement of Paris and a Master of Requests and unofficially accompanied a ceremonial embassy to England before receiving his first diplomatic appointment as French ambassador to Venice in 1672. Since his father was still alive, Jean-Antoine still bore the name Count d'Irval. But during his embassy to Venice his father died, his older brother acquired the more prestigious title of President de Mesmes, and Jean-Antoine took the title of Count d'Avaux, a name that was to be well known in diplomatic circles for more than thirty years.

D'Avaux's two year stay in Venice was not particularly important in diplomatic terms; he seems to have spent much of his time arranging to send artists to France, inquiring into the techniques of glass and lace manufacturing, and acquiring paintings and books for people like Colbert. But his diplomatic experience was undoubtedly a factor in his selection as one of the three French plenipotentiaries to the peace conference at Nijmegen which was gathering to put an end to Louis XIV's Dutch War. During the more than two years he spent in this Dutch town, d'Avaux was able to make a number of important contacts among the more than twenty ambassadors gathered there. He also started to acquire the knowledge of northern and western European countries, statesmen, and French policy which was to serve him so well during the next three decades. And he had the coveted honor of signing two treaties on behalf of France. The signing of the Franco-Dutch peace treaty in 1678 far from ended all points of conflict, particularly when the growing influence of the Prince of Orange in the government of the Netherlands threatened the renewal of war even before the treaty was ratified. Consequently, to the surprise and perhaps dissatisfaction of some Frenchmen who had hoped to get the appointment for themselves or for a relative (particularly Secretary of State Pomponne), the experienced Count d'Avaux was appointed as Louis XIV's extraordinary ambassador to the Netherlands.

The embassy did not start very auspiciously. In a most unorthodox move, d'Avaux was ordered to proceed to The Hague even though the Dutch had not yet ratified the peace treaty. His quick journey led nowhere as he could not be officially received and, under the circumstances, few men were willing to talk with him. The beginning of his embassy was made even less promising by the fact that his appointment was widely believed to be provisional. Nevertheless, d'Avaux was destined to remain ten years in this post which was often a nerve center of French diplomacy at a time when Louis XIV's dominant position in "international" affairs seemed almost unchallenged. Following the Sun King's orders, d'Avaux allied himself to the republican leaders who opposed William of Orange. Unfortunately, this had the effect of severely limiting his effectiveness because William soon made it clear that he would regard anyone who had contact with the French ambassador as an enemy. The conflict became so intense that d'Avaux even recommended armed intervention to reestablish republican control of the Dutch government, an idea which Louis XIV fortunately did not take seriously. It was at this time that the infamous stealing of letters from one of d'Avaux's couriers occurred. William used the intercepted documents to try to destroy d'Avaux's cooperation with the republicans by exposing the latter's "treasonable activities." D'Avaux publicy cried out against the criminal act of stealing the letters and added for good measure that they were deciphered incorrectly. Curiously, the incident resulted in increased cooperation between the ambassador and the republican leaders. Later d'Avaux warned Louis of William's plans to invade England. After William's departure, d'Avaux was ordered to request his passports and return to France at the end of November, 1688. The War of the League of Augsburg was beginning.

After his return to the French court, d'Avaux scarcely had an opportunity to renew old acquaintances and become reacquainted with his homeland before he was appointed as Louis XIV's ambassador to James II on the latter's ill-fated attempt to regain his throne by invading Ireland. The enterprise was brought to an end at the Battle of the Boyne, the battle whose anniversary still serves as an excuse for conflict between northern Irish Catholics and northern Irish Protestants today. The sight of oranges (as in apples and oranges) and orange flags is still enough to make Irish Catholics see red. Fortunately for d'Avaux, Louis did not hold him responsible for the disaster and even went so far as to invite him regularly for those coveted visits to the Chateau of Marly which showed that a man was in the Sun King's good graces.

During the early years of the War of the League of Augsburg, the number of important French diplomatic positions abroad declined precipitously and d'Avaux remained at home. He fit well into the French court for he was a very pleasant person. Saint-Simon described him as handsome, polished, gallant, and with a graceful bearing, all desirable qualities for one of the Sun King's ambassadors. His ability as a skilled diplomat is suggested by a description of him by one of the French secretaries of state: "Monsieur d'Avaux is a true genius and is very good tempered; he takes the large perspective, has much shrewdness and great experience in public affairs. He understands perfectly the interests of the princes of Europe, and he writes and speaks well." Of course, d'Avaux was not always such a paragon of diplomatic virtues. He occasionally lost his temper, and his suggestion that Louis XIV attack the Netherlands in 1688 hardly shows that he took a large perspective in international affairs. But there is no doubt that Louis XIV thought he was a more than satisfactory diplomat because in November, 1692, the king named him ambassador to Sweden.

until March of the following year. Despite innumerable difficulties, of which his own financial problems were but one, he succeeded in reestablishing fairly good relations between Louis XIV and Charles XI, particularly in relation to the Swedish mediation for the Peace of Ryswick. His health was broken but he stayed in Stockholm until the Swedes signed a treaty of alliance guaranteeing the peace. He was then allowed to return home to enjoy his honors including the position of Counsellor of State in Ordinary which the king had given him while he was in Sweden.

In 1701, despite his advanced age, d'Avaux was once more called upon to serve his king — by replacing the ill French ambassador at The Hague. The political situation was tense because Louis XIV had recently accepted the will of Carlos II naming Louis's grandson Philip as heir to the Spanish Empire. D'Avaux was given full powers to treat with the States General, but he soon recognized that the key to the political situation lay in London, not The Hague. Immediately after his arrival, the States General recognized Philip as King of Spain, but his successes stopped there. He returned to his old advice that Louis should attack the Dutch as soon and as strongly as possible in order to forestall their preparations for war. D'Avaux was recalled and took leave of the States General in August. He was to have no more official positions abroad, although he was called upon to give advice in France and engaged in a few behind-the-scenes attempts to establish a separate peace between France and the Netherlands. He died in Paris in 1709 at the age of sixty-nine, a man who can truly be said to have been a career diplomat who was a credit to his emerging profession. Despite the existence of men like d'Avaux, we must remember that, in general, diplomacy "remained an irregular occupation for amateurs and aristocrats" until the end of the *ancien régime*.[28]

Preparation, Personalities, And Effectiveness

Today ambassadorial appointments are widely sought after. Americans have been known to contribute thousands of dollars to presidential candidates in the hope of being made ambassador even to minor countries like Luxembourg. But was there such a desire in the seventeenth century? The theoretician Rousseau de Chamoy certainly thought so. He argued that men sought ambassadorships:

> because of the honor attached to the position, the quality and importance of the problems which are confided in him, the personal relations which he has with the princes and ministers of state where he serves, the opportunities afforded him to become known to his own sovereign, and the examples whereby ambassadors have been able to gain the highest dignities of the state and the church after their service.[29]

There are numerous examples of individuals who requested such appointments. But the overwhelming impression one gets from reading private and even some official correspondence is that offers of ambassadorial appointments were more likely to be turned down than accepted. Even when they were accepted, the reason was as likely to be because of pressure from the prince or ministers as the desire to be an ambassador.

The reasons given for refusals were similar throughout Europe, and many of them were quite valid. Perhaps the main problem was the financial burden which an embassy imposed on an individual. Even if his salary were going to be sufficient to pay his expenses, he seldom received it promptly. It was not unusual for a man asked to undertake a mission to refuse to do so until the arrears from an earlier one were paid. But, whether a man represented Denmark, the Netherlands, Venice or the emperor, the embassy often cost the envoy more than he was paid. In fact, fear of financial complications was probably the most important reason for refusal. For instance, even at the critical point in the life of Simon Arnauld de Pomponne when he was about to be rehabilitated and forgiven for earlier transgressions against Louis XIV by undertaking the embassy to Sweden, Pomponne refused the position when he was told that his pay would be only 6,000 écus a year. He said that if he had to choose between displeasing the king and impoverishing his children, he would choose the former. Pomponne finally agreed to go when his salary was raised to 8,000 écus and he was authorized to maintain his embassy on a modest scale in regard to his household and equipage.

There were other equally understandable reasons why embassies were refused. One of Matthew Prior's favorite sayings was: "Men are forgot when abroad." This was often the case! In courts of absolute monarchs, the prince himself was the source of most benefits, and being out of his sight meant that a man was dependent upon others to put forward his requests for offices and emoluments. Potential ambassadors often feared that a friend would not press their cause so strongly when they were not there to put face-to-face pressure on the supporter. The same Arnauld de Pomponne mentioned earlier illustrates the problem and the remedy he tried to take for it after he had moved from the embassy in Sweden to the same in the Netherlands. In 1670 Pomponne requested permission to leave The Hague in order to meet LouisXIV who was at Lille, although he hoped "for no other advantage from this trip than that of being seen." [30] As it turned out, Pomponne actually received tremendous benefits from his embassies. He was appointed secretary of state for foreign affairs while still abroad. Regents in the Netherlands hesitated to go abroad as diplomats because of the danger that they would lose their influence in their town or province. An even worse problem than not getting benefits was that ambassadors were peculiarly vulnerable to attacks by their enemies at home. Potential ambassadors feared that if their mission were not going well or even if it were, they might suffer because of their not being able to defend themselves in person before the monarch.

Ambassadorial positions were also refused on grounds of poor health, inexperience, and unwillingness to leave current duties. Some men avoided service simply by failing to depart after their appointment. Some states, like Venice, found it so difficult to find ambassadors in the seventeenth century that they resorted to extreme means to force men to go. But such devices did not always work. When one Venetian noble was named ambassador to France in the late 1690's, he simply declared that he preferred to pay the fine levied on him and to suffer banishment for refusing rather than accept the appointment.[31] His choice is more understandable when one recognizes that, for many seventeenth century men, an embassy itself was nothing more than what the Dutch statesman John de Witt called "a gilded exile." When the English Lord Dartmouth was told that Queen Anne wished him to become ambassador to Venice, Dartmouth replied that "if the Queen thought it for her service that I should be out of the way, I need not go so far, having a house in Staffordshire, that I could easily and willingly retire to."[32] Dartmouth's lack of interest was not surprising because, as was common in other courts, the reason most nominees agreed to serve was to put the government "under an obligation to provide for them at home." Dartmouth was already well established at home so he had no need for diplomatic experience since, as one of his fellow Englishmen wrote, "Foreign services may sometimes prove a good stirrup but never a good saddle."[33] In other words, for most men ambassadorships were a means to an end, not the end itself.

Despite the difficulties involved, governments did of course eventually find men who would serve as ambassadors. But it is appropriate to ask a number of questions about these "amateurs and aristocrats" who held such sensitive positions. What kind(s) of training, if any, did they have to prepare them for diplomatic work? How did they know how they should behave? What kinds of personalities did they have? Can any generalizations about their effectiveness be made?

Recent studies of the modernization process in early modern governments have shown a key distinction between modern and premodern bureaucracies. Modern bureaucracies commonly require specific pre-entry training before an individual can acquire a position whereas premodern bureaucracies rarely require such training, relying instead on inservice training.[34] This inservice training worked quite effectively in some parts of seventeenth century governments, particularly the armed services. The different ranks of navy and army officers provided a natural hierarchy in which individuals could be given training and increasing responsibility as they moved up. Unfortunately, in diplomacy there was no recognized hierarchy through which individuals moved. Whereas generals and marshals had with few exceptions moved up through the officer ranks in a somewhat regular way, few ambassadors had previously served as envoys, residents, or diplomatic secretaries.[35] The high social status required of ambassadors precluded the possibility that they could accept the low level diplomatic jobs which would have given them the opportunity to learn by apprenticeship. Ambassadors often attached young nobles to their households as unofficial junior diplomats. But the practice was too haphazard and the ambassadors too unwilling and too pressed for time to be able to make the inservice training effective. Therefore around the end of the seventeenth and the beginning of the eighteenth centuries, a number of governments created "schools" with the specific responsibility of preparing men to become diplomats. In other words, there were attempts to move the training of diplomats from the "premodern" to the "modern" level, although the statesmen involved would have been unlikely to use such words to describe their acts. They merely recognized the problems caused by the lack of training of ambassadors and tried to do something to improve it — one more example of the role practical necessity played in the development of diplomatic institutions and practices.

Perhaps the most famous attempt to establish a training institution was that of Torcy, the French Secretary of State for Foreign Affairs, who persuaded the Sun King to establish the Political Academy *(Académie Politique)* in 1712. Previous efforts to create such an institution had been hindered by the exigencies of the War of the Spanish Succession, but Torcy was finally able to scrape together the funds to establish scholarships for some young men and to allow others to participate at their own expense. The Academy was inadequately funded, however, and too dependent on the support of one man. When Torcy was dismissed shortly after the death of Louis XIV, the Political Academy itself was disbanded. But Torcy's institution was hardly unique. There had been a politico-military school founded in the reign of Philip II of Spain which trained Spanish diplomats, but it had petered out by the reign of Philip IV. There were other training institutions established about the same time as Torcy's. The Pontifical Ecclesiastical Academy in which churchmen who are destined for the papal diplomatic service still receive their training was founded at Rome in 1701 by Pope Clement XI. A few years later, Peter the Great of Russia began to send young men at his expense to Königsberg and other places to learn languages and be otherwise prepared for diplomacy. In 1747 Frederick II of Prussia set up a temporary training school to produce men for subordinate diplomatic posts.[36] Although, with the exception of the papal Academy, these attempts were ephemeral, it is worthwhile to examine their curricula briefly in order to discover what areas of study were thought to be important.

The long lists of subjects with which some early modern theoreticians thought diplomats should be acquainted suggest that an ambassador had to be a "Renaissance Man" who was well instructed in everything from religion to natural philosophy, from literature to politics. These lists were essentially the same as those drawn up for any of the men who held public trusts (ministers) and had little effect on their performance. But the practical statesmen like Torcy who were involved in the establishment of the various "political academies" were quite aware of the subjects which would be of practical value to aspiring diplomats. The theoretical manuals themselves which were designed to serve as "textbooks" for aspiring diplomats were available, including such famous ones as De Vera's volume entitled *The Perfect Ambassador* published in Spanish in 1620 but best known in the French edition of 1642 and Abraham van Wicquefort's *The Ambassador and His Functions*. But there is little or no evidence that they were included in the curricula of the academies. Torcy assumed that the works on international law (or what was then called "public law") by men such as Grotius or Puffendorf were valuable.[37] "Modern" diplomatic history was to be studied by making extracts from the actual documents deposited in the diplomatic archives. Foreign languages were the third subject Torcy considered important. Statesmen in other countries agreed with this selection, especially the emphasis on languages. In fact, the only significant English attempt to train diplomats in the early modern period emphasized the study of French and Italian. The scheme established chairs of modern history at Oxford and Cambridge Universities in 1724 whose occupants were to appoint and pay the language teachers. The program was moribund within three years but the importance of language study was clearly recognized. Since these attempts to provide formal diplomatic schooling occurred so late in our period and since they had so little actual effect, it is appropriate to ask: how did ambassadors in fact learn how to behave during most of our period?

A most important factor determining the way an ambassador behaved abroad was his experience at his own court. A great lord who was used to a position of importance at home could not be expected to become a whimpering supplicant at another. Indeed, this was one of the reasons why individuals of high social standing were thought to be desirable as ambassadors! But any man of importance would have observed the behavior of diplomats at his own prince's court and have formulated certain assumptions about how to behave. Indeed, many seventeenth century ambassadors seem to have formed opinions similar to those expressed in a nineteenth century drama where a pretend diplomat says: "An ambassador must . . . always give the impression of being busy. . . ." or "Madame, a diplomat fears nothing!"

Advice on how to behave officially was often included in the instructions ambassadors were given before departure and in conversations with the sovereign or his ministers.[38] They also could get practical advice from their predecessors and others who knew the foreign court well. In some cases there were even individuals like secretaries abroad who could help. For instance, Louis XIV maintained a sort of "master of ceremonies for the French embassy" in Rome for more than forty years, one of whose primary functions was to advise French ambassadors how to behave when they arrived. These kinds of advice were not sufficient for a diplomat who had to discover several different modes of behavior if he were to be successful in his mission. For example, ambassadors had to decide when to draw a distinction between the behavior required of them in their public and private characters. There was, of course, a difference between the two. As Wicquefort pointed out, ambassadors are the greatest actors in the world because they play such important roles, but sometimes they must drop the role and behave like ordinary human beings. The difficulty was to know when to play each role. An English theoretician wrote in 1730, "It is rare to find an ambassador who can readily distinguish on every proper occasion, his public from his private character." He goes on:

> An ambassador is not at liberty to resent an injury done to his private character in any degree; but every affront or indecency offered to his public character must be strongly insisted on [objected to] until an adequate satisfaction be made agreeable to his instructions and supported by the law and custom of nations.[39]

Making a mistake in such a situation might spell the difference between the success or failure of his mission. But this sort of behavior problem was extremely simple compared to some of the other occasions when a slight nuance of expression or phrasing could be disastrous. In these cases it was the true abilities and personalities of the ambassadors which were important, not any formal instructions they might have been given.

Any generalization about the personalities of seventeenth century ambassadors is subject to the same weaknesses (and perhaps strengths) as are generalizations about "national character" today. Obviously it is foolish to say that all Germans like to obey orders, that all Americans are expert mechanics, or that all Frenchmen are romantic. Yet anyone who has lived and/or traveled in these countries is aware that, although the generalizations do not fit everyone, there are enough differences between nationalities to give the stereotypes at least a modicum of accuracy. The same thing is true of generalizations about the personalities of seventeenth century ambassadors. Thus, a few examples might serve to give an impression which is valid for many others.

Stereotypes existed in the seventeenth century just as today. A particularly interesting example is a description of the French by an Englishman:

> They are very exact here in all the trifling duties of life. People take a great deal of care to inform themselves about a person's health after a small fatigue [illness], and it is a point of civility to send him a small compliment upon it. An honest man is not more scrupulous in returning a pledge left in his hands than a Frenchman is in returning a visit. To make and receive visits is one of their chief occupations, and they think their time well employed in that way. A life which they pass with company is, in their opinion, a life agreeably spent and in order. Man, they say, is made for society. . . . They almost think every man an owl or a philosopher who has any inclination for solitude, not being able to comprehend how it is possible for anyone not to be pleased with conversation where a great many polite and obliging things are said. They are likewise very watchful for any opportunity of employing a thousand little far-fetched ways [of behaving] that have become natural as it were custom and by which they pretend to please. All this put together makes up that magnificent name which they call the *Art of Living* . . . which they look upon as the great concern of life. They don't seem to live for any other end.[40]

If this description of the French is accurate, it is no wonder that French ambassadors had a reputation for being among the most successful in that calling of all Europeans. The personality traits described here can almost be called the essence of a good early modern ambassador.

Without putting too much faith in stereotypes, it is perhaps instructive to imagine how effective a Frenchman would be in Spain. There it was important for a man to be punctual in returning visits and

> extraordinarily humble in his comportment for the Spaniards, more than any other people, love to be respected in their own homes and cannot abide an insolent carriage in a stranger. On the other side, courtesy and moderation will gain mightily upon them. . . . Moreover, a respectful and humble carriage is a mighty advantage to gain intelligence and knowledge; it is the key that opens the breast and unlocks the heart of anyone: He who looks downward sees the stars in the water, but he who looks only upward cannot see the water in the stars; therefore there is much more to be gained by humility than otherwise.[41]

Obviously a French ambassador would do well in Spain. But consider the problems an English diplomat would have there if a French generalization about the English were true:

> Generally speaking this nation is haughty, arrogant, suspicious, and so vain

that I don't even think there can be any vanity left for the Spanish. Their conduct is insufferable to all gallant men. It is necessary to be very modest and very docile in order to live even passably well with those people who at least appear to be respectable. . . .[42]

Without pushing the thought too far, it might not be inappropriate to say that at least some of the conflicts between states might have been a reflection of the clash of cultures which occurred between an ambassador and his hosts abroad.

On the other hand, it may be that the nuances of behavior which spelled the difference between success and failure were not culturally based nor could they be taught. Rather, successful behavior may have depended more on the personalities of the men themselves than on their national background, an argument strengthened by the fact that all countries had both successful and unsuccessful diplomats. For instance, the Austrian ambassador Franz Paul von Lisola was generally recognized as succeeding almost wherever he went. The same can scarcely be said for von Harrach, the Austrian ambassador in Spain at the end of the seventeenth century, who was competing with the French ambassador Harcourt to influence the Spanish court in the succession question. The stiff, phlegmatic Harrach, filled with the pride and punctiliousness typical of the imperial court, crudely expounded the Austrian claims to the Spanish throne and alienated the German born Queen of Spain who was expected to support her Austrian relatives. Harcourt, on the other hand, "employed the silent influence of bribes, promises, and personal flattery, and was ably seconded by his lady, a woman of the most accomplished and winning manners. His house was open to all; and his table, at once the scene of elegant conviviality and princely magnificence, attracted even those who were adverse to his cause, and formed a striking contrast with the formal and inhospitable establishment of the imperial ambassador."[43] Whether the eventual French success was due completely or even largely to Harcourt's finesse is impossible to determine, but it certainly had some role. Of course, there were also unsuccessful French ambassadors. The count of La Vauguyon who also served in Spain seems to have been a rather unsympathetic person who was furthermore an unscrupulous fellow in all senses of the term.

Perhaps it is appropriate to mention some aspects of the personality of one other French ambassador whose good sense and ability to understand men and their foibles must have stood him good stead abroad. One day during a game of backgammon Louis XIV challenged one of his opponent's plays. He demanded the opinion of the courtiers present but they maintained an embarrassed silence. Suddenly the king saw the Count de Gramont, an ex-ambassador, and cried:

— "Ah, you are going to settle this!"

And the king signaled Gramont to come closer. Immediately, the Count declared:

— "Sire, you have lost!"

— "What?" exclaimed the king. "I haven't even explained it to you yet. . ."

— "That doesn't matter, Sire. Don't you see that if the play was even doubtful these gentlemen would not have failed to champion your case?"

Such outspokenness could have been disastrous in an ambassador, but Gramont was a sufficiently good judge of men that he knew when he could get away with outrageous acts of speech and when he could not. Another example involved a Monsieur de Béchameil who thought he looked like Gramont's nephew who was one of the handsomest men at the French court. Béchameil was extremely vain about the supposed resemblance. One day Gramont bet that he could give Béchameil a kick and that Béchameil would thank him for it. The wager was taken. Gramont casually walked up behind his victim who was strolling in the garden and gave him a kick in the seat of the pants. Béchameil turned around furiously, but Gramont, with a charming smile, said quickly:

— "Oh! It's you, Monsieur? I am so sorry! I thought you were my nephew! There is such a resemblance . . ."

Béchameil, consoled and delighted, smiled and thanked Gramont whose wager was won.[44] Obviously Gramont fit in well at courts which, like that of France, enjoyed practical jokes, but he had to hold himself in check when on his embassies to Cromwell and later James II.

Athough an ambassador's personality was important in determining whether he fit in at the court to which he was accredited, the purpose of his mission was not only to get along with his host. He was also to carry out negotiations, discover information, and do other necessary diplomatic acts.[45] This raises the question: how effective (or ineffective) were seventeenth century ambassadors? There is no simple answer. Goals were often so complicated and involved or even so hidden in inuendo and unrecorded oral instructions that it is next to impossible to determine whether an ambassador was successful in any specific negotiation, much less in general. Furthermore, since diplomatic goals of different states were often in conflict, the success of one ambassador often meant the failure of another even if both were excellent men. Thus it is dangerous to assume that failure of a policy meant that the ambassador was ineffective any more than that a policy's success meant that he was effective. It is better to ask whether an ambassador was able to discover accurate information, make accurate judgments about his host's policies, write his reports carefully and regularly, and fulfill his other diplomatic responsibilities.

It is better to ask whether an ambassador was able to discover accurate information, make accurate judgments about his host's policies, write his reports carefully and regularly, and fulfill his other diplomatic responsibilities. Using this criteria, some ambassadors were obvious failures. What other judgment can be rendered about the papal nuncio at Paris in 1676? This nuncio loved his leisure. He did not write or even dictate his letters but merely ordered his secretary to write on certain topics. He did not even read letters addressed to him, but simply had an assistant summarize their contents. What must be said about the effectiveness of the Dutch ambassador to France who reported about a meeting of Louis XIV and some of his ambassadors which was going to take place in 1671? The Dutchman wrote that he had no fear at all about the results of the meeting when in fact it was at this time that Louis XIV firmly decided to go to war against the Netherlands.[46] A recent study of French diplomats in Vienna shows how even the men who were reputed to have been the best diplomats of the seventeenth century completely misread and misinterpreted the condition of the emperor's army. In 1682 Emperor Leopold had begun to create a modern professional army which fought quite successfully against the Turks. The Frenchmen in Vienna were so impressed by the confusion of the Austrian officials that they attributed Austrian successes either to the presence of the emperor's German allies or the weakness of the Turks. The French government was thus able to dismiss the possibility that Austrian troops would do well in a future war against France. It is true that the French government itself welcomed and shared this interpretation, but it does not excuse the failures of the men on the scene in Vienna.[47] French ambassadors in England were also lulled by their own experience in a way which hindered their understanding of the role England could or would play in international relations. They were able to recognize that, unlike France, government in England depended largely on the court and Parliament, and they observed these quite well. The ambassadors were unable to extend beyond these boundaries to discover the vital forces and resources which were so important for England's later role in international relations. They shared this failure with most seventeenth century ambassadors who tended not to believe that such things as economics were matters of importance. It can even be said that they shared the failure, if such it be, with their whole society. With the exception of England, the Netherlands, and Venice, most countries' social morés assumed that men as high born as ambassadors should not deal with such lower class activities as commerce and industry.

An ambassador was particularly expected to be accurate about whether or not war, especially involving his own country, was going to break out. As might be expected, the results were disastrous when ambassadors failed in this. Even a cursory reading in the diplomatic and political correspondence of 1671 and early 1672 shows that it was common knowledge throughout Europe that France and England were going to attack the Netherlands. For instance, the Venetian ambassador in Spain reported in January, 1672, that the French ambassador spoke publicly of "the irrevocable attack" of his master against Holland.[48] Yet throughout most of 1671, the Dutch ambassador in Paris refused to believe that the attack would actually come. The Dutch back home seemed to be guilty of the same act of sticking their collective heads in the sand and ignoring the coming war. But, before criticizing the Dutch too strongly, we should remember that rumors of war were a constant part of conversation among diplomats and other people in the seventeenth century, and the rumors often did not come true. For instance, an English diplomat recorded a conversation he had with Prince William of Orange in May 1680: "At night the Prince took me aside and talked of all our affairs. He begins to think that it is very likely the King of France will fall upon Flanders this summer." [49] Many other individuals agreed with the Prince, but of course Louis did not go to war against the Spanish Netherlands in 1680. What this means is that we must be very careful when attributing foresight to ambassadors who reported that they expected war to break out and then it did. In the case of Louis XIV, almost everyone was always expecting him to go to war, even when he had no intention of doing so. Finally, ambassadors who were cautious might well have predicted war even when they really did not expect it. After all, a diplomat who warned of war when it did not break out was much less likely to be punished than a diplomat who did not predict war when it did really occur.

One final question about seventeenth century ambassadors should be examined — how faithfully did they carry out the orders they received? On the surface, obeying orders would appear to be a crucially important sign of diplomats' effectiveness or at least the effectiveness of their state's diplomatic machinery. But the men who wrote theoretical works about diplomacy were on solid ground when they qualified the general principle. They recognized that occasionally the man on location had to decide that he should not carry out certain orders. For example, Wicquefort wrote: "The ambassador should not fail to carry out promptly the orders of his Prince when they are expressed and reiterated unless he is sure that it would cause more damage and that he would make himself more criminal by carrying them out than by failing to obey them." [50] Whether they read the theoreticians or not, a number of ambassadors did decide not to obey orders on occasion. For example, Jean-Antoine d'Avaux[51] became very nervous during the first four days of June, 1684, because despite explicit and repeated instructions to deliver a memoir to the government of Amsterdam before the first of June, he had not done so. D'Avaux held back for reasons which he explained very fully in a letter to Louis XIV on June 3. The primary reason was that he believed it would be better to hold off delivering the memoir telling how Louis intended to treat the town of Luxemburg after he took it until after Louis actually took the town. Fortunately for d'Avaux, he received news of the capture June 4 and delivered the memoir the next day. The Sun King's only comment on his ambassador's failure to obey instructions was to note that he assumed the memoir had been delivered as soon as d'Avaux heard of the capture. Later, when he was in Sweden during the War of the League of Augsburg, d'Avaux felt safe in adding a condition to the peace proposals Louis sent him, despite the fact that this was not in his instructions. This time he defended his act on the grounds that it could be disavowed later if necessary or desirable. Disobedience like these actions by d'Avaux was relatively rare among seventeenth century ambassadors. The fact that he was an old and trusted servant of his sovereign probably made them more acceptable. A less experienced or confident ambassador was not likely to challenge instructions from his prince.

There were some states whose ambassadors seem to have been particularly susceptible to taking policy making into their own hands. Chief among these was the Netherlands. This was particularly the case when ambassadors were themselves members of the States General and were thus used to being decision makers at home. It was particularly difficult for them to avoid assuming that their position on the spot gave them special rights to decide policy. An example is Conraad van Beuningen, Dutch ambassador in England, who tried several times to get a peace settlement with France "in flat contradiction to his instructions" and another time, without any instructions, "to induce the emperor and Spain to a settlement with Louis XIV." [52] As a result, it was not unusual for the States General simply not to be able to trust their own ambassadors. The Spanish kings ran into similar problems. At one point during the negotiations for peace at Ryswick, the Spanish government had given its ambassador repeated instructions to secure a truce or a peace. The ambassador, who wanted the fighting to continue, continued to obstruct peace until his secretary was bribed into exposing the ambassador's instructions. The Spaniard was then forced to acquiesce in his government's desires but only because of the pressure from William III who also wanted peace.[53] There are other cases like these but, for the most part, ambassadors did in fact carry out their instructions as best they could.

FOOTNOTES

[1] L. Rousseau de Chamoy. *L'Idée du parfait ambassadeur*, ed. by L. Delavaud, Paris, 1912, p. 12.

[2] A. van Wicquefort. *L'Ambassadeur et ses fonctions*, Vol. I, The Hague, 1681, p. 10.

[3] J. de La Sarraz du Franquesnay, *Le Ministère public dans les cours étrangèries; ses fonctions et ses prérogatives*, Paris, 1731, pp. 30-31.

[4] C. Cole, ed. *Memoirs of Affairs of State*, Trans. by C. Cole, London, 1733, p. 86.

[5] O. Krauske. *Die Entwickelung der ständigen Diplomatie vom fünfzehnten Jahrhundert bis zu den Beschlüssen von 1815 und 1818*. Leipzig, 1885, pp. 170-71.

[6] This question and the analysis apply equally well to ordinary or extraordinary envoys. Wicquefort. *Ambassadeur et ses fonctions*, see note 2, Vol. I, p. 10; among the modern scholars note C.-G. Picavet. "La 'Carrière' diplomatique en France au temps de Louis XIV," *Revue d'histoire économique et sociale*, Vol. 11, 1923, p. 386; E. Satow. *A Guide to Diplomatic Practice*, 2nd edition, Vol. I, London, 1922, pp. 241-42; Krauske. *Entwickelung der ständigen Diplomatie*, see note 5, pp. 165-66.

[7] See above, Chap. III pp.   . M. A. M. Franken. *Coenraad van Beuningen's Politieke en diplomatieke aktiviteiten in de jaren 1667-1684*, Groningen, 1966, p. 262.

[8] F. Krämer, ed. *Lettres de Pierre de Groot*, The Hague, 1894, p. 19, 6 November 1670.

[9] A. Munthe. "L'Administration des affaires étrangères de 1648 à 1720," in S. Tunberg, et al. *Histoire de l'administration des affaires étrangères de Suède*, Trans. from Swedish by A. Mohn, Uppsala, 1940, pp. 144-167.

[10] See below, Chap. VII, pp.

[11] A. de Galtier de Laroque. *Le Marquis de Ruvigny*, Paris, 1892, p. 153; J. M. Kemble, ed. *State Papers and Correspondence, Illustrative of the Social and Political State of Europe*, London, 1857, p. 141.

[12] C. E. Engel. *Le Chevalier de Gramont*, N.P., [1963], pp. 193 & 224-27.

[13] Huntington Library, San Marino, California. Stowe Collection, 28 November 1670.

[14] The title *internuncio* was used in the seventeenth century for papal representatives who substituted for nuncios. R. A. Graham, S. J. *Vatican Diplomacy*, Princeton, 1959, pp. 120-26; I. Cardinale. *Le Saint-Siège et la diplomatie*, Paris, 1962, pp. 93-96.

[15] C.-G. Picavet. *La Diplomatie française au temps de Louis XIV (1661-1715): institutions, moeurs et coutumes*, Paris, 1930, p. 77; Kemble, ed. *State Papers*, see note 11, pp. 2 & 92; D. B. Horn. *Scottish Diplomatists, 1689-1789*, Historical Association Pamphlet, London, 1944, pp. 11-12.

[16] P. S. Lachs. *The Diplomatic Corps under Charles II & James II*, New Brunswick, N.J., 1965, p. 51; R. Przezdziecki. *Diplomatie et protocole à la cour de Pologne*, Vol. II, Paris, 1937, p. 144.

[17] M. Lane. "The Diplomatic Service under William III," *Transactions of the Royal Historical Society*, 4th ser., Vol. X, 1927, pp. 103-05; H. L. Snyder. "The British Diplomatic Service during the Godolphin Ministry," in R. Hatton and M. S. Anderson, eds. *Studies in Diplomatic History*, London, 1970, p. 48.

[18] Munthe. "L'Administration des affaires étrangères," see note 9, pp. 228-34.

[19] Franken. *Beuningen's Politieke*, see note 7, p. 260; A. D. Ortiz. *The Golden Age of Spain, 1516-1659*, Trans. from Spanish by J. Casey, New York, 1971, p. 43; Horn. *Scottish Diplomatists*, see note 15, p. 8.

[20] Archives des Affaires Etrangères. Paris. Mémoires et Documents, Fonds France, Vol. 373, fol. 148.

[21] W. J. Roosen. "The True Ambassador: Occupational and Personal Characteristics of French Ambassadors under Louis XIV," *European Studies Review*, Vol. 3, 1973, p. 122; Graham. *Vatican Diplomacy*, see note 14, pp. 123-25; Cardinale. *Le Saint-Siège et la diplomatie*, see note 14, p. 93; Snyder. "British Diplomatic Service," see note 17, p. 49.

[22] Roosen. "The True Ambassador," see note 21, pp. 122-28.
[23] Snyder. "British Diplomatic Service," see note 17, p. 63; Archives des Affaires Etrangères. Paris. Correspondance Politique, Espagne, Vol. 81, fol. 83, Harcourt to Tallard, 26 March 1699.
[24] See below, Chap. IV, pp.
[25] D. B. Horn. *The British Diplomatic Service, 1689-1789*, Oxford, 1961, pp. 170-71; J. Klaits. "Men of Letters and Political Reform in France at the End of the Reign of Louis XIV," *Journal of Modern History*, Vol. 43, 1971, pp. 584-85.
[26] See above, Chap. III, p
[27] "Figuriborum"—someone who takes great pains caring for his appearance. The information for this biographical sketch is drawn primarily from: E. Mallet, ed. *Négociations de Monsieur le comte d' Avaux en Hollande*, Paris, 1754, 6 vols.; J. A. Wijnne, ed. *Négociations de Monsieur le comte d' Avaux, ambassadeur extraordinaire à la cour de Suède*, Werken van het Historisch Genootschap, new ser., Utrecht, 1882-83, 3 vols.; O. N. Gisselquist. "The French Ambassador, Jean Antoine de Mesmes, Comte d'Avaux, and French Diplomacy at the Hague, 1678-1684," Ph.D. dissertation, University of Minnesota, 1968, 374 pp.; *Dictionnaire de biographie française*, Vol. IV, Paris, 1948, cols. 837-41.
[28] H. M. A. Keens-Soper. "The French Political Academy," *European Studies Review*, Vol. II, 1972, p. 355.
[29] Rousseau de Chamoy. *Idée du parfait ambassadeur*, see note 1, p. 17.
[30] L. Delavaud, ed. *Le Marquis de Pomponne, ambassadeur et secrétaire d'état, 1618-1699*, Paris, 1911, p. 47.
[31] Public Record Office. London. SP 101/23, Newsletter from Paris, 24 January 1698.
[32] *Bishop Burnet's History of His Own Time* as quoted in Horn. *Scottish Diplomatists*, see note 15, p. 7.
[33] Quoted in Snyder. "British Diplomatic Service," see note 17, pp. 50-51.
[34] J. A. Armstrong. "Old-Regime Governors: Bureaucratic and Patrimonial Attributes," *Comparative Studies in Society and History*, Vo.. 14, 1972, p. 3.
[35] See discussion of ranks below, Chap. IV, pp.
[36] Keens-Soper. "French Political Academy," see note 28, p. 338; Ortiz. *Golden Age of Spain*, see note 19, p. 44; Cardinale, *Le Saint-Siége et la diplomatie*, see note 14, p. 134; Horn. *British Diplomatic Service*, see note 25, p. 133.
[37] J.-J. Jusserand. "Grotius étudié par les secrétaires d'ambassade français en 1711," *Bibliotheca Visseriana*, Vol. 8, 1929, pp. 3-4; Keens-Soper. "French Political Academy," see note 28, pp. 340-42; G. Mattingly. *Renaissance Diplomacy*, Boston, 1955, p. 211.
[38] See below, Appendix,
[39] [W. Keith]. "Observations on the Office of an Ambassador," in *An Essay on the Education of a Young British Nobleman*, London, 1730, pp. 50-51.
[40] B. Muralt. *Letters Describing the Character and Customs of the English and French Nations*, Trans. from French, 2nd edition, London, 1726, pp. 96-97
[41] J. Howell. *Instructions for Forreine Travell*, 2nd edition, London, 1650. The reprint edited by E. Arber, Westminster, 1903, is used here. p. 29.
[42] A French ambassador in England, quoted in R. Ternois. "Les Français en Angleterre au temps de Charles II, 1660-1676," *Revue de littérature comparée*, Vol. 34, 1960, p. 204.
[43] W. Coxe. *History of the House of Austria from . . . 1218 to 1792*, 3rd edition, Vol. II, London, 1847, reprinted New York, 1971, pp. 463-64.
[44] Engel. *Le Chevalier de Gramont*, see note 12, pp. 192-94.
[45] See discussion of diplomatic functions below, Chaps. VI and VII.
[46] F. de Bojani. *Innocent XI, sa correspondance avec ses nonces*, Vol. I, Rome, 1910, pp. 136-37; Krämer. *Lettres de Pierre de Groot*, see note 8, pp. 45-46.
[47] R. Place. "The Self-Deception of the Strong: France on the Eve of the War of the League of Augsburg," *French Historical Studies*, Vol. VI, 1970, pp. 459-473.
[48] *Calendar of State Papers . . . Venice*, Vol. 37, London, 1939, p. 155.

[49] H. Sidney (later Earl of Romney). *Diary of the Times of Charles the Second,* ed, by R. W. Blencowe, Vol. II, London, 1843, p. 58.

[50] Wicquefort, *L'Ambassadeur et ses fonctions,* see note 2, Vol. II, p. 98.

[51] See above, Chap. III, pp.   Mallet, ed. *Négociations d'Avaux en Hollande,* see note 27, Vol. III, pp. 62-67.

[52] Franken. *Beuningen's Politieke,* see note 7, pp. 262-271.

[53] S. B. Baxter. *William III and the Defense of European Liberty, 1650-1702,* New York, 1966, p. 355.

CHAPTER IV

Second Class Diplomats:
Low In Prestige, High In Importance

Ambassadors were expensive! This combined with the fact that only certain courts had the right to send and receive representatives of ambassadorial rank meant that in the seventeenth century many more diplomats bore low titles than bore the title of ambassador. Whereas it was pointed out earlier that the traditional grouping of the period put ambassadors and nuncios in the first rank of diplomats,[1] there was much less agreement about the second. In earlier centuries, "envoys" and "residents" were considered to be about equal in prestige and constituted the basic second class titles. By the late seventeenth century, however, a variety of other titles had come into use whose relationship to the first two was unclear. Indeed, even the relationship of envoy and resident to each other became unclear.

In the following discussion, although the offices will be dealt with according to their different names, the reader should remember that the seventeenth century did not draw clear and sharp distinctions between residents, chargés d'affaires, agents, envoys, etc. We should not draw such distinctions today either because doing so gives a spurious order to a situation which was then essentially disorganized and confused. Even more than in other aspects of early modern history, generalizations about sub-ambassadorial diplomats should be regarded as tentative and susceptible to exceptions. This is true not only because of the confused "system" itself, but also because we seldom know many details about lower level diplomats except their names (if even that!). They were often not of sufficiently high status for much information to have been recorded (or kept) about them. Finally, the situation was not fixed. The relative positions and/or importance of titles were different at different times and places.

Envoys and Residents

In the last half of the seventeenth century second rank diplomats, particularly envoys, were becoming more important. This is shown by the fact that during this time special ceremonial procedures were being established for them.[2] At first the procedures were very unsettled but, as was so often true of early modern diplomacy, tradition and pragmatism were combined to develop useful practices. Certain parts of the ceremonial traditionally used for ambassadors were combined with that previously used for residents. Gradually, envoys acquired a position which was lower than ambassadors but higher than simple residents. The situation was further complicated by making some men envoys extraordinary rather than ordinary and giving some of them the additional title of minister plenipotentiary. As was usual in affairs of ceremonial, each court established its own rules for second class diplomats, but they were influenced by other countries. Practice was not consistent even at a single court. In France for instance, lower ranking individuals were not allowed to present their letters of credence to the king nor even to have an audience with him. Yet in 1680 a man holding the lowly rank of papal "auditor" was allowed such an audience with Louis rather than just with the secretary of state for foreign affairs which is all he had expected. In some courts there was a real ceremonial distinction between envoys who gave their letters of credence directly to the reigning prince and the residents, chargés d'affaires, agents, and plenipotentiaries who merely gave the letters to the minister for foreign affairs.[3] Since the distinction did not significantly affect their functions, many statements about envoys apply equally well to the lower ranks.

It was pointed out earlier that more seventeenth century diplomats bore low titles than bore the title of ambassador. We should also note that many more second rank diplomats were called "envoys" or some variation thereon than any other specific title. For instance, as King of England, William III named twelve ambassadors, but he had forty-two envoys extraordinary! His other diplomats were six residents, four secretaries, and three agents. The same sort of numerical distribution appeared in appointments of the Swedish and other courts.[4]

Why was such a large proportion given the title of envoy? Two answers have already been suggested. First, only certain important rulers and states had the right to send ambassadors. Less prominent rulers or states were forced to use a lower title, and envoy was the most prestigious of those available. Second, envoys were cheaper than ambassadors; as a result even sovereigns who had the unquestioned right to use ambassadors often chose to send envoys instead. But, there were other reasons as well. Since envoys were of lower social status than ambassadors, there were many more qualified candidates willing to serve as envoys than there were to become ambassadors. In some states, like the Netherlands, the elaborate life style of ambassadors was not easily reconciled with the bourgeois attitudes of Dutch burghers who were more willing to accept the lower ranking position. The Marquis de Ruvigny who represented Louis XIV in England on several occasions never held a title higher than envoy extraordinary although he was widely referred to as the "French ambassador." He himself claimed to prefer the title of envoy as it was less of an encumbrance and had fewer obligations than the title of ambassador. It has also been argued that Ruvigny was refused the higher title because the Sun King would not so honor a Protestant even though he had to make use of the Protestant's services. Envoys were occasionally sent as temporary substitutes to await the arrival of a slower moving ambassador. Such was the case after the peace treaty of Turin was signed between France and Savoy in 1696. The choice of a Savoyard ambassador to France was a delicate matter which was well worth reflecting about so Victor Amadeus sent an envoy extraordinary to reestablish relations, make reports, etc. until an ambassador could arrive. But most envoys were intended to be their master's permanent representative at the court to which they were sent. A final reason for sending envoys was that it enabled them to avoid quarrels over precedence which would hinder important diplomatic work. Louis XIV did not send an ambassador to the Hapsburg court at Vienna because the emperor refused to let a French ambassador take precedence over the ambassador of the emperor's Spanish relatives. This occurred despite the fact that Philip IV of Spain had publicly acknowledged the right of French ambassadors to precedence in all courts after the d'Estrades-Watteville conflict in 1661.[5] By sending an envoy rather than an ambassador Louis avoided conflict because it was universally recognized that ambassadors took precedence over envoys no matter what the relationship of their masters.

Relatively little is known about the social background of envoys, but the skimpy evidence suggests that the variety was much greater than for ambassadors. English envoys under William III tended to be young, not very wealthy men, but Queen Anne tended to prefer more socially acceptable individuals like James Vernon, envoy extraordinary to Denmark in 1702, whose father was a secretary of state. English envoys were often rather colorful individuals. For example, George Stepney (who filled a number of posts, primarily in Germany) was unable to enter into a serious correspondence with a young London widow because he was deeply involved in an affair with a married lady in Dresden which he claimed involved ''danger, expense and adultery.''[6] Curiously, their unorthodox lives even struck some French observers, the nationality which today is reputed to be quite casual about immorality. In a memoir for his successor, a French ambassador described Abraham Stanyan, the English envoy extraordinary in Switzerland in 1708:

> This man is completely wrapped up in himself, and he depends greatly on the liking which the Protestants of these regions have for the English. Furthermore, he flees work; his morals are extremely loose; and he does not set a good example for anyone either by his conduct or by any religious acts. He shows his animosity towards France so strongly that one can say that it

almost becomes insolence — this is evident not only in his speech but even in his public writings. He has no influence in Switzerland except in the canton of Berne. He would not be worth any attention at all if it were not for the importance of those people by whom he is employed.[7]

Nevertheless, despite the English envoys' poor reputations, it has been argued that at least under William III, most of the hard diplomatic work abroad was done by envoys rather than by the ambassadors.

It is appropriate to note that English diplomats spoke equally harshly when evaluating French envoys. For instance, François de Pas, Count of Rébenac, was described as "ambitious and arrogant, and by his contemptuous and haughty attitude did much to quicken the animosity of the Elector against the French." Despite his personality, Rébenac was named to replace his father as ambassador to Spain upon the latter's death. Other French diplomats never acquired a higher title than envoy. Charles-François d'Iberville, born in 1653 to a modest Norman family, became a clerk in the secretariat of foreign affairs under Colbert de Croissy in 1678. Ten years later he was made resident at Geneva. After the Peace of Ryswick a decade later, he was named envoy at Mainz. While in this position he traveled to Trier, Cassel, and in the Palatinate trying to persuade German princes to accept the Partition Treaties. When his tour at Mainz was cut short by the War of the Spanish Succession, his next appointment was as envoy extraordinary to Genoa in 1706. In 1710 he was sent to Spain. He finally served as envoy extraordinary in London from 1713 to 1717.[8]

One aspect of d'Iberville's career was typical of many second rank diplomats — the long periods of time he spent at this posts. Unlike ambassadors for whom a sojourn abroad of ten years was quite unusual, lower ranking diplomats often spent very long periods in the same post. Count Camillo Balliani died in Paris in 1702 after having been the representative of Mantua to the French court for almost forty years. A Swede represented his kings in England from 1661 until his death thirty years later — the last twenty years as envoy extraordinary. Another man represented the Swedish crown in Poland for twenty-six years, successively holding the titles of "secretary with commission," agent, and finally resident.[9] It was this last title of "resident" which had originally been considered equal to "envoy" but which had gradually lost status by the end of the seventeenth century. Nevertheless, the title was used often enough that it should be examined briefly.

Some seventeenth century rulers simply stopped calling any of their diplomats "residents." This was at least partly the result of the title's having been degraded when some minor German princes "gave or even sold the title to persons who had no diplomatic functions at all." Nevertheless, even the most prestigious ruler in Europe, the Holy Roman Emperor, continued a tradition more than a century old of keeping residents in Poland throughout the period. Their presence was constant, sometimes hidden, other times more open; but they were always there to keep affairs under surveillance, to maintain correspondence with Vienna, and to serve as informers and guides to the ambassadors who appeared sporadically. Other courts also maintained residents for low level contacts whose services could be supplemented by more prestigious diplomats when necessary. Frederick William of Prussia, the Great Elector, kept a "stable resident" at the court at Warsaw for years, only giving him the quality of envoy in 1685. In the meantime, whenever important negotiations were necessary, the Great Elector sent John Hoverbeck to Warsaw time and again. By his death in 1682, Hoverbeck had spent almost fifty years dealing with Polish affairs. His son had even been trained to take his place, but he ended up serving in Denmark. Although their numbers were relatively small, the English also continued to appoint residents including Sir George Etherege to Regensburg under James II. Etherege's dim reputation as a dramatist just barely outshines his even dimmer career as a resident. Queen Anne was still appointing residents as late as 1713, although it is questionable whether the desire to appoint John Drummond as resident in Brussels truly reflected the needs of diplomacy. Rather, Bolingbroke, one of Anne's ministers, seems to have wanted to give Drummond the resident's post and also the position of consul at Ostend in order to help Drummond reestablish himself financially after his firm had gone bankrupt. Bolingbroke wanted to do this to show his personal appreciation for Drummond's support of him and the ministry on previous occasions.[10] The hope of making a profit from a diplomatic position was most unusual to say the least. Most residents suffered the same financial problems which plagued other ranks of diplomats.

Diplomatic Secretaries:
Their Rank and Functions

All the types of diplomats discussed so far have had one important characteristic in common: they were all to a greater or lesser extent official representatives of their sovereign. In other words, they were given letters of credence[11] which gave them the right to speak and act on behalf of their masters — using a seventeenth century term, they had a "representative character." The position of diplomatic secretaries in this matter was not clear. The two extremes were: 1. *secretaries of embassy* who were appointed separately from the ambassador or other diplomat whom they served; they were given separate letters of credence which enabled them to act officially on their own; 2. *secretaries of ambassador* who were private individuals picked and paid by the ambassador with no official position of their own. From the viewpoint of the sovereign, there were advantages and disadvantages in both situations. Most secretaries, of course, preferred to have an official position.

What were the benefits of utilizing secretaries of ambassador to the ruler? They did not have to be paid separately; the government did not have to find men willing to take the position nor to find replacements,[12] nor worry about personality conflicts between an ambassador and his secretary, nor suffer from conflicts over authority between diplomats. However, the costs and problems of using secretaries of ambassador were high! Horror stories abound about the misuse which secretaries who had been left stranded by the departure or death of their ambassador made of their skills, knowledge and papers. These secretaries, who had often been hired at the lowest possible wages, were greatly tempted to sell secrets even while they were still employed. One can imagine how much greater the temptations became after their income had stopped and they were falling into poverty. As a result, some secretaries (especially those who had been hired abroad for their linguistic abilities) worked first for one employer and then moved on to work for another who might well represent a sworn enemy of the first. Others sold copies of ciphers to the highest bidder and engaged in other nefarious activities.

Under such circumstances one would assume that any government which wished to keep control of its diplomatic servants would utilize only secretaries of embassy or develop some method for controlling ambassadors' secretaries after their employment ceased. A number of states did just that. As early as 1669, the Swedes used the title "secretary with commission" for men who were in effect secretaries of embassy. At first such appointments were made sporadically, but by 1688 a regulation formally established the office for the purpose of assuring the stability and continuity of Swedish legations abroad. The posts were not filled regularly in the 1690's but in 1703-1704 "secretaries with commission" were appointed for Holland, France, England, Vienna, and Prussia.

The English also had secretaries of embassy who were appointed and paid separately from the diplomat who headed the mission. William III himself decided whether an ambassador needed a secretary of embassy, while Queen Anne seems to have decided after consulting her Lord Treasurer. In both reigns, after a secretary of embassy was approved, the ambassador participated in the actual selection. The essential elements of the process are illustrated by a letter from a secretary of state to the Earl of Manchester, a newly appointed English ambassador to Venice:

My Lord,
I did not omit to lay before the King your Lordship's desire to have a Secretary of the Embassy to go with you to Venice; and by the last post I

received an answer from Mr. Blathwayt that His Majesty has been pleased to agree to it; and I have accordingly given directions for the preparation of the Privy-Seal for Mr. Stanyan whom I understand from Mr. Montague your Lordship has picked for this employment.[13]

The Privy-Seal was the document which authorized the Treasury to pay the individual named therein.

Surprisingly, the French, who are often thought to have been leaders in seventeenth century diplomatic practice, were behind in using secretaries of embassy. The title "secretary of the king" which a number of French diplomats bore had nothing to do with diplomacy and was a purely honorific title with no duties attached. With a few minor exceptions, French secretaries were classic examples of secretaries of ambassador rather than of embassy. As a result, they were often untrained in diplomatic procedures, inefficient, and/or unable to perform their tasks satisfactorily. Toward the end of the Sun King's reign, his Secretary of State for Foreign Affairs, the Marquis de Torcy, started the French Political Academy, one purpose of which was to create a specially trained corps of men who would serve as secretaries to diplomats. At first the Academy seemed to be a success, but it lost its prime supporter when Torcy was relieved of his office after the death of Louis XIV. The Academy was dissolved in 1721. There was another attempt to reestablish the system in the 1770's but it did not work then either. The French Revolution arrived with France still using the old system of secretaries of ambassador.[14]

The problem was magnified toward the end of the seventeenth century. Diplomats from most countries often hired several different men who were in effect personal secretaries or secretaries of ambassador. For instance, the Spanish ambassador in London in 1691 had a regular secretary, a language secretary, and four clerks. The French ambassador to England in 1713 had four secretaries, while Louis XIV's ambassador in the relatively unimportant post of Switzerland from 1698 to 1708 had six secretaries to maintain his daily correspondence. Obviously all the problems inherent in secretaries of ambassador would apply to these other three, four, or six secretaries even if the first held the official position of secretary of embassy. Indeed, the situation might even be worse! The secretary of embassy might be required to hire and pay an assistant out of his own salary, a fact calculated to make the assistant's position even more insecure than that of a regular secretary of ambassador. Some historians have argued that experienced ambassadors rarely thought very highly of their private secretaries, but considering the conditions of their employment, it is a wonder that the secretaries performed even as well as they did.

Just what did a diplomatic secretary do? On the one hand, he was essentially a clerk who performed the drudgery of actually writing letters and other documents by hand. He also served as a messenger to carry documents to and from the host government, attended his master at ceremonies, helped run the household, and was a general flunky. On the other hand, a secretary was also called on to perform a number of more important tasks, especially when his diplomat master was indisposed or not in town. For instance, during the absence of the French envoy extraordinary to England in 1716, his secretary received a letter from the French Council of the Marine about insults made to French fishermen on the coasts of France and England. The secretary gave a copy of it to the British secretary of state along with a request that such insults be stopped. Another time the secretary gave two Frenchmen visiting in London a certificate that they were French and Catholic and were in England on their private business. Of course, the issuing of passports was a never ending task.[15] At other times secretaries were called on to travel. This could be rewarding as when Matthew Prior was given the honor and responsibility of taking news of the signing of the Peace of Ryswick and a copy of the treaty of London. He was received with joy and rewarded with a gift of two hundred and ten pounds, a magnificent sum, for his efforts. Other diplomats, particularly those stationed in Germany, sent their secretaries to neighboring courts to carry messages or to acquire whatever information they could. In 1652 the Venetian ambassador in Paris sent his secretary to London where he remained for three years, eventually acting as if he were actually a resident although he had never been officially accredited to Cromwell.[16] In summary, it is appropriate to describe a seventeenth century diplomatic secretary as a sort of office manager and clerk for the diplomat who headed the mission.

Matthew Prior — Diplomat and Poet

Secretaries and higher ranking diplomats often voiced the same plaint — boredom. Yet one gets a somewhat different impression from a poem Matthew Prior wrote describing his life as a diplomatic secretary, "the Englishen Heer Secretaris" at The Hague:

While with labour assid'ous due pleasure I mix,
And in one day atone for the bus'ness of six,
In a little Dutch-chaise on a Saturday night,
On my left hand my Horace, a Nymph on my right.
No Memoire to compose, no Post-Boy to move,
That on Sunday may hinder the softness of love
For her, neither visits, nor parties of tea,
Nor the long-winded cant of a dull refugee.
This night and the next shall be hers, shall be mine,
To good or ill fortune the third we resign.

We can undoubtedly dismiss his derogatory statements as poetic license; he would not have sought new secretarial positions so assiduously if he had truly disliked duties such as sending informational memoirs and interviewing French Protestant refugees who had information to sell, a position to plead, or who wished to go to England.[17]

Matthew Prior, or Matt as his friends called him, was one of several seventeenth century Englishmen who were able to combine diplomatic and literary careers — George Stepney, Paul Rycaut, and George Etherege. Born of low social standing, Matt probably would have gone nowhere except for a chance encounter with Charles Sackville, sixth Earl of Dorset. In his youth, Dorset had engaged in wild capers such as startling respectable folk by running naked through the streets in the wee hours of the morning and scolding them for staying out so late. As he grew older, Dorset became a patron of men of letters. Thus, after he discovered a tavern boy, Matt Prior, with a volume by the ancient Roman author Horace in his hand, Dorset soon became Matt's sponsor, sending him to school and then to Cambridge University. Matt did well academically at Cambridge, but, as could be expected of a man whose tastes had been partially molded in a tavern, he also engaged in other types of pursuits. In later years he told of visiting the mother of his friend George Stepney who was still at Cambridge. She asked him how George was behaving and if he drank? Prior: "I said he sometimes drank moderately." She begged him to tell the truth: "Mr. Prior, you are with him constantly, and I can believe you. Did you ever see him drunk in your life?" Answer: "No, indeed, madam, for I was always drunk before him."

The Glorious Revolution brought Matt's friends to power, resulting in his appointment as secretary to the new English envoy extraordinary at The Hague. There Prior was involved primarily with the ordinary routine of a diplomatic secretary, despite the excitement of the war against Louis XIV. His early letters tended to be dull recitations of official news, but he soon learned to enliven them with gossipy anecdotes. Such examples include conflict between the wives of the Swedish envoy and the Imperial resident over the purchase of a new carriage, or the public whipping of a serving maid who smuggled letters to prisoners. More importantly, Prior made the acquaintance of men who could help his career, especially King William. When the envoy returned to England, Prior stayed on without official status. Later he was appointed official English Secretary with a salary of one pound a day, which he complained really meant that he was forced to spend eight to twelve pounds a week for postage alone. Little significant business developed so Matthew was able to return to poetry and the study of French in his spare time until the appointment of the Earl of Jersey as the new English representative at The Hague. This again started Prior on what must have seemed like a never ending pursuit of some other official position. In the end Jersey arrived and, after Prior made himself agreeable and helpful, the Earl recommended that Prior remain with him in the Netherlands. With Jersey as a patron, Matt's career advanced nicely. He went with Jersey as English secretary to the peace conference at Ryswick, was jointly appointed Secretary to the Lords Justices of Ireland, and, because of his command of French, was eventually made secretary to the Earl of Portland's magnificent embassy to Louis XIV.

Seldom did Prior's chauvinistic attitudes show through more clearly than during his first months in France. They took the form of ridiculing Louis XIV who, Prior wrote, "has very good health for a man of sixty and has more vanity than a girl of sixteen." "His house at Versailles," Prior continued, "is something the foolishest in the world; he is strutting in every panel and galloping over one's head in every ceiling, and if he turns to spit he must see himself in person or his Viceregent the Sun. . . ." What had started out as a temporary appointment in France dragged on through the departure of Portland, the embassy of Prior's patron, the Earl of Jersey, and yet the beginning of the Earl of Manchester's embassy. Finally in August, 1699, he returned to London to become an under-secretary of state under Jersey. Another quick mission to France the following October assured Louis XIV that William III did indeed intend to sign the Second Partition Treaty. Concomitantly, Jersey's resignation as secretary of state temporarily brought Matt's career in diplomacy to an end.

Meanwhile, Prior was more than satisfied by his being given a place on the Board of Trade and Plantations, the permanent position for which he had searched so long and which he thought he could depend on in the future. A single term as a Member of Parliament would not have been important except that a vote on the impeachment of the ministers supposedly responsible for making the Second Partition Treaty forced him to choose between his chief patron, Lord Jersey, and his childhood friends who were Whigs. The vote made him appear to be a Tory. In later years this decision led to his losing the position on the Board of Trade. Prior returned to favor with the government of Harley and Bolingbroke but eventually suffered disaster for his part in making the Peace of Utrecht.

After the War of the Spanish Succession had dragged on for nearly a decade, the English government decided to make peace with France and began negotiations with a secret French representative, the Abbot François Gaultier. By July, 1711, it became necessary to involve an Englishman in the negotiations, one who knew French well, preferably with diplomatic experience, and with the appropriate political views of the situation in England. The obvious choice was at hand: Matthew Prior. His written accreditation made him appear to be little more than a messenger: ''Monsieur Prior is fully instructed and authorized to communicate our demands to France, and to bring us back a response to them, Signed Queen Anne.'' The French wanted to negotiate rather than just send messengers, so Louis XIV proposed sending Gaultier and another man with full powers back to London with Prior. Unfortunately for the plans of the Tory government, the journey to London was not uneventful. John Macky, the English officer in charge of the channel packet boats, had noticed Prior's secret departure, notified Bolingbroke of the event, and was told to keep watch for his return. Macky did more than watch; he arrested Matthew and his companions despite the pass which the former produced. Macky also notified several enemies of the ministry of his actions, thereby making public the news that negotiations were in progress. Bolingbroke immediately ordered the trio's release and, enraged at the efficiency of an officer of the Crown, threatened to hang him. Macky fled to Antwerp where he remained in disgrace until after the death of Queen Anne. The three quickly moved on to London where the Frenchman was housed at ''Matthew's Palace'' which for a time became the center of admirable ''cloak and dagger'' negotiations. Visitors arrived stealthily, and even the Queen's ministers sneaked in by the back door. The preliminary peace between England and France, known as ''Matt's Peace,'' was signed September 25/October 6, 1711. Because of his low social position, Matt was refused an appointment as one of the plenipotentiaries to the conference at Utrecht; instead he settled down to a boring job as a customs commissioner.

As is well known to all students of diplomacy, beginning a peace conference does not necessarily mean that progress will be made. Such was the case at Utrecht. Eventually, it was decided that a high ranking Englishman had to visit France in order to break the impasse. Bolingbroke, accompanied by Prior, arrived in Paris in mid-August, 1712. After enjoying himself tremendously and settling the problems, Bolingbroke departed for London leaving Matt behind to execute a number of personal errands and to care for English interests as well as he could without having been given any official position. After suffering innumerable snubs, he finally received some credentials naming him minister plenipotentiary, a generally unrecognized title but at least one which gave him some official standing. Matt played a significant role in the negotiations which eventually led to the signing of the treaties ending the War of the Spanish Succession in late spring, 1713. At this time he could write to Bolingbroke in the light-hearted way characteristic of their correspondence: ''I congratulate you most sincerely upon the birth of your beautiful daughter, the peace, after all the pangs you have so long time suffered, from the ignorance of some of your Englishmen mid-wives.''

In the following months Matthew Prior played the on again off again role of a secretary when there was an English ambassador in France, and actual English representative when there was not. His discouragement grew mightily when he was left in Paris suffering financial difficulties, while his French opposite numbers were richly rewarded for their role in making peace. But, alas for Matt, worse was yet to come! The death of Queen Anne in 1714 and the fall of the Tory ministry was to be more than a simple change of government. "Reprisals" were to be taken against the former ministers and their supporters. Prior had good reason to fear that he would be among the victims. There was even gossip at the French court that Matt should fear for his life. Prior's state of mind was not improved by his relationship with the Earl of Stair who arrived as the new English envoy extraordinary in January, 1715. The personalities of the two men were hardly compatible though, of course, Matt did his humble best to win over a man who had received most of his diplomatic training on the battlefield and who used military tactics to solve all his problems — even courtship. In order to win a widow who had vowed she would never remarry, Stair had hidden in her house and then showed himself at her bedroom window. In order to save her reputation she married him. Within a short time of his arrival in France, Stair had so alienated Torcy that the French Secretary of State refused to speak to him.

Stair was just the man to carry out the brusk order he received February 1 to seize all of Prior's papers. The new ministry wished to examine them for evidence of mismanagement to be used against members of the previous ministry. Prior may have suspected that his papers would be seized, for written on the front of one of his letterbooks is the statement: "This book . . . contains the true copies of letters written by me." Signed M. Prior. Another note was added in what appears to be a different ink: "Errors in transcribing which I find to be many excepted." [18] Perhaps Matt added the last phrase in order to create a defense if there were an attempt to use the letters against him or his friends.

However, even in his worst dreams Matthew had probably never suspected what his fate in the next few months would be. Not only had he never been properly rewarded for his work in bringing about the Peace of Utrecht, but now his actions were going to be held against him as offenses. Although he was not accused of any crime, he was called to testify before a Secret Committee created by the House of Commons to investigate the making of the Peace. The Committee was anxious to discover evidence on which to base a charge of High Treason against Prior's friends, the former ministers. Knowing this, Matt drew upon all his diplomatic skill both in phrasing his responses and in not saying more than was absolutely necessary. He tried to nullify potentially damaging inferences insofar as was possible. For instance, when he said that he had received money in France from a Monsieur Cantillon, a questioner pounced on

Prior asking if Cantillon were not a papist. Prior countered the implied accusation that he was pro-Catholic by saying that of course Cantillon was a Catholic: "Else, Sir, he could not have been a banker at Paris, which he had been for several years before I knew him." For more than nine hours Prior was subjected to this sort of badgering. Through convenient forgetfulness and vague answers, Prior managed to protect his friends and thwart the Secret Committee. Unfortunately for himself, the Committee, dissatisfied with the proceedings, kept him imprisoned for more than a year, although he was neither accused nor convicted of any crime.

Matt was not hanged for his part in making the Peace of Utrecht, but in some ways he might just as well have been. His professional life was over. With his enemies firmly in control of government and his friends in prison or exile, there was no possibility whatsoever that Matt would ever again have a role in diplomacy or politics. Thus he turned again to the writing of poetry, which was to account for his fame in later centuries as much or more than did his diplomatic activities. At his death in September, 1721, some friends published an obituary notice which ended in a eulogy:

> He was a person of universal learning and the most refined turn of wit; a pleasing and instructive companion, a kind master and a dear friend. He had a great soul, but cloathed with humility and good nature: He was an able minister, and an admirable poet, a generous benefactor, and what adds to his praise, an honest and sincere man.

He was buried in Westminster Abbey in the Poet's Corner.

Diplomatic Secretaries —
Their Representative Character

In returning to our general discussion of diplomatic secretaries, one special point can be drawn out of the biographical sketch of Matthew Prior: the differences in his role as secretary when he had a superior present and when he himself was the highest ranking English diplomat present. In the former case he acted basically as a helper of the ambassador; in the latter case Prior himself bore the representative character. This was the normal practice in the seventeenth century, although there was a question as to whether a secretary automatically acquired a representative character on the death or departure of the regular diplomat. It is unlikely that many people would have believed such automatic succession occurred. Indeed, when Prior asked the English government what character he should assume at the public entry of a new English ambassador to France, he was quite upset at the reply telling him to appear as a private gentleman because "the commission of Plenipotentiary does not give you a representing character." Prior wrote to his friend Bolingbroke asking rhetorically: "Do me justice my Lord, did I ever desire to be a lion in Arabia any more than to be an ambassador at Paris?" And he goes on to note that he was quite aware that he did not have a "representing character." [19]

There were two conditions, however, in which a secretary could have a representative character: 1. when he was expressly given it when he was left behind after the death or departure of a superior diplomat and 2. when he was sent with just the title of secretary to perform diplomatic functions. In both cases the secretary was usually given a letter of credence giving him official status. This was necessary if he were to have any hope of dealing effectively with the host government. For instance, one man faced some major problems when he went to London in the 1650's without any position at all except that of being secretary to the Venetian ambassador in Paris. Cromwell's government resented his lack of official status, made it difficult for him to get audiences, and treated him in a generally unfriendly way.

Some states went so far as to give a secretary a brevet ahead of time which could serve as a letter of credence if the need arose. Sweden is the best example. An edict promulgated in 1688 explicitly stated that "secretaries with commission" were under the orders of their diplomatic master abroad; they were to receive their food and lodging from him and even to consider themselves to be his domestic servants. The edict went on to explain that a major function of the secretaries with commission was to assure the stability and continuity of Swedish legations abroad. They did this in two ways. First, when a diplomat was recalled, the secretary remained to carry on his duties. Before the superior departed, he was supposed to introduce the secretary to his correspondents and friends, the government ministers, and the other diplomats residing at the court. Second, Swedish secretaries with commission were responsible for the archives of the legation. The archives were supposed to be kept very complete and include a variety of material: rules of protocol and ceremonial, ciphers, the texts of treaties Sweden had signed with other countries, laws and regulations concerning commerce, copies of letters and instructions, and information on negotiations and conferences. The secretary was to keep these records safe and up-to-date so that if the former diplomat took the original documents with him, his successor would be able to continue the work of the legation successfully. Of course, there was a gap between the edict and its execution, but at least the Swedes were making an attempt to put their diplomatic institutions on a rational and practical basis.

Other courts only sent the secretary a formal letter of credence after the death or departure of his superior. Such was the case, for example, of Christian Rompf, secretary of the Dutch ambassador to France in 1668. When the ambassador died, the States General at The Hague decided that Rompf should remain in charge of affairs until a new ambassador was chosen. Rompf remained in France even after the arrival of the new ambassador, Peter de Groot. This caused some problems because of disagreements over his authority. Rompf claimed that he was still an official Dutch diplomat even after De Groot's arrival. De Groot disagreed and called Rompf's claims absurd because 1. Rompf "has no authority to write to the States General except by my order or in my name . . .; 2. credentials are not withdrawn, but they expire on the departure of the diplomat or on the arrival of another one; since his [Rompf's credentials] were only for the period when there was no ambassador, they expired at the moment of my arrival." Finally, De Groot argued that if the States General considered Rompf as their secretary rather than the ambassador's, then De Groot would hire another one. De Groot's position was upheld. Rompf remained as the ambassador's secretary, not departing until March, 1674, well after the war with Louis XIV had begun.[20]

Other cases where secretaries were left behind after the departure of an ambassador were numerous. John Doddington stayed on in Venice to represent England in 1670 in dealings about salt fish and other things which Doddington argued were not of great importance but which would "be lost for want of prosecution, if no one be left to follow them."[21] After the execution of Charles I, Mazarin did not feel it appropriate for the French ambassador to remain in London, but he also wished to avoid offending Cromwell and possibly drive him into a Spanish alliance. Thus the French ambassador was ordered to find some excuse for leaving informally without in any way giving the commonwealth government formal recognition. His secretary "was left in London to represent French interests and — a matter of some importance to Mazarin — to send word of any bargains that came up when the pictures and tapestries of King Charles's famous collection were sold."[22] Occasionally the departing diplomat himself gave his secretary some sort of commission, but the secretary was generally not officially recognized unless or until he received credentials from his home government.

The title "chargé d'affaires" was occasionally given to secretaries (although it was not limited to them) when they acquired their representative character. Although the title was about the lowest recognized diplomatic title, it was often a promotion for a secretary to receive it. A promotion might well have been necessary to persuade Poussin to go to London as "Secretary Chargés d'Affaires" in April, 1701, after the departure of Ambassador Tallard. Since England and France were veering into the War of the Spanish Succession, Poussin's situation was not very comfortable before he was brusquely ordered to depart a few months later. Some of the very small and poor states which were on the verge of not even having the right to send diplomatic representatives (for example, the Republic of Geneva, other Swiss cantons, certain German princes and city states) made representatives of their bankers, merchants, doctors, and other citizens/subjects who were already living abroad. Ordinarily these men did not have a clearly specified diplomatic character, but occasionally they were given the title of chargé d'affaires.

Unofficial Diplomats

Below the chargés d'affaires existed a netherworld of men whose authority as negotiators must be called suspect to say the least. Seventeenth century credentials seem unneccarily formal to us today. But then the documents really did help a government official to know if a man's claim to be a diplomat were legitimate. The question was particularly important for individuals claiming to represent small, poor and/or distant rulers. Problems also arose during wartime when secret negotiations between combattants were kept going almost as a matter of course, often through very questionable or unlikely intermediaries like the "Fat Abbot" Gaultier mentioned in the biographical sketch of Matthew Prior.

Two examples will illustrate the problem. In 1658-59 an Irish merchant named Nicholas Bodkin was able to insinuate himself into the negotiations leading to the Peace of the Pyrenees and a variety of other affairs involving the English Commonwealth, France, Spain, and Charles II before his restoration. At one time or another Bodkin convinced various decision makers that he was speaking on behalf of the Commonwealth, Mazarin, and Charles II. His plans involved Spanish efforts to make peace with England and the marriage of Charles II. In the latter he discussed the marriage of Charles to one of Mazarin's nieces, a suggestion which was actually within the realm of possibility. But Bodkin also suggested a Stuart marriage for Mazarin's nephew with Ireland as a dowry. It was impossible to take the proposal seriously, and Bodkin eventually lost credit with everyone. Another case occurred shortly after the French victory in the Battle of Steenkerk in 1692. One of William III's trusted associates, a former burgomaster, began unauthorized peace negotiations with the French ambassador in Switzerland, perhaps with the intention of overthrowing William's predominant position in the government of the Netherlands. The Dutchman was arrested and, since his guilt was obvious, sentenced to life imprisonment.[23] In neither of these cases was the imposter successful, but such self-appointed diplomats were capable of muddying the waters of diplomacy quite seriously before they were found out.

Unofficial diplomats were occasionally successful when their services were utilized by decision makers themselves. There was no counterpart among the major European states in the seventeenth century to Louis XV's eighteenth century "Secret of the King," wherein the King of France in effect maintained a separate and unofficial set of diplomats abroad. But, the situation was somewhat analagous in England under William III and Anne. In a sense, Matthew Prior's mission was unofficial when he remained in the Netherlands after his superior's departure in 1694. He complained to the Earl of Dorset: "I have only a verbal order to stay here till my Lord Faulkland comes over, so they have made me a minister without one syllable of a commission to act by; and ordered me to receive all their letters without one penny of money to pay their postage." [24] Prior's case was primarily a matter of the wheels of government turning slowly, but William also intentionally used unconventional methods and secret unofficial diplomats. He did so in an attempt to maintain secrecy and to be sure his orders were obeyed. The Tory ministers at the end of Queen Anne's reign did not trust the regular diplomatic representatives at The Hague who, in the ministers' opinion, were simply tools of their Whig opponents. Thus the Tory ministers used an English merchant living in the Netherlands to arrange a correspondence with the Pensionary of the States of Holland and to perform other secret actions for them. [25] But in general decision makers recognized that, except in wartime, officially accredited diplomats were more likely to succeed in whatever tasks they were put to than were unofficial ones.

Consuls and the Consular Service

Today many countries have combined the consular and diplomatic services, but there is still often a tendency for "diplomats" to look at mere "consuls" with disdain. Such an attitude may not be fair but it has a long and well-established tradition behind it. Men who held titles of "consul" and performed duties which we would today call consular came into existence at least as early as the fifteenth century. But for centuries they had little or nothing to do with diplomacy. Consuls were generally appointed and paid by the local colony of merchants with whose affairs the consul dealt. A consul's authority did not derive from his own prince's appointment but from the recognition of the local sovereign where he lived and, of course, by his fellow merchants.

In the middle of the seventeenth century, the consular services of several countries underwent significant changes. Henry IV had made French consulates in the Levant venal — that is, they could be purchased by whoever wished to become the officeholder. Around 1650 the old administration, centered in Marseilles, was replaced by a confusing situation in which authority and disciplinary powers were unequally shared by a Chamber of Commerce, the Parlement of Provence, the Royal Council in Paris, and the Marine. In England the change dates from 1649 when consuls first became state officials in the sense that they were appointed by the government and also in the sense that they had to change the priority of their interests. Previously, their loyalties and efforts were primarily designed to benefit the English merchants trading in the area of the consulate. In the last half of the seventeenth century, their local functions were subordinated to matters of "national interests": the search for political and military information, the promotion of trade in general, and supporting the work of ambassadors.[26]

Although consuls did not exactly become diplomats in the seventeenth century, the line between the work of the two groups was blurred in both directions. Each kind of officer performed functions which today would be considered to fall within the province of the other. One obstacle to the merger was the fact that consuls were traditionally used in areas important for trade, particularly seaports, which were not generally the places where diplomatic representation was necessary. French consuls were primarily in the Levant, the eastern Mediterranean, while most British consuls were scattered throughout the western Mediterranean. Another thing which prevented the consuls from becoming diplomats was that they remained essentially private persons rather than being made "public ministers" complete with letters of credence. When circumstances required it, foreign consuls in Russia, the Iberian Peninsula, and elsewhere combined the two functions. The Swedes even went so far as to make no real distinctions between diplomats and consuls. As early as 1649-52 the duties of both envoy and consul were united in the Swedish resident in Portugal. The same was true of some Swedes in England, Holland, and Russia. Nevertheless, consuls were not a basic part of a country's normal diplomatic establishment, and they usually did not consort with diplomats nor perform diplomatic functions in any organized way. They did so as individuals, not as a normal part of their job.[27]

FOOTNOTES

[1] See above, Chap. III, p
[2] See below, Chap. VII,
[3] C. de Martens. *Le Guide diplomatique*, 4th edition, Vol. I, Paris, 1851, p. 56; E. Satow. *A Guide to Diplomatic Practice*, 2nd edition, Vol. 1, New York, 1922, pp. 241-42.
[4] L. Bittner and L. Gross. *Repertorium der Diplomatischen ertreter aller Länder seit dem Westfälischen Frieden*, Vol. I, Berlin, 1936, *passim;* D. B. Horn. *The British Diplomatic Service. 1689-1789*, Oxford, 1961, pp. 43-45.
[5] See below, Chap. VII,
[6] Public Record Office. London. Stepney Papers 105/60 as quoted in C. K. Eves. *Matthew Prior, Poet and Diplomatist*, New York, 1939, p. 87.
[7] J. de Boislisle. *Les Suisses et le marquis de Puyzieulx, ambassadeur de Louis XIV*, Paris, 1906, p. 82. Unless otherwise noted, all translations are my own.
[8] L. de Saint-Simon. *Mémoires de Saint-Simon*, new edition, ed. by A. de Boislisle, Vol. IV, Paris, 1879, p. 278, note 3; L. de Sourches. *Mémoires du Marquis de Sourches sur le règne de Louis XIV*, ed. by G.-J. Cosnac and others, Vol. V, Paris, 1882, p. 372.

[9] A. Munthe. "L'Administration des affaires étrangères de 1648 à 1720," in S. Tunberg, et al. *Histoire de l'administration des affaires étrangères de Suède,* Trans. from Swedish by A. Mohn, Uppsala, 1940, p. 156.

[10] R. Przezdziecki. *Diplomatie et protocole à la cour de Pologne,* Vol. II, Paris, 1937, pp. 134 & 340; R. Hatton. "John Drummond in the War of the Spanish Succession: Merchant turned Diplomatic Agent," in R. Hatton and M. S. Anderson, eds. *Studies in Diplomatic History,* London, 1970, pp. 90-91.

[11] See below, Appendix,

[12] Secretarial appointments were not always easy to make. For instance one candidate in England had hopes of becoming a travelling tutor, "but if all else failed 'would reckon himself very happy to go to Vienna as secretary with an English ambassador.' " Horn. *British Diplomatic Service,* see note 4, p. 40.

[13] C. Cole, ed. *Memoirs of Affairs of State,* Trans. by C. Cole, London, 1733, p. 2, 12 August 1697.

[14] On the Political Academy see J. Klaits. "Men of Letters and Political Reform in France at the End of the Reign of Louis XIV," *Journal of Modern History,* Vol. 43, 1971, pp. 577-97; H. M. A. Keens-Soper, "The French Political Academy," *European Studies Review,* Vol. II, 1972, pp. 329-55; Archives des Affaires Etrangères. Paris. Ecole diplomatique, 1692-1833.

[15] See below, Appendix,

[16] E. R. Adair. "The Venetian Despatches," *History,* new ser., Vol. 20, 1935, pp. 128-29.

[17] For Matthew Prior's biography see Eves, *Matthew Prior,* see note 6; L. G. W. Legg. *Matthew Prior: A Study of his Public Career and Correspondence,* Cambridge, 1921; M. Prior. *The History of his Own Time,* several editions.

[18] Public Record Office. London. SP 105/28, Archives of British Legations.

[19] *Ibid.* fols. 103-107.

[20] F. Krämer, ed. *Lettres de Pierre de Groot,* The Hague, 1894, pp. 28-29.

[21] Huntington Library. San Marino, California. Stowe Collection, Doddington to Sir Richard Temple, 15 August 1670.

[22] C. V. Wedgwood. "European Reaction to the Death of Charles I," in C. H. Carter, ed. *From the Renaissance to the Counter-Reformation,* London, 1966, p. 410.

[23] F. J. Routledge. *England and the Treaty of the Pyrenees,* Liverpool, 1953, pp. 42-46; S. B. Baxter. *William III and the Defense of European Liberty,* New York, 1966, p. 310.

[24] In the seventeenth century international postage on letters was paid on arrival at the destination. Quotation is from Great Britain. Historical Manuscripts Commission. *Calendar of the Manuscripts of the Marquis of Bath Preserved at Longleat.* Vol. III, London, 1908, p. 21.

[25] M. Lane. "The Diplomatic Service under William III," *Transactions of the Royal Historical Society,* 4th ser., Vol. X, 1927, p. 106; Hatton. "John Drummond," see note 10, pp. 79-80.

[26] D. C. M. Platt. *The Cinderella Service: British Consuls since 1825,* Hamden, Conn., 1971, pp. 5-8; W. H. Lewis. *Levantine Adventurer,* London, 1962, pp. 21-22.

[27] Archives de Affaires Etrangères. Paris. Consulats. Vol. I, 1669-1790, *passim;* K. Mellander and E. Prestage. *The Diplomatic and Commerical Relations of Sweden and Portugal from 1641 to 1670,* Watford, 1930, pp. 66-72; Munthe, "L'Administration des affaires étrangères," see note 9, p. 168; Horn. *British Diplomatic Service,* see note 4, pp. 240-41.

CHAPTER V

A Typical Early Modern Embassy

A new ambassador was chosen! In principle the newly selected diplomat immediately went to the sovereign to thank him for the honor and was from that moment considered to be the ambassador (a most important consideration since his salary ordinarily began then!). Some courts even went so far as to address all correspondence concerning the post to the new man. Such a procedure made sense if the new ambassadors were to leave immediately for their posts as they were almost invariably ordered to do. Unfortunately, most found many reasons to postpone their departure but very few to hurry it. Delays of a month and more were the rule rather than the exception.[1] One should not assume, however, that the diplomats were simply procrastinating and enjoying their salaries without performing their duties. The preparations necessary prior to departure were very time-consuming.

High on the list of the new diplomat's responsibilities was the need to contact the representative from the court to which he was going. This enabled the representative to evaluate the new ambassador and to notify his own master of the appointment. Of course, the foreigner would probably have been keeping track of developments so intimately involved with his own master as the appointment of a new man to his master's court. How successfully he did so was problematical. On September 6, 1685, the French ambassador in London, Barrillon, had written that a "Sieur Gromstal" was to be sent to Paris. On September 10th Barrillon called him "Trombal." On the 13th the name was corrupted to "Tombal" while it had become "Franseval" on the 19th. It is unlikely that Barrillon's opinions about William *Trumbull* were very valuable since the two men obviously were not well acquainted.[2] Nevertheless, a newly appointed diplomat usually exchanged several visits with his counterpart for ceremonial purposes and to learn about the other country.

The ambassador's preparations for his new position fall into several categories: learning about his official duties and responsibilities, acquiring the servants and goods necessary for maintaining a diplomatic household, and finally, arranging his personal affairs for his absence. The new diplomat learned about his official duties from the instructions and other documents he was given and during interviews with ministers or even the prince himself. Ideally the ambassador also had meetings with individuals who had served at the post earlier and read relevant despatches, treaties, etc. Directly before his

departure the diplomat usually had a farewell audience with his sovereign in
which he was assured of the ruler's confidence and support. The meeting was
usually serious and formal, but a story about the Viscount of Guilleragues who
was departing to be French ambassador in Constantinople is amusing. At his
farewell audience Louis XIV discoursed:

> "I trust, Monsieur, that I shall find reason to be better satisfied with your
> conduct at Constantinople than I am with that of your predecessor."
> "And I trust, Sire," Guilleragues replied, "that you will not be making that
> same observation to my successor." [3]

The large size of the ordinary diplomatic households and the furnishings
which diplomats took with them indicates how difficult and time-consuming
the hiring of individuals, purchasing of supplies, etc. for the embassy was. Sir
Bulstrode Whitelocke, appointed as Cromwell's ambassador to Sweden in
1653, found that there were so many people who wanted to go with him that he
eventually appointed a private committee to relieve him of the task of selecting
individuals for "ordinary employments and service under him in his voyage."
The committee, made up of some of his "friends well known at Court, and
some of his own officers and gentlemen, and his son, wwas to handleε his
affairs relating to his embassy, to peruse the list of his retinue, to examine the
fitness of persons recommended to Whitelocke's service, to agree for wages,
advance money, etc., to take order for provisions and preparations for the
voyage." [4] Other men were unwilling to delegate authority over such details
and thus spent hours making decisions about personnel and furnishings.
Whitelocke's experience also illustrates the ways diplomats prepared their
personal affairs. He left sealed instructions for the selling of his estate in order
to prevent controversies and to provide an income for his children in case he
died while away. "He appointed servants to manage his affairs in the country;
and to his wife he left the command of all." He also gave his brothers-in-law
power to handle certain financial affairs while old friends living in his house
were to receive and answer his private letters and write to him in Sweden. Other
individuals were to correspond on public matters. Personal problems were
difficult enough for an ambassador in any case. They were even more difficult
to solve when his private affairs were not going well, even when he was home.
Béthune's attempts to arrange his affairs before leaving for Poland as French
ambassador were complicated by the fact that his mother and brothers were
trying to stop him from receiving his share of the paternal inheritance. [5] We can
wonder how much a diplomat's performance of his duties was affected by the
personal problems resulting from his being abroad for long periods in an age
when communication was difficult and procedures for dealing with such a

situation were not well established. Unfortunately, it is not possible to determine now just what the effect was. We can tell, however, that such problems provided ready excuses for a man who was hesitant to depart on his embassy.

We also know that many men hesitated to depart simply because they were concerned about the difficulties of the journey. Under the best of circumstances, travel was not easy and diplomats were frequently called upon to leave at times which were not even moderately satisfactory — winter, the stormy season at sea, or wartime. Depending on the circumstances, the minister might be ordered to take a specific route because his sovereign wished him to perform additional diplomatic tasks along the way. For instance, he could be called upon to meet with other servants of his master to consult with them about his "further proceeding and whatever else may be thought necessary for Our service." Or the traveling diplomat might be called upon to carry out certain negotiations at courts he visited on his journey. For example, the Frenchman Croissy negotiated at Berlin, Cassel, and Wolfembutel in 1715 while on his way from Paris to Stockholm. Other ministers were simply told to pay their respects to princes along the way if it were convenient. More often diplomats were simply told to choose their own route — whichever was most convenient.

The relatively primitive means of transportation often dictated the route. For example, it is obvious that anyone traveling to England had to go by boat. The English government usually furnished yachts, even to diplomats of relatively low status. A request was made on behalf of the Envoy Extraordinary from the Elector of Brunswick not only for a yacht but for a specific captain. Although boats were not absolutely necessary for travel to continental states, many other governments made ships available to diplomats accredited to them. For example, the Republic of Genoa furnished the Emperor's Envoy Extraordinary with a galley to carry him to Leghorn in 1703, while the Swedes provided a man-of-war to carry Whitelocke from Stockholm to Lübeck. Even when the host did not furnish the transportation, many diplomats chose to journey by sea when possible.[6]

The reasons for their choosing ships are easy to discover. Travel by ship was more comfortable; once the journey started the diplomat could leave details to the captain rather than having to fuss with them himself; once on board less supervision of his household and baggage was necessary; and one could be relatively sure of having food to eat and a place to sleep. It would be possible to continue listing the advantages of sea voyages but this would give the impression that all was well with them. In reality even sea journeys inspired great concern and even fear in seventeenth century ambassadors. One problem was that, except when oared galleys were used, primarily in the Mediterranean, one could never be sure of departure schedules. For instance, d'Avaux was hurrying to Sweden in 1693 and arrived at Dunkirk the 9th of January ready to take ship. He was still there two and a half weeks later waiting for good winds. Matthew Prior was unsuccessful in his attempt to bring news of the Treaty of Ryswick more rapidly than the regular mail packet boat because of the vagaries of weather. He had hired a little sloop off the Dutch coast before noon but could not move until the next evening because the wind was from the northwest. That night they "had what the seamen call a fresh gale and the landsmen a storm." After springing a leak, they were in danger until the next day when the English coast was finally reached. But it turned out that the packet boat which had left several hours later had actually arrived ten hours before Prior's little sloop and had had a less dangerous crossing.[7]

Other diplomats ran into other dangers. In 1702 an envoy was run aground off the Dutch coast. The seamen finally got the ship loose by pulling on an anchor dropped some distance away but the pilot had become too timorous to try to move during the night so the envoy's party had to hire a bark which happened to lie nearby to carry them to shore. That the dangers were very real is illustrated by the fate of poor Dr. William Aglionby, English Envoy Extraordinary to the Duke of Savoy. His galley was shipwrecked on the coast of Corsica and he himself narrowly escaped drowning. As it was he lost all his equipage and money, coming ashore half dead in his waistcoat and drawers. Several of his servants were drowned.[8] An English envoy to Denmark was actually lost when his ship went down during a December storm. It is easy for us today to ignore the dangers of the elements, but the diplomats of the seventeenth century were made all too aware of them by such misadventures.

Despite the dangers inherent in sea voyages, there were other reasons which persuaded diplomats that sea travel was worth their while. For instance, the diplomat's own master might provide the necessary ships, thereby decreasing his personal travel expenses, although he often had to hire additional merchant vessels to carry his retinue and belongings. When Louis XIV replaced his ambassador at Constantinople with the Viscount of Guilleragues, he was accompanied by an imposing number of ships: two navy ships, the Hardi and the St. Augustin, an unnamed "flute," four merchant vessels, and six miscellaneous small craft. Other ambassadors were not accompanied by such impressive flotillas, but many rulers did take advantage of the opportunity to show their naval power, impress their friends, and warn their enemies.

Perhaps the major advantage of journeying by sea was the opportunity to avoid certain types of problems, especially enemy territory or war zones. Diplomatic theory and practice were in accord that an "ambassador and his suite enjoyed their privilege of immunity [from arrest, interruption, etc.] from the moment they came within the jurisdiction of the prince to whom the mission was accredited. . . . '' But theory and practice were also in accord that this immunity was not a right of diplomats passing through third countries; rather any immunities they may have had were merely courtesies extended by other states.[9] Few diplomats were willing to trust themselves to the mercies of third states without first obtaining the appropriate ''passports'' which at this time were somewhat like safe-conduct passes or visas. All too often, especially during wartime, such passports were either impossible to obtain or were held up so long that they were no longer valuable. States were unwilling to grant safe-conducts to representatives of their wartime enemies for they realized that it was not likely to be to their advantage to do so. Some diplomats were willing to take the chance of traveling with only their diplomatic character as protection as did the Frenchman Bonnac when journeying through Poland to become French ambassador to Sweden. Bonnac was captured by some Polish troops, but fortunately the Polish king had him released. The Abbé de Polignac left France to become ambassador to Poland in disguise as a ''courier extraordinary'' because France was at war with the Maritime Powers. Few diplomats were willing to go so far as that because it was generally recognized that a diplomat in disguise forfeited his claims to any sort of diplomatic immunity. In the summer of 1711, Matthew Prior journeyed to France disguised and in a fishing boat to begin the negotiations which would end the War of the Spanish Succession. This was done to keep his mission secret from his fellow Englishmen rather than because he was trying to escape detection by the enemy French.[10] Taking a ship did not exclude the possibility of capture by enemies but at least it made the possibility less likely; and disguises were not necessary.

All too often, however, geographical and other circumstances dictated that the diplomat journey by land. The difficulties were many! For a start, the roads were generally awful. Even in France, which was generally reputed to have the best roads on the continent, a French ambassador commencing his journey was pleased to have avoided ''two or three shipwrecks on land,'' meaning that the roads were flooded. The roads elsewhere were usually in even worse condition. The situation in Italy can be inferred from an Italian proverb which circulated at the time: ''a galloping horse is an open sepulcher.'' Broken bones from falls while on the road were common among diplomatic entourages. Occasionally, when a prince knew that a diplomat was to arrive by land and wished to make a good impression, the roads would be improved before he arrived, potholes filled, and bridges repaired. More often, diplomats had to struggle with the same problems as ordinary travelers.

The vehicles used were often as primitive as the roads themselves. One diplomat arrived in Sweden to find that only very small country wagons drawn by one horse or two cows were available to transport his goods. The horses were also small and carried uncomfortable saddles made of bare wood; ths bihs were a piece of ram's horn and the bridle a small hempen rope. He was more fortunate than a successor who traveled the same route forty years later in the dead of winter. After trying carts and carriages, sleighs and sledges, none of which worked very well, he was forced to divide his party because there were not enough horses available to transport his forty packages of goods and twenty-eight people. Unfortunately the magnificent carriages diplomats took with them for use in the foreign capital were often unsuited for cross-country travel, but they were utilized anyway for want of anything better.

As VIPs most traveling diplomats were able to claim the best lodgings available in the places where they spent the night, even to the extent of evicting other travelers from rooms they had already rented. But even in the more populous and wealthy parts of Europe, the inns were seldom of the quality desired. The philosopher John Locke described a night in a French hostel: "Although traveling tires an Englishman, we were no sooner taken to our chambers but we thought we had arrived too soon, for the highway seemed a much sweeter, cleaner and more desirable place." "After supper we retreated to the place that usually gives relief from all sorts of moderate calamities, but our beds served only to complete our vexation as they seemed to be designed to prevent sleeping. I will not complain of their hardness . . . but the thinness of the coverings and the tangible quality of what was next to me, and the odor of all about me made me quite forget my supper. It was impossible I should have lasted till morning in that strong perfume had not a large, convenient hole in the wall at the head of my bed poured in plenty of fresh air." [11] At least Locke had found an inn. Another diplomat traveling from Lübeck to Hamburg in northern Germany found only a lamentable lodging with but two beds for his whole retinue. "The beds were made of straw and fleas mingled together; the antechamber was like a great barn, wherein was the kitchen on one side, the stable on the other side; the cattle, hogs, wagons, and coaches were also in the same great chamber", wherein the whole company spent the night in the straw.[12] Elsewhere in Europe, particularly in the vast reaches of Poland or Spain, diplomats frequently found themselves camping in the open because no housing except their coaches was available.

The times diplomats found more satisfactory lodgings, especially in towns, were likely to be something of a mixed blessing. True, the rooms and beds were more likely to be acceptable than those described above; and local officials often made formal visits bringing presents such as wine, clothing, and food. However, many seventeenth century innkeepers viewed travelers primarily as milch cows from whom the host should try to extract as much wealth as possible. Diplomats were particularly susceptible to such treatment since they were required to uphold their master's reputation and thus were loath to give the impression of being stingy. The combination of these factors resulted in each diplomat's passage leaving an infusion of wealth into the local economy. The amount was invariably increased as the locals invented new ways to extract gifts. For instance, the local church choir might come to serenade the ambassador and to receive a reward in return. Or a wedding party might casually pass before a diplomat's lodging and thus perchance receive a gift. The devices used to obtain money from a traveling ambassador were limited only by the imagination of the local residents.

But all the advantages were not on the side of the locals. Many diplomats or their retinues were quite willing to engage in frolicsome activities like tearing up the furnishings of the houses in which they stayed and other expensive forms of partying. The damage caused by the ambassador's suite was not always intentional as, for example, when Whitelocke was passing through Stockholm in 1654. His people's carelessness came close to causing as great a fire as that which destroyed London several years later. They built larger than normal fires which ignited the soot and soon a whole stack of chimneys was ablaze. Fortunately, the wind blew the sparks onto a tile roof whereas the houses in the other direction were built and covered with wood. Such incidents show that the journeys of diplomats were not unmitigated blessings for either the travelers or for their temporary hosts. A sense of humor was definitely an asset when traveling. Du Luc, a French ambassador, related how he arrived in Switzerland on a sledge covered with straw up to his neck to ward off the cold: "The good Swiss seeing me pass through their territory acted in their inimitable way, placing bets, some saying — 'It's a calf,' others — 'It's a pig.' I felt like helping the latter half win, but ambassadorial dignity stopped me from oinking." [13] Overall, the unpleasant quarters, insufficient food, and dinners of bad bread and foul wine fit only for the peasants must have made arrival at their destination a relief to ambassadors. However, it marked the beginning of a round of fatiguing activities connected with their diplomatic role.

In most cases the diplomat entered a capital city incognito. His first responsibility was to find appropriate lodgings for himself and his household. Although the tradition of permanent diplomatic representation had been established for more than a century, governments did not yet own embassy buildings abroad. This did not become established practice until much later. For example, the British did not buy a permanent embassy house in Paris until 1814.[14] Most diplomats rented houses abroad although a scant few purchased them; leases were on a private basis between diplomat and owner. Sometimes, when representation was continuous or nearly so, a diplomat might take over the house occupied by his predecessor. Such was the case for the Portuguese ambassadors to England. The first ambassadors reaching London after the revolt from Spain in 1640 "took up their residence in a house on the south side of Lincoln's Inn Fields, which served as the embassy for many years." It is probable that this was the origin of the name of "Portugal Street" which still exists today. Throughout much of the seventeenth and eighteenth centuries, French ambassadors to Venice resided in a palace in the quarter called "Cannareggio." Unfortunately for the ease of many diplomats, it was often not possible for them simply to take over their predecessor's lodging. Frequently there had been no immediate predecessor because relations had been broken temporarily or because the diplomat had taken so long to arrive that the lodgings had been rented to someone else. Other problems were raised by differences in rank of appointees to the same post. For example, ambassadors might preceed and/or follow envoys or simple residents. A house which was appropriate for one rank frequently was not appropriate for another. Finally, differences in household size often made a predecessor's lodgings unsuitable.

When possible a diplomat sent a trusted servant or friend ahead to make housing arrangements. More often he had to make them himself after his incognito arrival. In the meantime he might lodge in a furnished public house, as did the envoy of Brandenburg to France in 1698, or with his master's consul in the same city if there were one, as did the Duke of Manchester at Venice in 1697. In searching for a house, a diplomat had to take many factors into consideration: was the neighborhood appropriate, could it be arranged to provide for the needs of private living and official business, price, and others. Manchester complained that he was having difficulty in getting a house which "would be honorable and convenient" because he had to treat with nobles. Even though he agreed to their price, which was "very extravagant," they still delayed finalizing the agreement.[15] Housing problems were less severe for some lower ranking diplomats like a Danish resident in London who was invited to live in the house of the French ambassador. When all the problems were overcome and an ambassador finally moved in, his master's coat of arms was mounted over the door to distinguish the house from its neighbors.

If the diplomat actually had pressing business, he attempted to establish contacts with the host government immediately upon his incognito arrival. Often there was a delay before the diplomat officially notified the "Introducer of Ambassadors" of his presence. The Introducer then arranged the myriad ceremonial details of the ambassador's entry and first public audience with the sovereign.

In the late Middle Ages and Renaissance, the arrival of an ambassador was usually an event of great significance. Crowds of ordinary people flocked to greet him as did the official welcomers from the sovereign. Gradually the procedures were formalized and became almost a ritual. By the late seventeenth century, diplomats were seldom greeted officially upon their actual arrival, but pageantry and ceremonial were still desirable for a variety of reasons. Thus the tradition that a "newly arrived" ambassador should have a public entry was continued. The custom can be better understood if we remember that public entries were not limited to diplomats. Brides of kings and princes, the kings themselves on journeys through their realms, important religious officials, and others· were often given magnificent public entries which entertained the populace and provided them an opportunity to show their loyalty. In effect these entries were parades and served many of the same functions parades do today. But the entries of ambassadors served another purpose as well. The magnificence of his parade was thought to reflect the power and importance of his master, so the ambassador did his best to provide a "good show" while the hosts judged his master by his success or lack of it.

The criteria used for judging included the newness and richness of the clothing of the diplomat's household; the number, size and magnificence of his carriages; and the number and quality of his horses and mules. Usually these items were brought with the ambassador from his home, but occasionally they were purchased at his post specifically for the entry and later use. An idea of what was meant by "magnificence" in the seventeenth century can be shown by a description of one ambassador's traveling coach: it was of "blue velvet, with blue silk and silver fringe, and richly gilded; it would hold eight persons, and was drawn by six bay English horses, of a good size for travel, and very handsome." Ambassadors to Venice, of couse, could not use carriages but had to travel the "streets of water" in gondolas. In 1701 it was reported that Venice had at least thirty thousand gondolas, all black and all alike except that ambassadors and newlyweds were allowed to have gondolas decorated in livery and gilded. The richness of the ambassadors' gondolas was as great as the most magnificent carriages, and each diplomat usually had four or five of them.[16]

Obviously, all ambassadors wanted to have successfully impressive entries and to report on their success to their masters. After examining a number of these reports, the modern reader begins to feel that the entries were carbon copies of each other. Typical is La Vauguyon's letter to Louis XIV about his entry into Madrid in 1682:

I can assure Your Majesty that no ambassador has ever arrived with such brilliance at Madrid. My carriages are magnificent as they have retained the luster which they had at Paris . . . and the horses are more handsome and in better condition than when I accepted them from the sellers. Their harnesses, topknots, and reins were garnished with gold and silver. My livery was a very beautiful yellow cloth, covered with a four inch braid in bands colored like fire and dark separated by gold and silver; all had beautiful linen and lace with ribbons of different colors. The footmen wore tall plumes while the pages had bunches of feathers. All in all the whole made a marvelous effect, much better than I had imagined it would.[17]

The fact that the public were as interested in these details as rulers is illustrated by the fact that programs for entries were printed and sold. They told when and where the entry would take place and described in detail the carriages and costumes of the participants. Further indication of public interest is found in contemporary newspaper accounts and private diaries which frequently give detailed descriptions of the whole parade.

Since everyone pretended that the ambassador was newly arrived, he usually repaired to a preselected spot some distance from the capital. In France, for instance, ambassadors from Catholic princes spent the preceding night at the convent of Picpus, while representatives of Protestant princes stayed at Rambouillet. At the preselected spot he was met by the "Introducer of Ambassadors" and other high ranking representatives of the sovereign: Senators in Sweden, Earls in England, important members of the States General in the Netherlands. After appropriate discourse, the ambassador and his hosts entered the king's state coach for the final stage of the journey. The ambassador's coaches and household fell into line along with the coaches of members of the royal family and important officials, coaches sent by other diplomats already in residence at the capital, coaches and horses of the ambassador's countrymen, a contingent of important citizens of the capital city, the diplomat's baggage train, sometimes an honor guard, and other miscellaneous participants. Following a special route, the procession wound its way through crowded streets to a house where the ambassador and his suite were entertained.

Most rulers accepted financial responsibility for entertaining the ambassador for several days after his entry, a carryover from the late Middle Ages when rulers often paid all or most of the expenses of special embassies. The French actually had a special "Hotel of Extraordinary Ambassadors" where new ambassadors and their households were fed by officers of the king; that is, the officers furnished meats and vegetables which the ambassador's cook prepared. Also during these days, the king's "maître d'hôtel" offered coffee, chocolate, and tea to all those who came to visit the diplomat. The English diarist John Evelyn described the elaborate official entertainment of the Venetian ambassadors in London in 1685:

> The dinner was most magnificent and plentiful with music (kettledrums and trumpets) which sounded upon a whistle at every toast. The dessert was

served on twelve large platters piled so high that those who sat on opposite sides of the table could hardly see each other. The ambassadors did not touch these sweetmeats (which doubtless had taken several days to pile up in that exquisite manner) but left them to the spectators who had come to see the dinner. The spectators took but a moment to demolish all that curious work. Thus His Majesty entertained the ambassadors three days, which (for the table alone) cost six hundred pounds." [18]

Ironically the Venetian government was not so generous when it was their turn to host an English ambassador, the Duke of Manchester, in 1697. Although they were obligated to offer to lodge and entertain him, they wanted him to declare his intention to refuse the offer as his predecessor had done before the date for his entry was set. Manchester, however, "thought it time enough to let them know my mind after they had made the offer." [19] This was probably not a way to make himself popular with the Venetian government, but it may have impressed them with his forcefulness. More powerful states than Venice were likely to view the entertainment of ambassadors as an opportunity to demonstrate their wealth and power, although as cheaply as possible of course.

Later, the day of or the day after the entry was usually devoted to the First Public Audience with the sovereign. The significance of this audience has often been downgraded on the grounds that it was an "empty session" of florid, solemn speeches full of generalities and declarations. But there actually was often some real significance to the audience. First, as the diplomatic theoretician Wicquefort says, "The public audience marks the beginning of the employment of the ambassador and establishes him in the duties of his office although it is not absolutely necessary before he can begin to negotiate." [20] It was then that the letters which accredited him for the position of ambassador or resident were presented.[21] After the acceptance of the letters and recognition of his position, the diplomat was officially entitled to the rights and privileges due to his status. To be sure, diplomats usually enjoyed these rights and privileges even before their official reception, but these could be and occasionally were challenged.

There were at least three other significant aspects of the First Audience with the sovereign. First, the speeches were not always devoid of content. For instance, in his instructions to d'Estrades Louis XIV noted that the generalities and compliments to be voiced were left to the ambassador's discretion, but this statement was followed by two pages of very specific ideas about his policies which the king wished the ambassador to tell the States General. Second, as was true of other ceremonial occasions, something of the host's attitude toward an ambassador's principal could be gleaned from the host's willingness or unwillingness to grant the diplomat the honors he thought were his due. Third, since the audiences were public, diplomats hoped to make a good impression there just as they did in the entry.

In several seventeenth century states the Public Audience had very special significance. In many capitals official business could be conducted even before the audience had taken place but in Venice it could not. There the method was "so different from other courts, that til this [audience] is over one can make no proposition to them. . . ." [22] As long as the ambassador remained incognito he usually did not even have contacts with other diplomats in Venice. In Sweden the king had expressly ruled that an ambassador could have no personal contact whatever with a Swedish senator until after his Public Audience. This was significant as senators were often important sources of information. Of course, these rules, like most other regulations of early modern governments, could be ignored if the situation warranted it, but it was obviously more desirable to go ahead and have the audience and thus not have to worry about disobedience.

With varying details Public Audiences throughout the seventeenth century followed the same pattern. Important officials escorted the diplomat from his lodging to the sovereign's reception room with elaborate ceremony. After some conversation with government ministers, the ambassador was taken into the sovereign's presence where his credentials were presented and they exchanged speeches. After some informal conversation and introductions, the ambassador was returned to his lodging with the same ceremony as before. It was also common, especially for diplomats from distant lands, to offer gifts to the rulers at the audience. A Russian ambassador gave the newly restored Charles II clothing lined with sable, black fox, and ermine furs, Persian carpets, hawks, horses, and bows and arrows. A Moroccan offered the same king two lions and thirty ostriches. Charles laughingly said that he supposed it would be proper to send a flock of geese in return. Although these embassies and presents created great excitement, it is unlikely that they were as great a sensation as that which had occurred at the beginning of the fifteenth century when Tamerlane sent a Tartarian envoy to the King of Castile and presented him with two gorgeous Hungarian slaves. Tamerlane's assumption that the girls would be a welcome gift was wrong.

Public Audiences did not always pass smoothly. For instance, a Muscovite envoy to Sweden did not receive notice of his audience until ten o'clock in the morning, and by that time he was already too drunk to have an audience so it had to be postponed. A Frenchman's audience with the king of Poland at least had the virtue of not leading to any conflicts between the diplomat and the ruler. On arriving at Danzig in 1648, the Count of Arpajon learned of the king's death. Two months later he reached Warsaw and made his official entry. He was then taken to the royal palace where two marshals of the court met him and took him to the hall where the body of the dead king was still exposed awaiting the election of a successor. Only after this macabre audience was the ambassador conducted to another hall where he was received by the Polish Senate in solemn session.[23] Most Public Audiences were of course much more ordinary and traditional. Many diplomats described the audience in detail in their reports home, but others simply mentioned that it had taken place and proceeded in the "normal" manner. Many rulers were quite willing to let the matter rest with that.

The elaborate ceremonial of the First Public Audience with the sovereign was just the beginning of a whole series of official visits which the ambassador was obligated to make. The Queen, the Queen Mother, the heir to the throne, other royal children no matter how tender their years, the king's brothers, sisters, and other relatives, and important officials all expected and were accorded a visit by the newly arrived diplomat, even if they had little or no significant role in the government. The ceremonies were not as elaborate as that with the sovereign, but etiquette was often very strict in any case. In cases where these individuals did play a role in government, the visits occasionally did provide real opportunities for the diplomat to establish contacts which would be of significance for his work.

These royal visits were followed by others which usually had a practical value — to the representatives of other princes at the same court. Obviously an ambassador did not contact agents of princes with whom his own master was at war, but he did visit most of the others. There were some variations in local tradition, but usually the new arrival was called on by diplomats of a lower rank than his own (for example an envoy called on an ambassador), while he made the first visit to diplomats of the same or higher rank. Such visits were considered so important that orders about them were often included in the formal public instructions given diplomats before they left home. For example, many English instructions included this phrase: "You shall entertain a good correspondence and friendship with the ambassadors, envoys and residents of other princes and states now in alliance or amity with us, who shall happen to be at that court at the same time with you." These visits were punctiliously returned, and they frequently became the basis for continued contacts, both official and unofficial, for the rest of the time the minister was at his post.

Once the initial round of ceremonies was over, usually in a period of several weeks, the minister could settle down to conducting the business for which he had been sent abroad.[24] It usually did not take long for diplomats to become dissatisfied with their situation because of problems — financial, health, boredom, and others. Under such circumstances it is not surprising that diplomats were often anxious to obtain permission from their masters to leave their posts at least temporarily. Such leaves of absence were often quite necessary. Difficulties of communication and the lack of formal procedures made it very difficult for a diplomat to tend to his private affairs from a distance over a long period. These problems are illustrated in the seventy-eight letters John Doddington, secretary of the English embassy in Venice from 1669 to 1673, wrote to his brother Sir Richard Temple. The letters are filled with requests to Temple to perform tasks for Doddington like pay his debts, intervene with government officials about payments due him, buy and sell property, etc. The awkwardness of the situation is exemplified by the fact that on one occasion Doddington had to send Temple at least three different copies of his power of attorney because he did not know if any of them arrived safely in England.[25] Other diplomats were beset by similar problems which tended only to grow worse as their time abroad was extended. Thus seventeenth century diplomats almost invariably requested permission to return home, at least temporarily, within a year or so after their original departure.

Not surprisingly, such permission was often difficult to obtain. Governments could expect a number of problems if they agreed. Negotiations and other diplomatic affairs might suffer. The diplomat would undoubtedly submit claims for extra expenses, while it might well be necessary to pay a temporary replacement abroad. Furthermore, it might be difficult to get the man to return to his post just as there had often been difficulty getting him to leave in the first place. These problems plus the ordinary lethargy of early modern governments often meant that a diplomat waited long months before receiving the desired permission. The primary exception to this pattern occurred when the prince wanted his diplomat to return for some special reason of his own: to confer with his ambassador, to listen to firsthand reports, or even to show his displeasure by leaving a diplomatic position temporarily unoccupied (just as is occasionally done today). The only instance with which I am acquainted of a government's attempting to regularize the situation was a project elaborated by the Swedish chancellery in 1685. The plan was that Swedish diplomats residing abroad would periodically return to Sweden to confer with the home goverment, inform the home officials about the situation abroad, and themselves be informed about points of Swedish policy which could not safely be committed to paper. But the plan was not implemented.[26]

At this point in the discussion of what a typical seventeenth century embassy was like, it is necessary to discuss the ways in which a man's tour of duty abroad

was terminated. The first to be mentioned should be that most effective case —
death. By dying at his post, a diplomat provided one last service to his fellows;
attendance at his funeral gave them an opportunity to engage in important
conversations in an informal way. Funerals were so much a part of diplomatic
life that there were even formal printed invitations sent out:

> You are invited to attend the funeral of the high and mighty seigneur,
> Monsieur Evrard, Marquis de Salviati, Grand Master of the Hunt and Envoy
> Extraordinary of the Grand Duke of Tuscany to His Majesty [Louis XIV].
> The Marquis, who was a Commander of the Order of Saint Steven for the
> carabineers of His Royal Highness of Tuscany, Marquis of Borchegiano,
> etc. passed away in his mansion on the rue de Bourbon. The funeral will take
> place today, Friday, 8 July 1707, at seven o'clock in the evening in the
> Church of Saint Sulpice, his parish church. *Requiescat in pace.*[27]

The number and rank of individuals attending such a funeral depended on the
importance of the diplomat's principal as much or more than on his personal
qualities.

A diplomat's death could provide an opportunity for the host to honor the dead
man's master as when the Swedes furnished a man-of-war to carry the body of
an ambassador back to France in 1692. Or the occasion could lead to conflict
over debts, honors, etc. When the pope's nuncio, Varese, died in France in
1679, there were problems about who had jurisdiction over the remains, who
was to pay for transporting the corpse, etc. The quarrel was of such dimension
that three years later there were still some doubt whether the pope would send
his traditional present of swaddling clothes for the newborn son of the Dauphin
"because the question of the offense to the cadaver of Varese still had not been
resolved."[28] In other cases, particularly those of lower ranking diplomats,
burial simply took place in the country where they died.

The vast majority of seventeenth century diplomats ended their tour of duty
alive, so one can ask why they were recalled. There is no apparent pattern, but it
is evident that governments hesitated to recall their ambassadors except for
what appeared to be very good reasons. The expense and other problems of
finding replacements were often sufficiently important to encourage governments to leave men abroad who might be somewhat unsatisfactory. Furthermore, there were apparently no hard and fast rules regulating how long
diplomats would remain at a given position. Many men who were regarded as
resident rather than temporary diplomats remained abroad less than a year. An
informal survey shows that a large majority remained at a given post three years

or less. Yet there were other men, particularly from the less important powers, who remained in the same capital ten or even twenty years.

One of the most common reasons for recall seems to have been the desires of the diplomats themselves. A man might temporarily hold off requesting permission in the hopes of having his plea looked upon more favorably at a later date. But, if one can believe their plaints, bad health, the need to settle domestic and/or financial affairs at home, inability to afford the continued expense of serving abroad, extraordinarily long service abroad, or even the fear that they were no longer effective, eventually forced them to ask for their own recall. Depending on the needs of the home government, such permission might or might not be forthcoming. The Spanish government delayed granting permission to the Marquis of Liche, its ambassador in Rome, despite his being sick and broke. Eventually his wife threw herself in tears at the king's feet to try to obtain permission for his return. In such cases the diplomat could do little else than suffer and remain at his post. In a few rare cases, the diplomat might be given permission in advance to withdraw when he determined that his mission had been accomplished or he despaired of success, but such cases were very rare. I know of no case where a seventeenth century diplomat came home without permission, except when the government to which he was accredited ordered him to depart.

Cases where the host government actually expelled a diplomat were quite rare and were usually the result of some extremely unusual situation. For instance, shortly before her abdication, Queen Christina of Sweden was about to become a Catholic and was greatly influenced by the Spanish ambassador. She decided to show her friendship to Spain by breaking off the friendly relations which had existed between Sweden and Portugal ever since the Portuguese had successfully rebelled against Spanish rule in 1640, a fact not yet recognized by Spain. In the spring of 1654 she ordered the Swedish Introducer of Ambassadors to take a letter to the Portuguese resident and open it in his presence. "The contents surprised them both; Christina informed Silva e Sousa that his mission at the Swedish court was useless, because she had decided not to acknowledge the Duke of Braganza as King of Portugal, since this title belonged rightly to Philip of Spain; therefore he would do well to make preparations for departure and need not hope for a change after her abdication, because she intended to inform her successor, so that he would follow the same course." Duke Charles Gustavus, afterward Charles X and Christina's successor, and his ministers were astonished and embarrassed. They tried to get the letter back and wanted to pretend the affair had never happened. Charles "wrote to the resident, enclosing a letter to the King of Portugal, in which he expressed his good will and promised that the declaration should have no effect." Queen Christina's action was a useless gesture, although it may have helped to make her relations with Spain better after her abdication. Curiously, this same Charles X dismissed all foreign residents from his court, including the Portuguese, the following year on the grounds that they were "honest spies" whom he did not want around during his war against Poland. Silva e Sousa retired to Hamburg from where he continued to send news to Portugal and requested permission to return home. He was not allowed to do so until four years later.[29]

Spain and England became involved in a mutual expulsion of residents as a result of William III's negotiating the Partition Treaty dividing Carlos II's empire. In August, 1699, Alexander Stanhope, the English envoy extraordinary in Madrid, was given a letter protesting the Partition Treaty in very strong language. The following month the Spanish ambassador in England, the Marquis of Canales, presented an even stronger paper in which Canales threatened to take his case to Parliament. William III responded by calling this "insolent and seditious" and "unjustified by the law of nations." Then Canales was told to leave William's dominions within eighteen days, not to leave his house until his departure, and to be informed that His Majesty would receive no more written communications from the ambassador or his domestics. In November Stanhope was ordered to leave Spain under the same conditions, but the Englishman tried to gain a point by declaring that his own king had already ordered him to depart.[30] The English expelled French diplomats on two occasions: once after the Glorious Revolution and the other after Louis XIV recognized "James III" as King of England in 1701.

More commonly, especially when the problem was one of personalities or was not sufficiently grave to risk a rupture of relations, the host government would get rid of an unwelcome diplomat by asking his own government to recall him. Such was the case when Philip V of Spain asked Louis XIV to recall several French ambassadors. A more curious instance was when the English ambassador to Prussia, Lord Raby, had become most unwelcome in Berlin. Raby, a vain and contentious man, was having an affair with the wife of the prime minister. The Prussian king, who was also anxious to enjoy the lady's favors, demanded Raby's recall on the grounds that Raby's relationship with her was making the king himself appear ridiculous. But then the king unaccountably changed his mind and insisted that Raby stay at his post.[31]

Perhaps the most unusual case of all was when diplomats were removed at the request of a third party. Such apparently occurred when, after a secret treaty was signed between Louis XIV and Charles II in 1681, Louis wanted Charles to recall certain pro-Dutch envoys and replace them with pro-French men. Such changes were made in the English personnel at The Hague, Copenhagen, Vienna, Paris, and several German states. This type case was quite rare, however.

Other embassies were brought to an end by the outbreak of war. Curiously, such a rupture did not always result in a tense or even unpleasant relationship between the departing ambassador and his host. A final audience was usually dispensed with, but even this was not always the case. In 1684 the French ambassador reported that he had received a last audience with the king and royal family of Spain and had been given an especially beautiful present besides.[32] The departure could be even more amicable. After Louis XIV declared war on Carlos II in 1673, his ambassador Monsieur de Villars was ordered to withdraw from Spain but only after having attended the celebrations for Carlos' birthday. Villars was treated with all sorts of honors at his final audience and then left for Bayonne where the ex-Spanish ambassador to France was being held as a hostage for Villars' security. The two ambassadors were supposed to pass into their own countries in an honorable way but the return was marred by a "stupid adventure." According to French reports, the Spanish ambassador's retainers attacked Villars' people as they were crossing the river. "It was a rather ridiculous combat in which the ambassadors exposed themselves despite the fact that shooting was occurring on all sides and several valets were killed." [33] More normally when a resident was departing because of the outbreak of war, he simply requested or was given his passports and departed in a few days with little ceremony or conflict.

Just as is the case today, seventeenth century ambassadors were sometimes recalled to show displeasure with another country's policies even when there was no intention to go to war. For instance, in 1668 Louis XIV's ambassador to Stockholm was recalled to indicate Louis' displeasure over Sweden's helping to arrange the Peace of Breda and her participation in the Triple Alliance. For a period thereafter, France was represented in Sweden only by a simple resident. Another incident fourteen years later illustrates how complaints about ceremonial could be used for public consumption to hide the actual cause of a diplomat's recall. The Frenchman Bazin was recalled from Sweden even before he had his first audience, supposedly because the Swedes wished to receive him with just one senator instead of the traditional two. In fact, Bazin was recalled because Sweden had aligned herself with enemies of France. On other occasions diplomats were recalled because their services were needed at other posts or at home, because they were not doing a satisfactory job, because they had become so unpopular that they were no longer effective, because of a change of government or ministers at home which made the diplomat an inappropriate representative abroad, or for other miscellaneous reasons.

Under normal circumstances when the diplomat was finally accorded permission or commanded to depart, he undertook procedures which were in effect the reverse of those he had done on his arrival. He requested a final audience with the sovereign at which his letter of recall[34] was presented; he said good-by to the prince and thanked him for his help and kindnesses; his speech reflected the current state of relations between the host and his own master but was always very polite. The ceremony, dress, and procedures were much like those at the beginning of his mission and they served the same purposes.

Just as the diplomat had been incognito before his First Public Audience, so did he revert to that status after the "Final Audience," even though he usually remained in the capital several days or weeks. In addition to making the practical and personal preparations for his return journey, he also had to call on the ministers of the host government, other resident diplomats, and almost everyone with whom he had had official contacts. Whitelocke reported that it was necessary to be very exact in these visits, being certain not to omit anyone who had previously called on him. He managed to make as many as seven visits in one day but still the task took several days. Most diplomats also found their last days crowded by the needs of somehow arranging to satisfy their creditors, who were invariably numerous, while the money available was invariably scarce. In cases where a diplomat awaited the arrival of his successor before departing, his time was also spent informing the new man about the state of affairs, introducing him to appropriate individuals at the court, and helping him set up housekeeping. It is difficult to see any pattern in whether or not an outgoing minister awaited the arrival of his successor except to note that papal nuncios almost always did wait. Eventually the diplomat embarked on his journey, suffering all the pangs and fears of travel which had accompanied his original departure, but this time assuaged by his pleasure at the prospect of his return home.

The procedures followed at home by newly returned diplomats depended to a great extent on the type of government which they served. Venetians had to sign a book indicating their arrival date and then write and read their relation to the Senate within a stipulated time. Throughout much of the period, returning Englishmen and Swedes reported to government ministers; but at other times strong kings like William III or even Charles XI received them. French ambassadors, at least toward the end of the reign of Louis XIV, went to see the Secretary of State for Foreign Affairs who made arrangements for him to "salute" the king and give an account of his embassy. This practice was so common throughout the Sun King's reign that an ambassador's not having a conversation with Louis at the end of a mission was almost a sign of disgrace. Since records were not kept, we have little information on what was said. One must be suspicious of existing reports like that in which Pomponne reported that Louis had such an amazing knowledge about his mission that the king seemed to have concerned himself with nothing else during Pomponne's absence. French ambassadors also conferred with government ministers, wrote relations, tried to get their bills paid, and then often settled into the ordinary routine of courtiers at Versailles. Like their modern counterparts, seventeenth century diplomats occasionally had some difficulty changing from "His Excellency the Ambassador" to an ordinary courtier and supplicant at his own court. The hierarchical nature of society did help ease this problem, however, as did the responsibilities of the new positions which they frequently were given.

FOOTNOTES

[1] See, for example, France. Commission des Archives Diplomatiques. *Recueil des instructions données aux ambassadeurs et ministres de France . . . Hollande,* ed. by L. André and E. Bourgeois, Paris, Vols. XXI and XXII, *passim.*

[2] R. Clark. *Sir William Trumbull in Paris, 1685-1686,* Cambridge, 1938, pp. 8-9.

[3] W. H. Lewis. *Levantine Adventurer, The Travels and Missions of the Chevalier d' Arvieux, 1653-1697,* London, 1962, pp. 180-81.

[4] B. Whitelocke. *A Journal of the Swedish Embassy in the Years 1653 and 1654,* new edition, ed. by H. Reeve, Vol. I, London, 1855, p. 60. Anyone interested in the details of an early modern embassy should not fail to use this delightful journal kept by one of Cromwell's ambassadors.

[5] M. Rémusat. "Un Ambassadeur de France en Pologne (1674-1680)," *Revue de Paris,* Vol. 26, 1919, p. 568.

[6] Public Record Office. London. SP 100/14, 18 October 1710; British Museum. London. Add. MSS. 34,356, 29 December 1703.

[7] British Museum. London. Loan 29/335.

[8] Public Record Office. London. SP 92/26; [La Combe de Vrigny]. *Travels through Denmark . . . in the Retinue of the English Envoy, in 1702,* Trans. from French, London, 1707, p. 3.

[9] E. R. Adair. *The Exterritoriality of Ambassadors in the Sixteenth and Seventeenth Centuries,* New York, 1929, pp. 107-110.

[10] See above, Chap. IV, pp.

[11] J. Locke. *Locke's Travels in France, 1675-1679, as Related in his Journals and Other Papers,* ed. by J. Lough, Cambridge, 1953, pp. 277-80.

[12] Whitelocke. *Journal of the Swedish Embassy,* see note 4, Vol. II, pp. 352-53.

[13] H. Mercier. *Histoire pittoresque de la ville et des bains de Bade,* Lausanne, 1922, p. 36.

[14] J. L. Anderson. "The British Embassy in Paris, 1714-63," *History Today,* Vol. XXI, 1971, p. 52.

[15] C. Cole, ed. *Memoirs of Affairs of State,* Trans. by C. Cole, London, 1733, p. 7.

[16] F. M. Misson. *Nouveau voyage d' Italie fait en l'année 1688,* Vol. I, The Hague, 1691, p. 192.

[17] A. -F. Aude. *Vie publique et privée d' André de Béthoulat, comte de La Vauguyon, ambassadeur de France (1630-1693),* Paris, 1921, p. 158.

[18] J. Evelyn. *The Diary of John Evelyn,* ed. by W. Bray, Vol. II, New York, 1907, p. 249.

[19] Duke of Manchester. *Court and Society from Elizabeth to Anne,* Vol. II, London, 1864, p. 32.

[20] A. van Wicquefort. *L' Ambassadeur et ses fonctions,* Vol. I, The Hague, 1681, p. 484.

[21] See below, Appendix, pp.   for sample letter of credence.

[22] Manchester. *Court and Society*, see note 19, Vol. II, p. 247.

[23] R. Przezdziecki. *Diplomatie et protocole a la cour de Pologne*, Vol. I, Paris, 194, pp. 136-38.

[24] The various aspects of a diplomat's "business" are discussed in chapters VI and VII.

[25] Huntington Library. San Marino, California. Stowe Collection.

[26] See above, Chap. IV, pp.

[27] Bibliothèque Nationale. Paris. Fonds Français, NA 7487, Fol. 404.

[28] F. de Bojani. *Innocent XI, sa correspondance avec ses nonces*, Rome, 1910-12, 3 vols, *passim*.

[29] K. Mellander and E. Prestage. *The Diplomatic and Commercial Relations of Sweden and Portugal from 1641 to 1670*, Watford, 1930, pp. 95-100.

[30] See below, Appendix, pp.   for the relevant documents.

[31] H. L. Snyder. "The British Diplomatic Service during the Godolphin Ministry," in R. Hatton and M. S. Anderson, eds. *Studies in Diplomatic History*, London, 1970, pp. 53-55.

[32] Aude. *Vie de La Vauguyon*, see note 17, pp. 226-27.

[33] *Lettres de Madame de Villars à Madame de Coulanges*, new edition, ed. by A. de Courtois, Paris, 1868, p. 28.

[34] See below, Appendix, pp.   for sample letter of recall.

CHAPTER VI

Information: Important
Objective Of Diplomatic Activity

In the seventeenth century, just like today, the necessary raw material of diplomacy was information. Early modern decision makers needed ever increasing amounts of data before they felt able to decide what policies they should follow. Of course, the early modern diplomatic world was less complex than today's, and events moved with what would now seem excruciating slowness. In particular, the process by which diplomats gathered, arranged and sent home the data their masters needed usually proceeded at a snail's pace. The reasons for the lack of speed will become obvious from an examination of the process of letter writing and the postal service. These techniques were primitive as were the ciphers used to keep the messages hidden from prying eyes. Then the chapter will examine the career of one of the chief "pryers," the Englishman John Wallis, who spent his life unraveling the messages diplomats and their governments had worked so hard to encipher. Diplomats abroad corresponded with many different people back home which in part accounts for the great variety of kinds of information in which they were interested. The specialization characteristic of twentieth century diplomatic establishments did not exist in the seventeenth century; the ambassadors or envoys themselves were required to be "jacks of all knowledge." This chapter will end with an examination of the methods used by early modern diplomats to acquire information, both formal and informal, especially espionage.

Sending Letters Home by Mail and Courier

The early modern era was very unlike our own, at least insofar as devices for speeding communication are concerned. There were no telephones, typewriters or even efficient pens or pencils. Thus the actual writing of letters was a time consuming activity for seventeenth century diplomats. One or more days a week were committed largely or wholly to preparing and sending despatches. First the diplomat had to decide what to report, often using notes or some sort of diary in which he had recorded his thoughts and experiences. Then he had to write out his thoughts himself in longhand or dictate them to a secretary who also wrote in longhand since only elementary forms of shorthand had been invented by this time. The time consuming process was lengthened even more because of the necessity to make the copies as clean and neat as possible. Since letters provided almost the only contact between a diplomat and his master, the former had to try to make as good an impression as possible in order to maintain his reputation and hopes for future advancement. Even simple acts took time: sharpening the quill pens (which some writers did not do often enough to satisfy modern historians who must pore over almost indecipherable writing) and sanding the paper (occasionally with a kind of silver glitter to give the writing an attractive appearance). But the most important reason letter writing days were so long was the sheer volume of correspondence which diplomats maintained. Sending ten or more letters per post day was not uncommon. Fortunately, many diplomats found it possible to compose one letter which then served as the model for the others. If the diplomat had a trustworthy secretary, he was able to avoid the further tedium of copying the letters into a bound volume (simply called a "Letter Book"). The secretary also wrote the duplicates which, especially in wartime, were sent by an alternate route in order to increase the chances that at least one would arrive safely at its destination. The whole of this activity was complicated by pressures to complete the job before the "ordinary" left.

The use of the term "ordinary" occasionally confuses modern readers who picture seventeenth century diplomatic correspondence as being carried swiftly by mounted couriers dressed in handsome uniforms carrying bags marked with a "silver greyhound" or other appropriate emblem. The picture is false. Most diplomatic mail was carried by the "ordinary" mail service which early modern governments had recently established or reestablished. The reason why diplomats tended not to use couriers except when absolutely necessary was stated succinctly by the theoretician Rousseau de Chamoy: couriers were an expense which should not be incurred unnecessarily. They should only be used for carrying finished treaties, for extremely urgent and important affairs, if the ordinary postal service was entirely broken, or if the normal ways of sending letters were closed and it was impossible to get the letters through in any other way.[1] A diplomat who caused his master the expense of a courier except under these circumstances was liable to be reprimanded and even have to pay the charges himself.

On the occasions when couriers were used it was hoped that the despatches would arrive at their destination more rapidly than by the ordinary post and also that they would be less likely to be intercepted and read en route. Unfortunately the vagaries of travel were such that the speed of the courier (who usually went the whole distance himself) was not necessarily faster than the "ordinary." In 1661, for example, the French ambassador at The Hague, was informed that his despatch of June 2nd sent by the ordinary had arrived before that of June 1s: sent by courier; as a similar situation had happened previously the ambassador was warned not to send couriers who served only to cause the king a completely useless and unnecessary expense.

The hope of keeping despatches confidential by using couriers was also often in vain. The very fact that a message was so important that a diplomat chose to use a courier attracted attention and encouraged agents to try to discover the contents of his pouch. In theory it was widely agreed that couriers and despatches were protected by diplomatic immunity in the seventeenth century.[2] In fact interference was relatively common. This could be carried out under the guise of an ordinary highway robbery as happened to one of d'Avaux's messengers while he was the French ambassador in the Netherlands in 1684. William, the Prince of Orange, wished to discourage communication between the ambassador and the leaders of Amsterdam. The Prince surrounded d'Avaux with spies who informed him whenever d'Avaux sent a courier who might carry information about such contacts. On one occasion, one of d'Avaux's couriers started his journey from The Hague with the regular post horse; but the governor of Maestricht (one of William's supporters) delayed the messenger for a very long time and would not give him permission to leave with the regular mail. Meanwhile three groups of men were sent out to wait a quarter of a league from Maestricht. The "bandits" who caught the messenger after he was finally given permission to leave the town were actually Dutch soldiers. They stripped him and took his letters without stealing anything else except his boots and Jerkin; then he was given back into the safekeeping of his postilion who took him back to Maestricht. The man returned to The Hague where he informed the ambassador of his misadventure.[3]

Other couriers also ran into difficulties with "robbers," but some were openly stopped by government officials who examined the despatches. In these cases, the diplomat usually complained to his hosts who in turn replied that they would attempt to capture and punish the "robbers." Or the interference was blamed on the officials' over-zealousness and promises were made that the men would be punished and further abuses prevented. The major factor which prevented even more widespread interference with couriers was stated by an English ambassador in France whose man had been arrested. He said simply that the French would undoubtedly give satisfaction or they would find "their couriers and ambassadors' servants used just in the same manner in England." As so often happened in early modern diplomatic conflicts, the threat of retaliation alone was effective.

Since diplomats used couriers in the hope of having their despatches delivered successfully rather than to provoke an incident with their hosts or other rulers, their messengers occasionally resorted to unusual tricks to get through. This was particularly true during wartime because even theoretical immunity did not apply to couriers of an enemy. In the sixteenth century couriers had sometimes disguised themselves as priests, monks, pilgrims or merchants — people who were protected by canon law. But there were disadvantages to doing this in the seventeenth century. It was difficult for them to claim any sort of immunity if they had hidden their identity at first; and the strictures of canon law did not, of course, apply in Protestant countries. Thus a diplomat was more likely to depend on a man who had proven his ability to pass through enemy territory because of speed and stealth. Or the diplomat might depend on an individual of somewhat more importance than an ordinary courier — for example, his secretary or a traveling nobleman. In any case we know that despite the restrictions governments placed on the use of special messengers because of their expense, they were still used sufficiently often that the English government had established a special group of ''Forty Messengers of the Great Chamber in Ordinary'' for both internal and external affairs. The master of the posts in France received 3,000 livres during the year 1660 alone for the horses of couriers sent to other countries.[4]

The excessive cost, publicity, and other problems attendant upon the use of couriers combined to ensure that most diplomatic correspondence was actually sent via the postal ''ordinaries.'' The actual techniques of carrying the mail changed very little in the early modern period, but most governments had established post office systems by the mid-seventeenth century. Although service was generally interrupted during wartime, the agreements necessary for international postal service were usually reestablished shortly after the cessation of conflicts. The main difference between the postal services in 1648 and those is 1715/21 was the increase in the number of cities between which mail was carried and the frequency with which it was done.[5]

The speed at which the letters could be carried was limited. There had been no technological advances for the past several thousand years — at least for land carriage. Letters could move no faster than a horse could run over poor roads which were seldom as good as those which the Roman Empire had built 1500 years before. In a contract signed in 1505 a private individual promised to carry mail between Brussels and other places in Europe according to this schedule:

Innsbruck — 5½ days in summer; 6½ days in winter
Paris — 44 hours in summer; 50 hours in winter
Toledo — 12 days in summer; 14 days in winter
Rome via Innsbruck — 10½ days in summer; 12 days in winter.[6]

A century and a half later these times were seldom matched much less bettered. The ordinary took about two weeks between Madrid and Paris in the late seventeenth century, about the same time as the Brussells-Stockholm schedule. In the spring of 1673 letters from Stockholm to Paris took between 13 and 16 days while the same journey in 1697 was running 16-18 days in summer and often 20-24 or more days in winter. Letter post between Paris and The Hague could arrive in 2 days, Paris-London in 3 or 4 days, but Vienna-London took nearly a month. All these times are, of course, just the normal, scheduled times. Storms, floods, ice, snow, and dark of night definitely slowed the postmen in their appointed rounds.

A diplomat's letters ran into few difficulties, of course, while they were in the hands of postal officials working for his own master; but opportunities for problems were rife when the letters were in the hands of foreign postmasters. The postal agreements signed between various states were usually easier to negotiate and conclude than to enforce. The control of governments over their own officials in the seventeenth century was often tenuous so, of course, the influence of foreign governments was next to nil. A postal officer could cause difficulties on his own such as the conflict between the pope's nuncio in Spain in 1680 and a Spanish "lieutenant of the post for Italy." Their disagreement over the rate which the nuncio should pay and a variety of other problems finally led to an impasse when the lieutenant insisted on being paid at the departure and arrival of each post and the nuncio refused. The conflict was settled only after the nuncio appealed to the king's ministers for assistance. They assured the nuncio that he would be required to pay only the same rate as the king. In cases where the government was unwilling or unable to act, diplomats resorted to making special, private agreements with individual postmasters in order to secure preferential treatment for their letters. This was possible since official letters continued to make up such a large proportion of the mails, especially of the part going long distances.[7]

In cases where some government official deliberately decided to make a diplomat's life more difficult, there was little he could do except threaten reprisals if the matter became too serious. But even this latter action was hard to take if the difficulties were being made clandestinely or for an apparently good reason. The French ambassador in Sweden in 1674 found himself in such a situation. He was sure that the Swedish chancellor had deliberately advanced the time at which the ordinary mail boat sailed from Hamburg so that Louis XIV's letters which arrived two hours later would be held up six days. To have attempted to get them delivered earlier would have required using expensive "extraordinary" methods. The modern scholar must be suspicious of such accusations by seventeenth century diplomats, however. One of their major pastimes was making complaints about mail service which thus provided them with ready-made excuses for their own failures.

These difficulties were relatively minor compared to the major problem which arose from entrusting despatches to the care of foreign postal officials. Secret diplomatic letters were put into the hands of the very people who were most interested in knowing their contents. All seventeenth century governments were quite willing to take advantage of the situation. In fact the opportunity to use the public post as a device for discovering information about the state's own subjects and about diplomats seems to have been an important factor in the decision to create postal systems in the first place. In France it was an axiom of political theory about sovereignty and absolute government that correspondence confided to the public post could be searched without scruple both in peace and war, whether it originally came from within or without the kingdom. The same attitude existed in England where the Post Office had been regarded "as part of the machinery for detecting conspiracies" against the government since the early 1500's. A modern scholar goes on to note that "the secrecy of the post was violated on a greater scale during the seventeenth century than at any other time. Even the correspondence of ambassadors was not immune from inspection." [8] He should probably say that especially the correspondence of ambassadors was not immune! The legal right of the English government to open mail was based on the royal prerogative since Tudor times and given an unassailable legal basis in the Post Office Act of 1711. Comparable attitudes existed in the other European countries.

Most governments maintained special bureaus which were responsible for discovering and copying any important information which could be found in the mails. These have been called "black cabinets" or in England "the Secret Office;" numerous proofs of their existence not only in London and Paris but in the Netherlands, Austria, Venice, and Hanover can still be found in archives today. A series in the British Public Record Office is actually entitled "Intercepted." The first volume begins in 1726, somewhat later than the period with which we are dealing, but an introductory letter by the compiler of the volume throws much light on the practice by which they were acquired which was also followed in the 1600's. The series consists

of copies, translations, & extracts from the original correspondence of Foreign Ambassadors Resident in England. It is quite clear that the letters to and from the Foreign Ambassadors Resident in England, were intercepted before they left and as they arrived in England — they were opened and copies or extracts (& sometimes both) taken — and where the language used was other than English or French, translations were made as well as copies,

and sent to the secretaries [of State] or other Ministers, . . . [or] the King —
The letters after being copied etc were sealed up again & allowed to proceed
to their destination.

The compiler regrets that much of this valuable series of letters suffered greatly
from dampness because they were not thought to be important. An old official
remembered that when the papers were at the Old State Paper Office in Scotland
Yard, "they were thrown in a closet as papers of no consequence, and where an
immense quantity perished." [9] Nevertheless there are still numerous copies of
intercepted letters both at the British Museum and Public Record Office from
the last half of the seventeenth century. The French interceptions are usually
intermingled in the larger series of diplomatic documents at the Archives des
Affaires Etrangères. Dutch examples are even to be found in London where
they sent copies of the letters they intercepted.

Evidence of how widespread the practice of opening letters was is also to be
found in the correspondence, both official and private, of seventeenth century
diplomats. Untold numbers include comments like that of Mme. de Sévigné to
a French ambassador in Sweden: "Adieu, Monsieur Ambassador; if the bishop
of Munster sees this letter, I will be very pleased for him to know that I love you
with all my heart." [10] Matthew Prior was even more explicit in a letter to a
secretary of state. He said that he did not want to write about a certain matter
"by the post, because I must name the persons, and I take it for granted that our
letters are broken open." [11] The practice was so widespread that diplomats may
have been disappointed if their letters and therefore they themselves were not
considered important enough for their mail to be intercepted.

Under these circumstances, it is not surprising that diplomats and their
governments had developed a variety of techniques which, it was hoped, would
reduce the number of occasions on which their mail was actually intercepted.
Some techniques had been used for centuries and others were relatively new.
The most obvious way was to try to conceal the official nature of the despatch so
that it would be hidden among the ordinary private and business correspondence which most governments could not examine simply because they
lacked the necessary resources to censor all the mail their post offices handled.
The easiest and cheapest technique was simply to address letters to an individual whom a foreign government would be unlikely to suspect of being
politically important — for example, a banker or merchant — with whom
arrangements had previously been made to have the letters forwarded to the
appropriate minister. But, since fake addressees themselves might be unfaith-
ful, some diplomats even attempted to hide the true destination from them. For
instance, the French ambassador to Denmark in 1697 wrote to Louis XIV's

governor at Huningue that a man in Germany who had to write to the Marquis de Torcy, the French secretary of state for foreign affairs, would address his letters to a "Monsieur d'Orgemont" in care of Monsieur Thelusson, a merchant at Basel. The merchant was only told to forward such letters to the governor who in turn sent them to Torcy by the French post. The French ambassador in Sweden also addressed his letters to the same Monsieur d'Orgemont.[12] Using false addresses was not overly successful, however, because the individual mailing the letter in the first place was often recognized as a diplomat's servant and the address noted. Secondly, spies often discovered what false addresses were being used. Finally, the random opening of letters occasionally led to the contents being discovered.

In their attempts to maintain secrecy, writers of diplomatic despatches resorted to a variety of subterfuges which were designed to conceal their contents even when the letters were intercepted by unauthorized persons. The first of these was to try to seal them in such a way that they could not be opened without it being evident to the recipient who could then raise a cry against the guilty parties. The ordinary methods used for sealing in the seventeenth century were such that it was not an easy thing to open a letter secretly in any case. The brownish red wax made a very hard seal marked with an individual's own pattern which even today is very hard and breaks if bent. Since the letters were generally folded so as to be their own envelope, the wax was usually dropped at the outside spot where the last fold was held to the rest of the page. Occasionally, the wax was dropped on the page, the last edge folded over, and then another drop put on top into which the patterned seal was impressed. Either method was so effective that the normal way of opening was simply to tear the paper and leave the seal attached to the main part of the letter. The technique assured that it would be very difficult for anyone without a fair amount of time and skill to open the letter secretly. In other words, a groom caring for a messenger's horse, a chambermaid, or other such person would probably not be able to do so. Nevertheless few seventeenth century diplomats were as confident about the effectiveness of their methods as was Lord Denzil Holles, the English ambassador to France in 1663. Holles wrote to Secretary of State Arlington suggesting a way for all English diplomats to improve the security of their letters: "If you will be pleased to give order the covers [of letters] may be made up with Paste, (which is but starch boiled up to a height), and sealed upon as I do, making some little holes in the upper paper that the wax may take to both, I durst lay all my estate, and my head to boot, which I prize more, they are opened no way."[13] Most diplomats recognized that the "Black Cabinets" or "Secret Offices" with their fire and candles burning constantly and their expert letter openers could undoubtedly succeed in opening the letters without leaving evidence of their tampering.

Security minded writers attempted to prevent their despatches from being read even after they were opened. Some engaged in the rather simple trick of including a letter with another but with no address or signature so that it would appear to be only a copy of the first and thus not be read by a careless spy. Others talked about using invisible ink although it is doubtful that any actually did use it. By far the most common device diplomats used to keep the contents of letters secret was the cipher.

Ciphers and Cryptography

A distinction is sometimes made between ciphers (or cyphers) and codes. A cipher is a method of secret writing in which numbers, different letters or other characters are substituted for the actual letters. In a code numbers, letters, words, or other symbols are arbitrarily designated to stand for words or phrases. The distinction is almost meaningless for the seventeenth century because most governments used a combination of the two for their diplomatic correspondence. Throughout the period most diplomats were furnished with at least two different ciphers: one for use in ordinary correspondence and the other which was more difficult for the things which were more secret and more important to hide from enemies. But it was not unusual for a diplomat to have many more than two. They were used for correspondence with his master, with his fellow diplomats serving in other courts, with ministers, or even for his private correspondence with friends and relatives. An example of the last type of correspondence is the Countess of Sunderland's letter to the English ambassador at The Hague in 1680. The Countess was willing to write newsy tidbits to the effect that her Lord had been to visit Lady Scroop and "found her at dinner on a leg of veal, swimming in butter, which has so turned his stomach, that she will scarce recover his good opinion." Because she had left her cipher at Windsor, however, she did not feel she could "write more plainly" about more important topics.[14] Since diplomats' personal correspondence was often concerned with such delicate topics as their hopes for advancement and which individuals at home were helping or hindering their careers, it is quite possible that they were as anxious to use private ciphers to conceal their correspondence from their home government as from foreigners. In any case, the use of ciphers was so widespread and there was such a large demand for them that there were actually printed forms available. A person needed only to fill in his own choice of numbers to stand for the relevant letters, mark a few private names or places, and he had a perfectly workable cipher which would serve for most purposes.

Most ciphers used in the seventeenth century were of the rather elementary type in which one or more numerals were simply substituted for letters. They were somewhat improved by including such rules as: all numbers ending in 9 or 0 are nulls; the order of the letters is indicated by using number 61 next to the first, 62 next to the second, etc. The difficulty was that the men charged with enciphering or deciphering were prone to make mistakes as the ciphers became more complicated. Also, the ever-present pressure of time made using a complicated cipher less desirable. Thus most despatches were written in the simple substitution type cipher of one numeral standing for one letter with a few other numerals representing specifics like king of Poland, Parliament, the pope, etc.[15] Many writers did not even bother to encipher the whole letter but only did paragraphs, phrases, or even just words here and there.

Obviously, one of the main concerns for anyone using a cipher is the necessity to keep the key secret. In order to do this, diplomats normally took with them all the ciphers which they expected to need while abroad or, under exceptional circumstances, new ciphers were brought by special couriers. Furthermore, diplomats were expected to use great care to keep the cipher locked up when not in use, not to allow copies to be made of it, and occasionally even to do the work of ciphering themselves when very important matters were at stake. Unfortunately, all too often either diplomats abroad or officials at home were not very security conscious. Some ciphers were stolen. Others were simply lost.

But the question can be raised whether keeping the keys of ciphers secret was really very important in the seventeenth century. The theoreticians disagreed about the answer. Wicquefort, writing near the beginning of our period, thought: ''It is not very difficult to invent a million new ciphers, but it is almost impossible to find one which cannot be decoded by someone who has a little genius and much practice in doing it.''[16] Callières, however, writing half a century later, thought that ''experience shows that a well-made and well-guarded cipher is practically undiscoverable except by some betrayal, that is to say that the wits even of the cleverest student of ciphers will fail to pierce its secret unless aided by corruption.''[17] It is difficult today to say which of these men was right. We can note that many practicing diplomats seem to have taken it for granted that foreign agents would be able to decode any letters which came into their possession. It is also possible to examine the opinions of an individual who engaged in the deciphering process.

John Wallis — Decipherer Extraordinary

An Englishman, John Wallis (1616-1703), began deciphering documents almost as a joke shortly after he had earned several college degrees and been appointed to a chaplainship during the English Civil War.[18] He was rewarded with the living of St. Gabriel in London (1643) and that of St. Martin (1647). Cromwell was generous and Wallis became a professor of geometry at Oxford and Keeper of the University Archives. The restoration of Charles II in 1660 helped rather than hindered his career. He was made chaplain to the king and encouraged to continue his deciphering under the direction of the new secretary of state. He continued this work for successive English governments and even trained his grandson who became the first official decipherer of England on his grandfather's death in 1703.

Wallis apparently did his deciphering work at home so that it could not interfere with his other duties. Copies of the intercepted letters were sent to him by the appropriate official. For instance, in May, 1665, Mr. Wren, a secretary of the Lord Chancellor, sent Wallis two letters to be deciphered along with a rather fulsome note: The Lord Chancellor "knows that to your industry & sagacity the most accurate ciphers are as open as a common alphabet, & this cipher being as he conjectures a very mean one will he supposes give you very little trouble to unmask it." Apparently Wallis was something of an artist with the proverbial artist's temperament for he reacted vehemently when his work was questioned. In 1690 one of his decipherings was returned to him after the envoy from Brandenburg to England had been allowed to read and comment on it. The secretary noted: "The Envoyé of Brandenburg having made some small corrections in the Letter deciphered by you, which may be of use to you if any others of the same cypher should again be sent to you I have sent those letters to you by my Lord's Order, who desires, that when you have perused those corrections you will send the letters back to me again, for his Lordship." Four days later Wallis shot back a response noting that most of the "corrections" were those which he had made himself — only a few had been made by the envoy. Furthermore, Wallis noted, the envoy's "corrections" were not mistakes of the decipherer (that is Wallis) but were inaccuracies in the language of the original writer. Wallis's work was generally satisfactory as is evidenced both by his having been maintained in the position of decipherer for so long and also by the fact that the king himself was interested enough to be concerned that he be paid. In 1689, for example, he was awarded the rather sizable sum of 50 pounds.

In his autobiography Wallis throws some light on the question of whether or not deciphering was easy. He described how he could master almost all ciphers which had been made in the mid-seventeenth century. "But of late years," noted Wallis, *"the French Methods of Cipher* are grown so intricate beyond what it was wont to be, that I have failed of many; tho I have mastered divers of them." If a generalization can be made from this one man's experience, it would appear that the ciphers became more difficult as the century progressed. The lives and activities of decipherers in other countries are not so well documented as Wallis's, but there is sufficient evidence to indicate that every state which could discover, create, and afford such technicians did so.

If it is true, as it seems to be, that despatches were intercepted and deciphered rather easily, a number of questions arise. Why did seventeenth century diplomats and their governments put so much effort into trying to conceal the meaning of their despatches? And more important, how much effect did the interceptions actually have on policy decisions? There are several answers to the first question. As has been noted before, enciphering despatches was particularly helpful in preventing anyone (like a chambermaid, waiter, or coachman) who only had an opportunity for a quick glance to learn what it said. As everyone who has worked in archives today where he can only copy material by hand knows, such copying takes an extremely long time to make an exact transcript. It is much easier and faster just to summarize the gist of a document; but of course it is impossible to summarize a document in cipher. Furthermore, if on any rare occasion a government wished to use information directly which it had discovered in a deciphered document, a diplomat could always claim that it had been incorrectly deciphered and then return to the attack on the grounds that the government should not have had the document in the first place.

Answering the second question of how much effect intercepted information had on policy decisions is somewhat more difficult. But, we can note that during peacetime any diplomatic agreements can only come into effect when both sides "agree." Although it may be of some help to know how far the other side is willing to go on a particular question, there is no peaceful way of forcing the other side to agree to more than it feels is in its own best interests. Furthermore, since the most important despatches were sent by courier, a foreign government could never be sure that it had all the appropriate information.

As far as intercepted information during wartime is concerned, it is obvious (since diplomats are recalled or sent home at the outbreak of war) that the volume of correspondence is reduced just at the time when it is most valuable. In both peace and war the delays in deciphering would have reduced the value of the intelligence. We can also note that the inefficiency of early modern governments, made it very likely that they seldom had the funds and/or personnel necessary to examine all the diplomatic correspondence which might possibly have been of value. Finally, we can note that early modern states suffered from the same problems faced by all governments, companies, individuals, etc. which depend on spying for information: even more important than the information itself was the accuracy with which the decision makers were able to examine the great mass of often conflicting materials and determine which is correct. How well they succeeded can only be judged by examining specific cases.

Recipients of Diplomatic Letters

Anyone who learns that letter writing often took up the whole of an early modern diplomat's "mail" day and that he sent five, ten or more letters out with each ordinary might well wonder to whom all these letters were addressed. Obviously, the first and most important was the letter sent to his own master. When the sovereign was personally involved in the direction of foreign affairs, successful ambassadors usually undertook to write him on every possible occasion. Depending on the form of government, they usually also wrote the secretary of state for foreign affairs at the same time.[19]

There were exceptions, of course. Papal nuncios addressed their official correspondence to the cardinal secretaries of state. In the mid-seventeenth century it was not unusual for English diplomats to exchange letters with the king, but after the Glorious Revlolution direct correspondence between the monarch and "his" diplomats decreased significantly. For instance, Matthew Prior[20] wrote directly to George I from Paris, but he did this in desperation because of his bad position vis-à-vis the new English government. The role of secretaries of state under William III could hardly be called exalted. During the king's numerous absences on the Continent, English diplomats were ordered to communicate with William Blathwayt, the Acting-Secretary of State who accompanied the king. Of course, William was in effect acting as his own secretary of state for foreign affairs at this time. Under Queen Anne the secretaries of state were occasionally ignored. But normally Anne instructed her ambassadors to write "to one of our principal secretaries of state." Because of their unusual form of government, Dutch ambassadors had no "sovereign" to whom to write. But in the 1660's, for example, they wrote three kinds of correspondence: public, secret, and private. The first was sent to the States General and read aloud; the second was sent to the "griffier" (secretary) of the States General; while the third, the most confidential, was written to John de Witt, the Grand Pensionary of Holland.[21] But most states were not so unusual, and diplomats' primary letters went to the sovereign.

Diplomats who wrote a large number of letters were only following orders. For instance, they were often told to write regulary to their colleagues at other posts. A formal clause included in British diplomatic instructions was: "You shall constantly correspond with Our ambassadors and ministers in foreign courts for your mutual information and assistance in your respective negotiations.'' [22] Diplomats from most countries received comparable orders, sometimes with the colleagues and their posts specifically named. Princes ordered this mutual correspondence as a device for diffusing information more rapidly than it could have been had all information been sent to the home government and then forwarded from there. Furthermore, with the exception of the few states which were able to send their diplomats regular newsletters,[23] most central governments did not have the manpower to carry out such an undertaking. The value of correspondence between diplomats ranged from excellent to worse than useless. The correspondence kept diplomats abroad informed about developments which affected their own job, but at the same time it created a community of opinion which might make diplomat misinterpret developments or hesitate to express an idea which contradicted the consensus.[24]

The main reason so many diplomats were overwhelmed with letter writing was that they corresponded with a tremendous number of individuals on an unofficial basis. The seventeenth century was one in which all sorts of people engaged in letter writing as an avocation. Diplomats were no exception. For example, in 1697 the French ambassador in Denmark corresponded with more than a dozen French diplomats, each of the joint secretaries of state for foreign affairs (Torcy and Pomponne), Torcy's chief clerk and his secretary, the Dukes de Maine and Toulouse (Louis XIV's illegitimate sons), the secretary-general of the marine, the controller-general of finances, the chancellor, several French intendants, the minister of the duke of Wolfenbutel, the intendant general of commerce at Paris, and others. Although few samples have survived and those that do are generally well hidden in private archives, we know that diplomats also carried on extensive personal correspondence with relatives and friends.

Another time-consuming aspect of letter writing was that the letters were so long. Seventeenth century diplomats did not try to be concise. One of their most useful qualities was the art of speaking without saying anything; and, as a matter of habit, they wrote the way they spoke. A long letter can almost always be summarized in a few lines. At least some ambassadors were aware of this tendency and apologized for being so verbose. But they continued to write letters of fifteen, twenty or more pages.

Researchers are astonished when they come upon a letter in which a diplomat starts by saying that nothing of interest has occurred since his last letter and then actually stops rather than writing several more pages about this ''nothing.'' One of the devices which enabled diplomats to maintain such a large correspondence was the common practice of writing one letter and then repeating the same information, often word for word, to the several correspondents. We can suspect also that another technique was that used by an Englishman in Germany who wrote: "I wrote to you the other day when I was drunk. . . . " Perhaps this is why so little of the diplomatic correspondence can actually be called "literature." [25]

The Kinds of Information
Which Interested Diplomats

A natural question one might raise at this point is: what was it that diplomats were writing which was worth the trouble of sending so many letters and trying so hard to conceal their contents? The answer is that seventeenth century diplomats were interested in many different problems. The amount and variety of information which they wrote about cannot be overemphasized. There were relatively few newspapers or other media from which decision makers could gain information about the countries with which they were dealing so they were much more dependent on diplomatic reports than statesmen are today. In fact, many diplomats, particularly the lower ranking ones, were appointed primarily as information gatherers since they were rarely given any significant negotiations to perform. The acquisition and transmission of information had become one of the most important, if not the most important function of resident ambassadors in the Late Middle Ages; it still was during the sixteenth and seventeenth centuries. [26] It was not unusual in our period for diplomats to receive replies like that a French ambassador received after he apologized for writing too long a despatch and dealing with unnecessary topics. Louis XIV wrote him:

> You must not be afraid in such situations that you are straying too far from your subject because there is nothing which happens in the whole world that does not come under the cognizance and fall within the sphere of a good ambassador. [27]

Diplomats took such advice to heart and sent hundreds of notices on dozens of subjects. But, since much of the material was sent on separate pages or in the original pamphlet, journal, or other form, much has disappeared or at least become separated from the original despatches. We often can only guess what and when something was sent and to what, if any, use it was put.

Obviously, decision-makers primarily desired information about current developments in any treaty or other matter an ambassador was negotiating: proposals and counter-proposals, suggestions for different wording of articles, notices of whether certain parts had been accepted or rejected, etc. Diplomats of course reported on their formal contacts with the government to which they were accredited. They sent descriptions of audiences including copies of speeches they made to the prince and his responses. Closely connected with this

type of information were reports on the political situation of the host government. The British public diplomatic instructions (which were designed to be
shown or given to the host government and thus did not include anything
offensive) stated very explicitly:

> You shall diligently observe the motions of that court and endeavour to
> penetrate into all their councils and designs, which may have an influence
> upon any of Our concernments, and what treaties may be entertained by them
> with any other prince or state; and of what you can discover, and of all
> occurrences which may be of consequence and may in any way concern Our
> interest at home or abroad, you shall give frequent accounts to Us by one of
> Our principal secretaries of State.[28]

In practice such instructions were usually carried out well. Diplomatic despatches invariably contained news about possible treaties and alliances, political institutions of the host government itself, cabals and projects, changes in
government personnel with special emphasis on whether or not the new officeholder would be favorably disposed to the diplomat's country, and the other
types of political information for which ambassadors have been responsible
ever since. In other words, seventeenth century diplomats differed little from
their predecessors and successors insofar as their responsibility for sending
political information was concerned.

However, the emphasis on personal information about local rulers in the
seventeenth century was different from later centuries. Even when a ruler did
not participate actively in his government, the most minor details about his
health were thought to be of great importance because they could warn of his
death and a change of rulers with all the dangers and opportunities that implied.
In 1693, for instance, an ambassador in Sweden carefully reported that the king
of Sweden had suffered from a cold for the last several days but that it did not
appear serious. Such information was especially important when the prince was
old and a slight illness more likely to carry him off. But knowing of good health
was also important as when Matt Prior described Louis XIV in 1713: "The Old
Monarch at 75 eats and sleeps at Versailles as if he were at your age."

Equally significant were possibilities of pregnancies, especially when the
child was a potential heir to the throne. The Danish envoy wrote from London
on 8 June 1669:

> On Saturday last the queen found herself so ill that for the third time she was
> so unfortunate as to disappoint the king and all the court in the hope that they
> had entertained concerning her pregnancy. Various reasons are advanced for
> this occurrence. Some say that a tame fox, which the king was very fond of,
> always lay in his bedroom and that it had got loose during the night and had

come up into the queen's bed, waked her up, and frightened her so that she became ill. Others say that this episode with the fox occurred two or three days before the miscarriage. They relate that leeches had been placed on her arm on the advice of the doctor; and, as she had always had a natural antipathy to them, her fears were increased. Still others say that a drink made of very strong wine called *stum,* which the doctors consider very harmful in such cases, was the cause. Whatever may be the reason, the king was quite distressed over the misfortune and stayed out of the council meeting on Saturday because of it.[29]

Since there was so little true understanding of medicine and physicians were notoriously close to being witch doctors, diplomats regularly reported material which today is considered foolish.

Yet, in the case of a ruler like Carlos II of Spain whose lack of an heir potentially threatened the peace of all Europe throughout the last third of the seventeenth century, it is not surprising that ambassadors reported every scrap of information they could get their hands on. One ambassador wrote in 1688 that the queen of Spain believed she would never bear a child, but that a Dominican monk thought the Spanish monarchs were prevented from conceiving by a magical spell. He added that the king wore rough shirts which were supposed to help. The ambassador had had the shirt examined by two doctors, one of whom said it would make conception occur and the other the opposite. Today we know that the probable cause of Carlos's infertility was the same thing which had made his own life so miserable. He was the genetic disaster resulting from generations of inbreeding by the Hapsburgs. Ambassadorial reports described him with brutal frankness. His weak legs (he didn't walk alone until he was five), pale complexion, and overlarge Hapsburg jaw which kept his mouth hanging open were not improved by his blue eyes and blond hair. His health was always deplorable. He seemed decrepit in his cradle, was unable to chew properly because of his misshapen jaw, and could not digest his food. His whole life was but a prolonged struggle against death. Carlos, constantly dominated by his mother, his wives, and his confessors, never took much interest in affairs of government. On the rare occasions when he attended council meetings, he acted like a schoolboy who watched the slowly moving clock simply waiting until he could leave. All in all, Carlos was an appropriate monarch to reign in Spain where, a Venetian ambassador noted, the king had "more of the forms than the reality of power, like some idol of antiquity who is the object of adulation, though his ministers make the replies."[30] But this was the king whose life was so important that special couriers regularly carried news of his condition. His death was reported on numerous occasions before it really occurred at the beginning of November in 1700.

Even in death kings, queens, and princes were objects of diplomats' attentions. Detailed accounts of the last moments were sent including such things as the last words spoken, whether death came easily or not, who was present, how soon and in what manner the successor was proclaimed, and exact details of the autopsy and funeral.[31] In reporting so carefully about dying, diplomats were carrying out their masters' wishes and probably their own inclinations as well. Deaths of important people were objects of great public interest. When possible, rulers took great care that their deaths should occur in an appropriate way. They really had opportunities to do so if an English diplomat's description is accurate: "It is a misfortune to great people that they must be tempted to think death a worse thing than it is, by the weight their friends put upon it, either out of kindness or estentation; and as their physicians must not let them die without pain, so their friends will not let them leave the world without making them be troubled at it."[32] But, many well-born people avoided contact with corpses when possible. The kings of France traditionally never even looked at a dead person, no matter how closely related, and usually left a building where a death was imminent or had just occurred.

Diplomats also described in detail the courts and courtesans of princes, starting with individuals close to the throne and then anyone else of significance or interest. For instance, the Englishman Matthew Prior wrote from France: "The Dauphin [son of Louis XIV] is somewhat like our Prince George except that the latter only kisses the Princess [Anne] while the former kisses all the actresses from the opera without distinction. Monsieur [brother of Louis XIV] is a little marionette with a broken voice who talks much and says nothing." Prior went on to say that "The whole court is somber and sad; bigotry and caution reign there to the point that kneeling girls say their prayers in the galleries as if it were a convent, and the guardsmen put aside their arms and knot fringe like the young girls in England." [33] Prior's anti-French bias was showing here; other descriptions of courts were more objective.

Court news was often tidbits of gossip rather then diplomatically valuable material. For example, the French ambassador in London in the early 1660's regularly sent Louis XIV a large page filled with the most pungent news of the English court's daily life. Most of his sheets have been lost but they were important then. The French secretary of state reminded the ambassador on several occasions not to forget them as the king enjoyed reading the stories. In the later years of the century when King Charles XII of Sweden smashed his grandmaster's windows, broke the chairs which were used during sermons at the palace, and destroyed a peasant's boat, diplomats dutifully noted the "events." During the short period of peace between France and England after the Glorious Revolution, a significant part of the information English diplomats

in France sent home was about the exiled court of James II which Louis had
kindly let the ex-king of England establish at the Chateau of Saint Germain.
Even after Louis XIV had recognized William as king in the Peace of Ryswick,
English diplomats found it awkward to be at a court where James was still
treated like a king. Their tenseness found its way into their despatches,
although Prior showed a sense of humor when he wrote to one of the secretaries
of state: "You see still in the *Gazette de Paris* enclosed that the King and Queen
of Great Britain were at Saint Cloud, and it is the King of England who is at
Loo." [34] But William III's diplomats were unhappy about the unusual situation
of James II's presence in France and the danger he posed to William's government. Diplomats from other countries tended to treat the anomalous situation
pretty much the way they treated court and political news in general.

One kind of news was a cross between political and court news — the
generalizations which diplomats made about the people with whom they lived.
Insofar as stereotypes have any validity, a number of those which diplomats
made could have helped their home governments to understand how another
government worked (or did not work). A number of these generalizations
would scarcely have endeared a diplomat to his hosts if his comments became
known. A good example is a French diplomat's description of the people of
Genoa: "the genius of the Genoese in general is to be hypocritical, deceitful,
perfidious, fickle, presumptuous, foolhardy, troublesome, vindictive, and
selfish. And these last two qualities, or passions to name them more appro-
priately, they possess to excess." The diplomat went on to add that the Genoese
admired the virtue of Louis XIV and feared his power. They esteemed the
French but this feeling was overwhelmed by their hatred. Finally, they had a
general indifference for all foreigners which had as its basis only ignorance and
conceit. [35] Generalizations about other "nationalities" in the seventeenth century seem to have had a certain amount of accuracy. The Spanish were proud,
the Swedes slow to make decisions, and the Austrians had a tendency to wait
until the last minute before taking actions which they obviously had to take. The
generalizations made by diplomats were not always flattering, but they were
often realistic.

The value of any military information which diplomats could send is obvious. Since they were usually forced to leave when war broke out, they could
seldom acquire military information during hostilities. But there were exceptions. A man accredited to a neutral state could discover important data about
neighboring states at war with his master; and neutrals were always concerned
about military events which might affect them. A diplomat also warned his
master of any possibility that the neutral country planned to help him or his foe
without bothering about the technicality of a declaration of war. Thus, when

France and Spain were fighting in the Spanish Netherlands in 1684, the French ambassador in the Netherlands took care to notify the French commander about movements made by the Prince of Orange and Dutch troops. While such perfidy was not as common in the seventeenth century as in the twentieth, declarations of war were not always made before fighting began.

For the most part, however, important military information was acquired during peacetime. This took two major forms: information about foreign methods of organization, regulations, etc. which could be adapted for use at home and, second, information which would be of value to one's own commanders if hostilities arose later. The first type is well illustrated by a letter Jean-Baptiste Colbert sent to his brother Colbert de Croissy who was French ambassador in London:

> I will be very happy to see the memoir that you are writing about the English navy . . . in order that we can profit from their great experience in this type of war. If it is possible, I will be especially happy to learn how they determine the number of men for the crews. If you could get the plans for the battles they have had at sea, you would please me greatly by sending them to me; but I know that this is a delicate matter.

Colbert also wanted information about how the British navy's ships were built and rigged, how its officers and men ranked, how it formed for battle, etc.[36] Colbert made the same request of the ambassador in the Netherlands. The Dutch, on the other hand, desired and obtained information on how the French army was organized after the major reforms of the 1670's and 1680's.

The second type of valuable military information consisted of reports of how many ships, guns, men actually in fighting condition, etc. which a potential ally or enemy had. Diplomatic and military archives of most countries still contain the numerous estimates made on such matters. Unfortunately for decision-makers at the time, a number of the estimates were not very accurate. Despite the fact that diplomats were often military men themselves, their conservatism or preconceptions occasionally prevented them from accurately judging the value of new weapons or organizational changes[37], while their lack of diplomatic sophistication sometimes allowed them to be misled by their hosts. The importance of discovering military information might be a partial explanation why, in the later years of the seventeenth century when wars were occurring most of the time, a number of states increased the proportion of their diplomats who were military men. In later centuries this role would be filled by military attachés, but early modern embassies had not yet developed such specialized personnel.

Finally, note should be taken of the addiction which most seventeenth century ambassadors and envoys had to miscellaneous information. Much of it can be classed as simple curiosities. Yet recognizing the variety of topics which were thought to be interesting enough to include in a diplomatic despatch can increase our understanding of seventeenth century civilization. For instance, the disdain which well-born diplomats had for the ordinary people, "the rabble," shows in a number of ways. In 1697 Jean-Antoine d'Avaux wrote several times about the great famine which the Swedes were suffering. He noted the degree of suffering in a rather callous way including statements that the famine was particularly bad in Finland and Livonia, that there were 8,900 persons dead in Finland in the last week, and that there was barely enough wheat for those who had money to pay for it, much less for the poor. Another story which twentieth century westerners find somewhat callous involved an event in Constantinople. Although the Turks were notoriously corrupt administrators, they were efficient when it came to food markets, especially bakeries. A western diplomat reported an occasion when the chief of police made a surprise inspection, caught a baker selling bread under weight and immediately sentenced the wretch to be baked alive in his own oven. When questioned by a western ambassador about whether the punishment was perhaps too severe, the chief answered, "I entirely agree, but by inflicting this severe punishment we shall prevent others from offending for a much longer period because of their fear of being similarly treated; you Franks have to keep on punishing your criminals because your sentences are not severe enough to deter them from sinning again." [38] The remark is especially interesting in view of the barbarity of seventeenth century European punishment.

Other miscellaneous subjects were dealt with in diplomatic despatches: fires, unusually cold winters, terribly hot summers, pestiferous mosquitoes, a famous mathematician who was trying to persuade the Protestant princes to accept and use the new style calendar, a diplomat who left the Swedish king's service after thirty years and joined the Danes, map-making, and almost any other topic one can imagine. Mention should be made of incidents which remind us of how the seventeenth century, which seems "modern" in many ways, was still quite primitive in others. For instance, the continuance of superstition as well as the primitive (natural) conditions which still existed in London are shown by a Danish envoy's report to his chancellery in 1669: "Last week two seals were seen in the Thames across from Whitehall. Their presence is believed here to have some special significance, as seal have never before been seen so far up the river." [39] We can conclude this discussion by noting that only a few kinds of information were treated as secret and put into cipher: negotiations, political and military affairs, and evaluations of personalities. Even though seventeenth century people did not see the rest as important enough to be enciphered, this does not mean that the material is not very important to us today. With the exception of the Venetian despatches whose study was pioneered by Ranke a cantury ago, relatively little use has been made of diplomatic materials for the internal history of most countries. Since the diplomats were men whose specific duty it was to observe and report, it is to be hoped that modern historians will soon begin to make more and better use of their efforts.

Sources of Information— Audiences, Conversations, and Spying

How did seventeenth century diplomats acquire the information which they sent home? The conventional way was then and still is today largely from meetings with appropriate officials in the government to which they were accredited. Simply getting permission for such a meeting, however, was often a major difficulty. When the prince made himself available to envoys and ambassadors on a regular basis as the king of Denmark did twice a week, the difficulty was eased. But many princes were unwilling to discuss affairs informally and insisted that diplomats request a formal audience to do so. This involved an official called "the introducer of ambassadors," "conductor of ambassadors," or a similar title. Every court of any significance had such a man. Even the Spaniards who did not have a master of ceremonies in the early seventeenth century had acquired one by 1675. The Swedish government formally established the position in 1661 but recognized that it had been in existence long before. The office was usually considered to be very prestigious and was filled by a high born noble. His duties were numerous although obviously they primarily involved matters of protocol. The introducer arranged and was present at the entries, departures, and the audiences of diplomats with the sovereign. Furthermore, he gave advice on the ceremonial practiced at the court, intervened in disputes between diplomats, and kept records of every detail of every ceremony in order to be able to cite previous practice whenever a problem arose. It was officially necessary to go through him or a secretary of state to obtain an audience in most courts. It was also possible, however, to obtain the aid of a favorite. In any case, the procedure was usually complicated, time-consuming, expensive, and not worth the trouble in terms of the quantity of information actually acquired. It was often more valuable simply to call on the appropriate secretary of state or other official.[40]

An equally if not more important method of gaining information was through social contact with local officials and other knowledgeable individuals. The importance of this was shown particularly well by an English earl who wrote:

> The principal business of a foreign minister is to get into the secrets, and to know all *les allures* of the Courts at which he resides; this he can never bring about, but by an insinuating behaviour, as may make him sought for, and in some measure domestic, in the best company and the best families of the place. He will then, indeed, be well informed of all that passes, either by the confidences made him, or by the carelessness of people in his company; who are accustomed to look upon him as one of them, and consequently are not upon their guard before him. For a minister, who only goes to the Court he resides at in form, to ask an audience of the Prince or the Minister, upon his last instructions, puts them upon their guard and will never know any thing more than what they have a mind that he should know.[41]

The success a diplomat had in acquiring such a position depended on many factors including his own social rank and the rank of his master. The representatives of the emperor and the kings of France and Spain could gain relatively easy access anywhere. But the representatives of lower ranking sovereigns like German and Italian princes or the republics of Genoa or Venice seldom had sufficient personal rank nor was their sovereign's rank sufficient to get them into the "best company."

A further difficulty in maintaining informal contact was that a number of states, recognizing the potential problems of a diplomat's acquiring dangerous information, passed laws prohibiting contact between citizens and diplomats. An English representative wrote in 1702 that after his entry the Senate of Genoa allowed him to receive visits from the nobility for only three days. After that "I may meet them in any third place, but they cannot come to my house, such being the rules of the Republic."[42] A few years earlier a French envoy had complained that the law prohibiting contact between nobles and diplomats had just been renewed "or rather established" to apply to him alone despite the fact that, for the first time in forty years, Louis XIV had honored the republic by sending them an envoy rather than a lowly agent. Of course, the envoy ignored the fact that the Genoese were quite aware of the French antagonism which was shortly going to lead to the French bombardment of the city because of Genoese help to the Spanish. Thus it was natural that they should treat him in a negative way.[43] Venice and the Swiss had similar laws prohibiting contact between nobles and diplomats. The Swiss broke the law fairly often but the Venetians did not. The Venetian government had an unpleasant way of reminding its citizens about the law. Individuals who broke it were found dead in the piazza hanging upside down by one leg as a sign of their treason.

The prohibition of contact with a diplomat did not have to be issued by a legally constituted government to be effective. The French ambassador Jean Antoine d'Avaux was particularly successful in using his social life to discover information. However, the enmity he was ordered to maintain against William of Orange when he was serving in the Netherlands caused him great difficulties. After the French government destroyed the walls of the principality of Orange, the tiny enclave in southern France which was the basis of William's claim to be a "sovereign" prince, d'Avaux's situation became almost unbearable. D'Avaux described his position after William declared that he would consider anyone who had contact with the French ambassador as his enemy:

> Being thus excluded from all social intercourse, I found myself in a terrible position considering how difficult it is in a Republic to be well informed about what is happening when one does not have free and open communication with everybody. That communication not only produces acquaintanceships and friends from whom one draws much enlightenment, but it gives an opportunity to those who wish to come and reveal secrets to . . . an ambassador without fearing anything.[44]

D'Avaux's situation was not to improve until Louis XIV allowed him to form more friendly relations with William.

Even under normal circumstances, merely being attentive and ingratiating was not sufficient to enable ambassadors to discover all the information they wished. As was mentioned above, information was almost like an item of trade in diplomatic circles. In order to learn facts they wished to know, ambassadors had to give information to others. Sometimes they could just pass on material they had learned on the spot, but news from their homeland was far more valuable for "the trade."

While obtaining information officially or by social contacts was both acceptable and desirable in the seventeenth century, another method was equally acceptable in practice if not in theory — espionage and its corollary bribery. In fact, an early eighteenth century theoretician even stated that the most valuable "intelligence" was that "which is purchased by the minister's purse and industry."[45] But one of his French counterparts argued that other methods were preferable to bribery and were more likely to be accurate.[46] Callières went even farther to argue, rather unrealistically in view of the constant financial problems early modern diplomats suffered, that an ambassador should be ready to spend large amounts for buying great secrets; "and," Callières continued, "he must be even prepared to do it at his own expense when the emoluments of his master are insufficient."[47] The extent to which such expenditures were necessary or desirable depended in part on the status of relations between the diplomat's master and the court to which he was accredited. If relations were friendly, it was usually rather easy to get good information, while unfriendly relations meant that reliable information was more difficult to acquire. Even when friends and ministers openly passed along news, they expected and were given "gratifications" as rewards and signs of appreciation.

Whether or not the host court was friendly, it was generally assumed that diplomats were "honorable spies." This was particularly true for the lower ranks. Spying was the primary role of some agents; they were given diplomatic credentials and some official business of no real significance as a cover. But even ambassadors were explicitly ordered to spy on occasion. For example, an English ambassador at The Hague was specifically requested to "learn underhand what you possibly can about the States [General's] inclinations" on a certain topic.[48] There was some feeling among theoreticians that diplomatic and spying activities should be kept separate and occasionally they were. For instance, the famous author of *The Ambassador and His Functions,* Abraham van Wicquefort, was used by the French secretary of state as a secret agent in the Netherlands, apparently without any connection between him and the French ambassador there. Although there were some cases where secret agents were sent abroad without an ambassador's knowledge, the practice was never as widespread as the one of having diplomats establish their own "spy rings."

Considering the nature of espionage, it is not surprising that there never was much evidence even of its existence, much less of how it functioned and who participated. Even that little has largely disappeared. In rare cases we have descriptions of a spy ring which a departing diplomat left for the use of his successor which tell what certain individuals had done, how much they were paid, and what could be expected of them in the future. For example, Matthew Prior described his spies in France. They included "Brocard, as we call him, [who] is Tr(ant), an Irishman encouraged by Mr. Vernon; his pretended business is merchandise of English things, as stockings, hats, etc., under which notion he gives our friends at Saint Germain [the exiled court of James II] an account of things in England . . . he costs us between two and three hundred pounds a year." Johnston, called "Baily," was disguised as a parson. He was "a cunning fellow and a true débauché" worth two *louis* a week. "My widow Langlois and her two daughters" would be helpful although Matt thought "the old woman is as cunning jade as lives, and will pump him [the successor] in his turn if he is not upon his guard; if he visits her, as he should do, he may learn something about most of the rogues and the priests in Paris who have any dealings at Saint Germain.''[49] More often, such information about a diplomat's spy rings was not written down for fear of discovery.

Evidence is usually limited to passing comments about people and events whose origins and/or outcomes cannot be discovered. In 1704 the Venetians ordered their ambassadors in Constantinople to find ''a skillful Greek'' who spoke Russian to go into Russia without any official character to penetrate secret movements and discover affairs. A French secretary referred to a chaplain whom his ambassador had planted in the entourage of the emperor's envoy before he left. The secretary had heard no word from the chaplain, but he had another ''canal'' to keep him informed about the envoy's activities.[50] Every diplomat worth his pay acquired a string of low level individuals — dancers, musicians, chaplains, physicians, and the like — who brought or sent information for which they hoped to be paid.

All diplomats did their best to acquire sources closer to the government. Those who were richer, smarter, or luckier succeeded. Jean-Antoine d'Avaux wrote from Sweden in 1697 that those Swedes in the government who were favorable toward France could not give him an exact account of what happened at the chancellery, a valuable kind of information. So d'Avaux found a man named Lyenstedt, the brother-in-law of a Swedish senator, who could render this service and also could tell d'Avaux about the king's plans and the Senate's resolutions. Since this was a very dangerous activity, Lyenstedt demanded and was promised that the affair would be kept secret. D'Avaux knew that this man was invaluable as an informant because he had given the French ambassador other information earlier. A ''gratification'' was necessary to be sure that the information came regularly, about three thousand livres immediately and a like amount in five or six months. Ambassadors from other countries also made use of Swedish gentlemen for the same purpose. A number of ambassadors were able to make what they considered to be the great coup of getting a prince's mistress to spy for them. In the late 1690's, the French-born mistress of Victor Amadeus, the Duke of Savoy, helped the French ambassador because she had hopes of escaping the Duke's clutches. She even wrote the ambassador messages while sitting on her toilet because that was the one place she could be fairly sure of avoiding interruptions. A mistress of Charles II of England apparently performed similar services.[51] Despite these examples, there seem to have been few of the *femme fatale* spies who are so commonly found in twentieth century fiction.

One belief which the seventeenth and twentieth centuries share is the idea that diplomatic spying is and was necessary and profitable. Evidence to support such a view abounds. This evidence is very convincing, especially since so many people seem to want to believe that the espionage which has been so popularized in fiction like the James Bond series has some basis in fact. Scholars have often supported the idea that diplomatic spying was worthwhile. A book on early modern *Secret Diplomacy*, originally published in 1937, was republished in 1963 with little change except in the title. The book's purpose was to show "that undercover diplomatic and espionage operations have been universally practiced by all governments and that such 'spying' and bribing have played a far greater role in history than is commonly believed." [52] Scholars have also often uncritically accepted early modern diplomats' own reports about the success of espionage activities. For instance, Jean-Antoine d'Avaux seemed most successful in his espionage in the affair when the States General of the Netherlands was considering sending eight thousand men to aid the Spanish in 1682. D'Avaux noted that "although no question had been treated in the States General with more secrecy and with such precaution and oathtaking during the previous ten years, I was nevertheless faithfully informed every day of what happened in the Assembly of Holland as well as in the Council of the Towns; that enabled the King to take appropriate measures for what he had to do." [53] What stronger evidence could one ask for?

Yet there are grave deficiencies in this view of the value of espionage. In general, the *Secret Diplomacy* book makes a major issue out of the fact that ambassadors used codes and secret agents. Codes and their value, or lack thereof, have already been discussed. [54] One must also question the usefulness of secret agents as well as the other aspects of diplomatic espionage. There were numerous cases where diplomats and spies never discovered important developments, despite their strenuous efforts and claims that they were succesful. For instance, Cromwell's ambassador to Sweden claimed to have been very close to Queen Christina and to have understood her motives. Yet he apparently did not even suspect that she was going to convert from Lutheranism to Catholicism or that religion was going to play a role in her abdication. In 1670 the Spanish and Dutch envoys went to Dover to see whether anything was negotiated by Charles II and his sister, Henrietta of Orléans, sister-in-law of Louis XIV. But they both returned to London when they "saw that nothing was planned there except a visit. . . ." Yet this was when the kings of France and England actually negotiated the now famous secret treaty of Dover in which Charles promised to help Louis against the Dutch and also to proclaim his conversion to Catholicism. The tables were turned on Louis XIV fifteen years later when his ambassador in London gave him no indication that England and the States General were going to renew their treaty of alliance. There are innumerable such instances of espionage failure, but they are usually ignored because they are not dramatic and exciting. Failures in espionage often remain unnoticed because diplomats seldom mentioned their failures in their despatches whereas they emphasized their successes.

Furthermore there were many occasions when governments' security systems simply did not work and developments became public knowledge. Such was the case when the negotiations between England and France which led to "Matt's Peace" became known when the French negotiators were arrested in England.[55] Carlos II's request to marry Louis XIV's niece was known all over Europe, despite the Spanish belief that it was still a secret. The terms of the supposedly secret treaty between England and Portugal were well known in the spring of 1703. The negotiations in the same year between the emperor and the duke of Savoy for the treaty whereby the duke was to desert Louis XIV and join the Allies were equally public knowledge. The *Gazette de Hollande* even published a surprisingly accurate account of the treaty several days before it was concluded. In such cases it is obvious that spying was not necessary to discover what was happening.

The reason information acquired by espionage was not really very valuable is still as true today as it was in the seventeenth century. Decision-makers could not be certain whether or not such information was accurate. It is all too easy to be a Monday morning quarterback when reading old espionage reports, finding one which predicted an event accurately, and then saying, Ah Ha!, the decision-maker had been told that such and such an event was going to happen. Therefore, since he did not take appropriate measures, he must have been stupid, treacherous, or incompetent. In recent years, such accusations have been hurled at Franklin Roosevelt who supposedly knew that the Japanese attack of Pearl Harbor would occur on December 7, 1941. However, this approach ignores the fact that decision-makers like Roosevelt, Leopold, and Louis XIV received a plethora of reports, many of which they knew had to be incorrect (for instance, when the reports were contradictory). Yet the problem they faced was that, unlike the Monday morning quarterbacks, they did not know which ones were inaccurate or even that any were accurate. There were and are a number of reasons for such uncertainty.

Rumors were always rife about any important event which affected diplomacy. A key one in the seventeenth century was that Carlos II of Spain was on his deathbed. This rumor circulated regularly for more than a quarter of a century. Other rumors about decisions to start or end wars, break or establish diplomatic relations, make or break treaties, etc. circulated (and were reported by spies) with great frequency. The rumors involved different countries according to the level of diplomatic tensions at any given moment. Even information from apparently well informed sources was often false. The pope's representative in Paris wrote to the cardinal secretary of state in Rome that the Venetian ambassador had visited him about midnight. The Venetian had just received a letter announcing the creation of a number of new cardinals and gave the pope's representative the list of names. When the representative questioned its veracity, the Venetian assured him that the list came from the podesta of Padua who had been informed by a courier going from Rome to Germany. But the information was false! It was also not unknown for supposedly official information to be carefully falsified, before an informant gave it to an ambassador. For instance, d'Avaux was given a copy of a despatch from the Dutch resident in Moscow which had been cleverly garbled in order to give the French an incorrect impression of the state of Russo-Dutch trade negotiations.[56] Since d'Avaux was a more capable diplomat than many others, the fact that he could be fooled illustrates very well the problem of utilizing secret information.

Closely related was the problem of double agents. Both Callières and Wicquefort warned about such agents. We know they existed, but very little solid information about them still exists. Callières warned about double spies who worked for both parties and also about the fake spy who actually gave false information at the direction of his own master. In order to judge the accuracy of the information, Callières warned that the diplomat should test all news by examining the informer's motivation, sources of information, etc. Wicquefort was somewhat more realistic, however, when he warned about princes who have their men gain the confidence of the ambassador by giving him some information in which the true part makes the false news also seem correct. If it is found out, however, even the correct information is suspect thereafter.[57]

It should now be apparent: rather than being underemphasized as a factor in diplomacy as the authors of *Secret Diplomacy* believed, the importance of espionage has been over-emphasized. This is probably the result of a widely held but simplistic view of international relations which interprets large scale events as being the result of small scale personal actions taken by rulers, mistresses, secretaries, etc. It ignores the importance of larger forces. Such a view also ignores the fact that, as mentioned above, decision-makers were always forced to make judgments as to which "facts" really were facts when they guided the foreign affairs of their states. Finally, the overall position of a state, the power available to it in the military terms, common interests between states, and the like were undoubtedly much more important to the outcome of negotiations and other diplomatic relations than any "facts" discovered by espionage. Secrecy and/or breaches of security were simply not very important.

FOOTNOTES

¹ L. Rousseau de Chamoy. *L'Idée du parfait ambassadeur*, ed. by L. Delavaud, Paris, 1912, p. 40.

² E. R. Adair. *The Exterritoriality of Ambassadors in the Sixteenth and Seventeenth Centuries*, New York, 1929, p. 170.

³ See above, Chap. III, pp.   , for a biographical sketch of d'Avaux. The story of the courier is told in E. Mallet, ed. *Négociations de Monsieur le comte d'Avaux en Hollande*, Vol. III, Paris, 1754, pp. 61-62.

⁴ V. Wheeler-Holohan. *History of the King's Messengers*, New York, n. d. [about 1934], pp. 10-17; J. de Boislisle, ed. *Mémoriaux du conseil de 1661*, Vol. II, Paris, 1905, p. 300.

⁵ A typical mail schedule was that of the city of Cologne in 1673. On Sundays and Thursdays the post left for Vienna, Regensburg, Nuremberg, Spire, and other places in Germany. On Tuesdays at 11 am it left for Wesel, Cleves, Munster, and Osnabruck while at noon it departed for Hildesheim, Hamburg, Denmark, and Sweden. At two in the afternoon it departed for Holland, France, Spain, and England. On Friday mornings there was a post at 11 am which went to the same places as that of Tuesday morning while between 2 and 3 in the afternoon another left for Holland, Brabant, and France. Saturday morning saw a post leave for Hildesheim, Stockholm, Danzig, and Copenhagen. Equally frequent arrivals were scheduled at Cologne. Sunday mornings about 10 the post came from various places in Germany while that from France, Spain, Brabant, Holland, and England was scheduled for between noon and one. Monday evenings one post was scheduled from Italy and another from Hamburg and Sweden. Thursday between 10 and 11 am came that from Cleves, Munster, Hildesheim, Hamburg, Sweden, and Denmark while that from Holland arrived about one pm. Friday evening came mail from various places in Germany and Saturday evening that from Mainz and Coblentz. Public Record Office. London. SP 9/201 (30). Similar postal networks connected almost all of the important cities in Europe if only via a number of intermediate stops rather than by direct service.

⁶ J. Devos. "La Poste au service des diplomates espagnols accrédités auprès des cours d'Angleterre et de France (1555-1598)," *Bulletin de la commission royal d'histoire (belge)*, Vol. CIII, 1938, pp. 211-12.

⁷ F. de Bojani. *Innocent XI, sa correspondance avec ses nonces*, Vol. III, Rome, 1912, p. 60; D. B. Horn. *The British Diplomatic Service, 1689-1789*, Oxford, 1961, pp. 232-33.

⁸ J. Walker. "Secret Service under Charles II and James II," *Transactions of the Royal Historical Society*, 4th ser., Vol. XV, 1932, p. 226. See also A. de Boislisle. "Le Secret de là poste sous le règne de Louis XIV,"

Annuaire-bulletin de la société de l'histoire de France, Vol. XXVII, 1890, p. 229; K. Ellis. *The Post Office in the Eighteenth Century,* Oxford, 1958, p. 62.

[9] Public Record Office. London. SP 107/1A

[10] L. Monmerqué, ed. "Lettres et pièces inédites tirées des manuscrits de M. de Pomponne," in his *Mémoires de M. de Coulanges,* Paris, 1820, pp. 496-97, 1 May 1666.

[11] L. G. W. Legg. *Matthew Prior: A Study of his Public Career and Correspondence,* Cambridge, 1921, p. 290, 10 June 1699.

[12] Archives des Affaires Etrangères. Paris. Correspondance Politique, Danemark, Vol. 58, fol. 24, 15 March 1697; J. A. Wijnne, ed. *Négociations de Monsieur le comte d'Avaux, ambassadeur extraordinaire à la cour de Suède,* Werken van het Historisch Genootschap, new ser., Vol. II, Utrecht, 1882, p. 308.

[13] W. L. Grant. "A Puritan at the Court of Louis XIV," *Queen's University Bulletin* (Kingston), no. 8, 1913, p. 7.

[14] H. Sidney (later Earl of Romney). *Diary of the Times of Charles the Second,* ed. by R. W. Blencowe, Vol. II, London, 1843, pp. 81-82.

[15] See below, Appendix, pp.   for sample ciphers.

[16] A. van Wicquefort. *L'Ambassadeur et ses fonctions,* Vol. II, The Hague, 1681, p. 223.

[17] F. de Callières. *On the Manner of Negotiating with Princes,* Trans. by A. F. Whyte, Notre Dame, Indiana, 1963, p. 142.

[18] This biographical sketch is based on D. E. Smith. "John Wallis as a Cryptographer," *Bulletin of the American Methematical Society,* 2nd ser., Vol. XXIV, 1917, pp. 82-96; C. J. Scriba. "The Autobiography of John Wallis, F.R.S.," *Notes and Records of the Royal Society of London,* Vol. 25, 1970, pp. 14-46; British Museum. London. Add. MSS 32,499.

[19] See above, Chap. II, pp.

[20] See above, Chap. IV, pp.

[21] M. A. M. Franken. *Coenraad van Beuningen's Politieke,* Groningen, 1966, p. 259; B. C. Brown, ed. *The Letters and Diplomatic Instructions of Queen Anne,* New York, 1935 [republished 1968], p. 218.

[22] J. F. Chance, ed. *British Diplomatic Instructions 1689-1789; Sweden, 1689-1727,* London, 1922, p. vii.

[23] See above, Chap. II, pp.

[24] C. H. Carter. *The Western European Powers, 1500-1700,* Ithaca, 1971, pp. 112-13; R. Place. "The Self-Deception of the Strong: France on the Eve of the War of the League of Augsburg," *French Historical Studies,* Vol. VI, 1970, pp. 459-73; C.-G. Picavet. *La Diplomatie française au temps de Louis XIV (1661-1715): institutions, moeurs et coutumes,* Paris, 1930, pp. 112-13.

[24] The quotation about being drunk is from the British Museum. London. Add MSS 34,095, fol. 106; C. S. Blaga would argue that much diplomatic correspondence should be called literature. "Le Dix-huitième siècle," Vol. I of *L' Evolution de la diplomatie,* Paris, 1938, p. 67.

[26] D. E. Queller. *The Office of Ambassador in the Middle Ages,* Princeton, 1967, p. 88; J. E. Neale. "The Diplomatic Envoy," *History,* Vol. XIII, 1928-29, p. 206.

[27] J.-J. Jusserand. *A French Ambassador at the Court of Charles the Second,* New York, 1892, pp. 198-99, 22 February 1663.

[28] Chance. *British Diplomatic Instructions, Sweden,* see note 22, p. vii.

[29] C. Lindenov. *The First Triple Alliance: The Letters of Christopher Lindenov, Danish Envoy to London, 1668-1672,* Trans., ed. and introduction by W. Westergaard, New Haven, 1947, p. 127, 8 June 1669.

[30] N. Barozzi and G. Berchet, *Relazioni degli ambasciatori veneti,* Vol. II, Venice, 1860, p. 131, as quoted by A. D. Ortiz. *The Golden Age of Spain, 1516-1659,* Trans. from Spanish by J. Casey, New York, 1971, p. 318, n. 7.

[31] See below, Appendix, pp.   for sample report.

[32] Savile. *Letters to and from Henry Savile, esq., Envoy at Paris,* ed. by W. Cooper, London, 1858, p. 80.

[33] Great Britain. Historical Manuscripts Commission. *Calendar of the Manuscripts of the Marquis of Bath Preserved at Longleat.* Vol. III, *Prior Papers,* London, 1908, p. 195, 1 March 1697/8.

[34] Jusserand. *French Ambassador,* see note 27, pp. 42-43 & 86; Wijnne, ed. *Négociations d'Avaux de Suède,* see note 12, Vol. III, Part 1, pp. 257 & 331-32, 21 May 1698 & 2 July 1698; Great Britain. HMC. *Manuscripts of Bath at Longleat,* see note 33, p. 259, Prior to James Vernon, 30 August 1698.

[35] Archives des Affaires Etrangères. Paris. Mémoires et Documents, Fonds divers, Gênes, Vol. 24 (1682-84), fol. 7.

[36] P. Clément, ed. *Lettres, instructions et mémoires de Colbert,* Vol. III, Part 1, Paris, 1861-73, pp. 110 & 204.

[37] W. J. Roosen. "The True Ambassador: Occupational and Personal Characteristics of French Ambassadors under Louis XIV," *European Studies Review,* Vol. 3, 1973, pp. 124-29; Place. "Self-Deception of the Strong," see note 24, shows how French diplomatic-military observers who reported on the Hapsburg armies in eastern Europe were prevented by their own preconceived perceptions from accurately evaluating the Hapsburg improvements.

[38] *Memoires du chevalier d'Arvieux, envoyé extraordinaire du roi.* Vol. I, Paris, 1735, p. 78.

[39] Lindenov. *First Triple Alliance,* see note 29, p. 154.

[40] See above, Chap. II, pp.

[41] Chesterfield. *Letters of Philip Dormer Stanhope, Earl of Chesterfield,* ed. by J. Bradshaw, Vol. I, London, 1892, p. 155.

[42] British Museum. London. Add. MSS. 34,356, Blackwell to Blathwayt, 30 September 1702.

[43] Archives des Affaires Etrangères. Paris. Mémoires et Documents, Fonds divers, Gênes, Vol. 24 (1682-84), fols. 12-13.

[44] Mallet, ed. *Négociations d'Avaux en Hollande,* see note 3, Vol. I, pp. 5 & 122.

[45] [W. Keith]. "Observations on the Office of an Ambassador," in *An Essay on the Education of a Young British Nobleman,* London, 1730, p. 52. See discussion of bribery for information in Chap. VII.

[46] A. Pecquet. *Discours sur l'art de negocier,* Paris, 1737, p. 92.

[47] Callières. *Negotiating with Princes,* see note 17, pp. 27-28.

[48] Sidney. *Diary,* see note 14, Vol. II, p. 64.

[49] Legg. *Matthew Prior,* see note 11, pp. 77-78.

[50] Archives des Affaires Etrangères. Paris. Correspondence Politique, Angleterre, Vol. 210, fols. 51-52, 2 May 1702 (?).

[51] Comte d'Haussonville. "La Reprise des relations diplomatiques entre la France et la Savoie au moment de la paix de Ryswick," *Revue d'histoire diplomatique,* Vol. 13, 1899, pp. 359-61; H. Forneron. *Louise de Keroualle, Duchess of Portsmouth, 1649-1734,* 2nd edition, London, 1887, pp. 140-49; Wijnne, ed. *Négociations d'Avaux de Suède,* see note 12, Vol. II, p. 7, 2 January 1697.

[52] J. W. Thompson and S. K. Padover. *Secret Diplomacy: A Record of Espionage and Double-Dealing: 1500-1815,* London, 1937, p. 6.

[53] Mallet, ed. *Négociations d'Avaux en Hollande,* see note 3, Vol. I, p. 109.

[54] See above, Chap. VI, pp.

[55] See above, Chap. IV, pp.

[56] Bojani. *Innocent XI,* see note 7, Vol. III, p. 111; A. Lossky. "Dutch Diplomacy and the Franco-Russian Trade Negotiations in 1681," in R. Hatton and M. S. Anderson, eds. *Studies in Diplomatic History,* London, 1970, pp. 32-35.

[57] Callières. *Negotiating with Princes,* see note 17, pp. 114-16; Wicquefort. *Ambassadeur et ses fonctions,* see note 16, Vol. II, pp. 16-17.

CHAPTER VII

The Variety of Diplomatic Duties

During the past five centuries for which states have been exchanging "modern" diplomats, the kind of work they have performed has varied according to time and place. Some ambassadors have been little more than postmen who took a message and returned with an answer. Others have for all practical purposes controlled the government to which they were accredited. There was great variety in the age of Louis XIV, but, not surprisingly, the vast majority of diplomatic activities fell into the middle ground rather than reaching the extremes.

Anyone who has ever written a job description knows that it can either reveal or conceal what the person holding the job actually does. One of the easiest ways to conceal is to write in such broad generalities that almost any activity seems to be part of the job. Descriptions of the functions of early modern diplomats can fall into this trap if the discussion is based on the works of the theoreticians. Antoine Pecquet, for example, saw the major duties of diplomats as being peace, war and the reconciliation of two or more princes. Callières and Wicquefort divided the functions of an ambassador into two principal categories: (1) discovering the business of others, in other words being an "honorable spy," and (2) conducting the business of his master.[1] These phrases are too broad in themselves to tell us what diplomats actually did but they do provide a basis for dividing a diplomat's functions into two parts: one (discovering the business of others) which was discussed in the previous chapter and the second (his master's business) to be discussed here.

The discussion of the large number of topics which interested early modern diplomats in the last chapter gives some hint of the variety of activities in which they engaged. Here it seems appropriate to clarify these duties by classifying them in rather broad categories. While an early modern diplomat would never have actually separated his activities according to these categories, he would undoubtedly have recognized them as aspects of his job and also recognized the terminology. The conducting of negotiations probably seemed most important to historians. Closely connected to negotiating was a tool by which diplomats tried to influence decision makers — bribery. When bribery did not work, diplomats, as a sort of reverse bribery, tried to influence decision makers by interfering in the domestic affairs of the country where they were serving. This kind of interference was also reflected in the obligation many diplomats felt to try to protect their countrymen and coreligionists abroad. It would be impossible to end a discussion of early modern diplomatic duties without evaluating the ceremonial activities which were such an important part of diplomatic life at that time.

Negotiations

Chief among the functions a high ranking diplomat could perform for his master was negotiating a treaty or some other kind of settlement. Although there was no hard and fast rule, important negotiations were seldom entrusted to anyone bearing a rank lower than envoy. It is this aspect of diplomatic history which historians have studied most carefully. As a result, there are innumerable works following in painful detail each minute step of a specific negotiation, each proposal, response, counter-proposal, breakdown and reestablishment of communications, etc. There would be little benefit from doing that kind of a study here. Rather, this section will examine the general kinds of techniques and procedures which were used in early modern negotiations. Although the objectives of diplomacy have changed somewhat, many of these techniques have remained basically the same for centuries.

In the seventeenth century the word "negotiation" meant more than just talks leading to a truce or treaty. It included attempts to achieve the whole range of diplomatic goals a sovereign set for himself. Maintaining good relations which were in danger of breaking down; trying to get a foreign court to carry out agreements which it had made earlier; trying to have an advantageous person elected as pope, king of Poland, or emperor; preventing two other states from coming to agreement; and the like were all thought to be different kinds of "negotiations." Some countries had specific types of problems in which their diplomats regularly engaged. For instance, Spanish diplomats were constantly instructed to try to persuade foreigners to abide by Spain's rules about trade with her American empire. Nuncios were, of course, deeply involved in religious matters such as persuading kings to introduce papal decrees into their kingdoms. But, as was noted above, studies of specific negotiations have been so widely disseminated that it is not necessary to belabor their variety further here.

While carrying on negotiations, diplomats obviously developed their own ideas of what their masters' policies could or should be. It was not obvious what, if anything, they should do about their ideas. Callières stated unequivocally that diplomats were the servants and not the authors of foreign policy.[2] Most decision-makers and diplomats would probably have agreed with Callières if the question were asked directly: do ambassadors have a policy making role? But matters were not so simple in practice. Every time a diplomat decided what pieces of information should be reported, how to phrase his despatches, etc. he consciously or unconsciously influenced his master's policies. But many men, especially ambassadors, were unwilling to be only agents rather than decision-makers. This was especially true for representatives of states like the Netherlands where they were participants in policy making at home. For instance, the Englishman Horatio Walpole tried hard to prevent England's signing any agreement with France after 1715 unless the Dutch also agreed. A Danish envoy in London, who was mostly a sender of information rather than a negotiatior, often gave very specific advice to King Christian V of Denmark on matters involving Denmark and England, particularly on the conflict over salutes in the Sound.[3] Even the ambassadors of that archtypical absolutist Louis XIV occasionally participated in the decision-making process. From time to time the Sun King actually asked experts (including his ambassadors) for advice on important policy questions. In such cases the ambassador's recommendation might well be followed, or an explanation of why it was not might be sent to him. Some French diplomats volunteered suggestions such as when Saint-Olon, the French envoy to Genoa, argued vehemently in 1684 that the Sun King should either capture or punish that city. He argued that it was important for Louis to control the sea in order to "give the law" to the princes bordering it. The French fleet did in fact bombard Genoa, but we do not know how much the decision to do so was influenced by Saint-Olon. Jean-Antoine d'Avaux at different times advised the king: (1) that if the French government did not treat the "new converts" (after the revocation of the Edict of Nantes) so badly fewer would flee the country, (2) that Louis could take certain steps to avoid war, and (3) that he should not try to capture certain towns as that would merely delay peace. However, every suggestion was accompanied by the ambassador's assurances that he was always ready to submit to the king's judgment. In many cases the king simply ignored the proffered advice, and in many cases diplomats stopped making suggestions.[4]

Bribery

In the opinion of contemporaries, a key part of seventeenth century negotiations was the distribution of "gratifications" to individuals well placed in a situation where they could influence the course of negotiations. Even the moralistic theoreticians argued that it was permissable for ambassadors to corrupt the ministers of the court where they resided if it were necessary for their masters' interests. Callières thought that the best way for a diplomat to gain the favor of a prince was to gain the "good graces of those who have most influence upon his mind" be they ministers, favorites or relatives. To do so required gifts — which ought to be carefully planned. The giver should know beforehand that the gift would be received in the right spirit and above all that the gift would not be refused.[5] An English theoretician was even blunter:

> A proper application of money is many times useful and often necessary; but to conceal the channels through which it is conveyed is a secret of as much importance to the giver as to the receiver; and it is a nice part of the ministerial [i.e. diplomatic] art, to execute things of that nature with a good grace.[6]

Today most people assume that the giving and/or taking of a gift by a public official is simply a bribe, but the seventeenth century did not see it quite that way. In an age when salaries were often paid late or not at all, presents were considered to be something in the line of fees or perquisites to which a man of importance was entitled as a matter of course. Furthermore, this was an age in which presents of all kinds were frequently exchanged between rulers, ministers, diplomats, and members of public assemblies. Although both givers and receivers undoubtedly knew when some gift was on the border of being legitimate, it is difficult for us today to know when courtesy stopped and corruption began.

Stories abounded in the seventeenth century and many are still repeated today about how some important decisions were made because of bribery. An excellent example is the claim that the French were able to purchase Dunkirk from Charles II because the French ambassador "bribed the Duchess of York, who was the daughter of the influential Chancellor Clarendon, with 'clock dials set with diamonds and other precious stones'. . . ."[7] Another claim was that Sweden withdrew its support of the Netherlands before Louis XIV began his Dutch War because "the Swedish nobles who governed the country were bribed handsomely to reverse their policy and support France."[8] The list could be extended indefinitely.

One must not infer from these examples that only the French distributed "gratifications" in order to persuade foreigners to make decisions favorable to their cause. Every state which had the funds to do so used bribery on at least an occasional basis. For instance, Spanish ambassadors in Rome regularly doled out pensions in the hope of keeping as many cardinals as possible favorable toward the Hapsburgs. When William III of England was concerned that the king of Sweden might "be prevailed upon to take resolutions very prejudicial to the public welfare," in other words to aid the French in the War of the League of Augsburg, he directed his envoy in Sweden to discover whether Count Oxenstierna would be amenable to receiving a present in order to help the Swedish king make the "right" decision. Apparently Oxenstierna was amenable as the envoy was ordered on 6/16 June 1691 to make an immediate payment of one thousand pounds to Oxenstierna's wife. The envoy was even promised that his bill for the sum would be punctually paid by the English treasury.[9] The payment was undoubtedly made to Oxenstierna's Lady because the English knew "that there is a certain delicacy to be observed in all commerce of this kind. . . ."[10]

However, there is evidence that the role of bribery has been greatly exaggerated as a factor in seventeenth century diplomacy. First, seventeenth century sovereigns were generally short on money but long on calls for their generosity. They often did not even have money to pay their soldiers, much less gratifications and pensions to foreigners. Second, diplomats and ministers of all countries who saw their apparently well-laid plans go awry were often anxious to lay the blame for failure on someone else's accepting a bribe, rather than admit that their own planning or skills were deficient. Third, underlying factors like changing power relationships, military or economic reorganization, economic weakness, and the like were frequently not evident to a man involved in day-to-day negotiations. Just as the physicians of the day who did not know the cause of a death often blamed poison, so too did polititicans and others who did not know the underlying cause of a negotiation's failure blame bribery. A fourth reason the importance of bribery has been exaggerated is people's failure to recognize a basic fact of how foreign policy is made. Ministers and princes had three options when faced with a possibility of taking an action. They could do it, not do it, or postpone a decision. Whatever the possible action — be it making an alliance, declaring war, or sending troops — there was always some foreign diplomat who had desired the action chosen and who quite possibly had passed out "gratifications" to persuade the prince and/or his ministers to make that choice. The diplomat therefore assumed that bribery led the decision makers to do what the briber wanted when in fact the officials were simply willing to take money for doing what they would have done anyway. In a sense this was recognized in the seventeenth century. Diplomats were often told that the purpose of a "gratification" given to ministers was to have them make decisions which were in the service of their own master or for a prince to make decisions which were in his own interest. That this was usually the case is shown by the fact that, although bribery was occasionally effective in actions of minor importance, it seldom, if ever, worked when a prince's fundamental interests were involved.

Another reason for bribery's ineffectiveness was the diplomats' tendency to bribe the wrong people. Diplomats were invariably confronted with the problem of discovering which of the numerous people surrounding princes and/or their ministers were actually in a position to affect decisions. Everyone claimed to be influential and diplomats had to guess who actually was. Often they guessed wrong.

Perhaps the worst problem diplomats faced occurred when the receiver of a gratification committed deliberate fraud. For example, an official might be a kind of double agent. It was not unusual for enemy diplomats at The Hague each to believe that the same member of the Dutch government was in his camp. It was difficult for a diplomat to know if his "man" were actually carrying out his promises since so much business was done secretly. It was easy for an official to take money from opposing foreigners without either finding out about the other. The most difficult fraud to discover, however, was that in which a minister worked in concert with the prince. In 1676, for instance, the Duke d'Estrées, Louis XIV's ambassador in Rome, reported how his brother had visited Cardinal Cibo, the pope's secretary of state. With customary secrecy, Cibo accepted the king's "benefits" as he had before. D'Estrées was confident that Cibo was a man of merit who would "not fail to do his duty toward His Majesty." But the ambassador was wrong. Cibo did not commit positive acts against France as some of the Sun King's other pensioners did, but the Cardinal Secretary did betray Louis passively. Cibo told Pope Innocent XI the secrets which the d'Estrées brothers told him and allowed decisions to be made against Louis's interests by abandoning the affairs of France in reality, although not in appearance, to the "tender mercies" of the papal Camarilla. This does not mean that Cibo was a weak character. Rather he played, with premeditation and duplicity, a role he had worked out in advance with his master the pope.[11] As a result of all these types of problems, we can be sure that the statement made by a Dutchman about a French ambassador in London in fact applied to most diplomats who tried to advance their cause by the use of bribery: "it can be presumed that Monsieur Colbert spent more money there than his negotiations gained from the expense."[12]

Influencing Internal Affairs

The morality of trying to influence the course of events by bribery was questionable in the seventeenth century, but another technique was easily accepted — trying to influence public opinion in the host country. Of course, the publics which were to be influenced were tiny compared to the mass publics with which we are acquainted today. Early modern diplomats were concerned with what could be called the political public — individuals who had high social and political status (the two often went together in the hierarchical societies of the seventeenth century), who knew what was happening in diplomacy, who lived close to the centers of decision-making, and who had the leisure to be concerned. The size of the political publics varied from an estimated twelve thousand people in the United Provinces to several thousands in Poland and England to several hundreds in France and Spain. The capital cities themselves were small in area. Paris was not more than a mile and a half in diameter, and most of the decisions were made nearby at Versailles. The chief English decision-makers generally moved and lived in the area of Whitehall and Westminster in London. Even in the Netherlands, many of the important people were concentrated at The Hague, a town which was so small that it was called "the most cosmopolitan village in Europe." Under these circumstances, small numbers and restricted geographical area, members of the political public could well hope to know personally the elites, the few actual decision-makers. All this is another way of saying that high politics in general and diplomatic activities specifically were still carried out on a small enough scale that they could be discussed in terms of the personalities of decision-makers who, being at the apex of the social hierarchies, were naturally popular subjects of conversion. The decision-maker elites were, not surprisingly, concerned for their reputations among their contemporaries. When this fact is coupled with the fact that there were very few sources of reliable information about such things as diplomacy,[13] the opportunities for a clever diplomat were wide open. By providing information (or propaganda as it would be called today) which had the appearance of authenticity, the diplomat could put pressure on the decision-makers to act the way he wanted. If the political public were convinced that a certain action was or was not desirable, the decision-maker might well take it so as not to appear foolish or stupid in the eyes of his contemporaries.

Although their propaganda techniques were not nearly as sophisticated as those developed in the twentieth century, seventeenth century diplomats were quite ready to take advantage of their opportunities to influence the political publics' opinions.[14] The theoreticians argued that diplomats should engage in propagandizing, and the instructions given diplomats show that the decision-makers agreed. For example, the English Secretary of State Bolingbroke was very concerned about the attitudes of the people surrounding Charles XII during the period the Swedish king was a guest-prisoner in Turkey in the town of Bender. The English were in the process of making "Matt's Peace" which was widely interpreted as a desertion of her allies. Thus Bolingbroke told the English diplomat accredited to Charles that

> We easily imagine that the steps which Her Majesty has taken towards
> finishing this ruinous war are the subject of general conversation even as far
> as Bender, and that you [will] meet with people ready enough to find fault
> with the measures which the Queen, by the perverseness of her allies, has

been obliged to pursue and to lay the blame, which is owing to their [the allies] conduct, at Her Majesty's door. But you are sufficiently apprized of the situation of her affairs and the just grounds of her proceedings to be able to confute those false reasoners and will without doubt, as a servant of the Queen, take all opportunities to vindicate her honor whenever any reflexion is aimed at it, since it would be as unbecoming a minister of hers to suffer anything of that kind to pass with silence as it would be injurious and affronting in any person who should offer to put him to the trial.[15]

This diplomat at Bender and others told to influence public opinion were not given specific instructions about what the "opportunities to vindicate" their masters' honor were, but the diplomats knew what was meant. Obviously, explaining their masters' position in conversations with a wide variety of people was most important. Passing items to the "newspapers," what today would be called giving out press releases, was also a popular device.

The most common procedure was to arrange privately to print the diplomat's message on sheets or pamphlets for free or inexpensive distribution. Examples abound. In 1700 the French representative in London printed a memoir which the French ambassador in the Netherlands had presented to the States General. It was distributed in England (both in French and English) several days before it had been officially forwarded to the king. Seventeenth century governments had no qualms about censorship as was illustrated by the fate of the English "manifesto of war against Holland" which the English envoy published in Spain in 1672. "After it had been sold openly about the streets for one day," the Spanish government (which was pro-Dutch) "caused it to be suppressed" and gave strict orders that "no more copies . . . be issued."[16] That such attempts to influence public opinion were often objectionable to the host government is illustrated by the treatment of the Spanish ambassador in London shortly after the restoration of Charles II. Charles was seriously considering a marriage with Catherine of Braganza, a princess of the family which was currently ruling in Portugal but which the Spanish still considered to be rebels. The Spanish ambassador had argued forcefully against the proposed marriage. Finally, in desperation, he distributed hundreds of copies of the memorials on the subject which he had presented to the king containing the arguments against the alliance as well as counter offers made by Philip IV of Spain. Charles was so outraged that he ordered the expulsion of the ambassador from England; eventually he relented and allowed the ambassador to return to court. But there is evidence that the propaganda efforts were counter-productive and even contributed to Charles's decision to make the Portuguese marriage.[17] Charles II was surprised and outraged in 1661 by this printed attempt to influence public opinion. By 1715 princes were unlikely to be surprised by such activities because they had become common — although a prince might still be outraged!

It is difficult to determine what if any effect diplomats' propaganda had on the making of foreign policies in the seventeenth century. We can just say that the diplomats and their sovereigns usually thought it was worth the effort.

It is but a short step from trying to influence public opinion or bribing ministers on legitimate diplomatic matters to becoming involved with the internal affairs of the host country. In the twentieth century such interference is considered to be one of the worst sins a diplomat can commit. Early modern theoreticians agreed: "The ambassador must not interfere in the domestic affairs of the state where he is negotiating." [18] But, both in theory and practice in the seventeenth century, a diplomat was allowed and encouraged to become involved with domestic affairs if his host desired the diplomat's aid or advice, if the interests of the two principals were very closely linked, or if his master's interests required it. Understandably, evidence about such interference is often lacking, but we do know that some ambassadors in effect controlled the governments to which they were accredited. The best example in our period was during the War of the Spanish Succession when the king and queen of Spain spoke to the French ambassador "about everything, even about the favors which the king must distribute." The Dutch ambassador at Constantinople from 1686 to 1725 carried considerable weight in the sultan's government and his sister was high in the favor of one of the sultanas. Interference in domestic affairs often took indirect forms like trying to influence choice of the individual office holders, giving financial support to a political party or clique, trying to create a party favorable to one's interests, and even fomenting rebellion.[19] But diplomats did not intevene only for political purposes. The popes had long opposed the Spanish tradition of men and boys running before the bulls on festival days, and in 1680 the nuncio tried to have it outlawed. He was not very successful; the tradition still exists today.

A diplomat's intervention in another country's domestic affairs was not necessarily in opposition to the goals of the host government, particularly in cases where, as Wicquefort said, the interests of the two principals were very closely linked. This particularly showed up when ambassadors engaged in military activities which today would not be considered appropriate to their status. Some actually participated in battles. During the years when he was officially Swedish ambassador in France, Otto Wilhelm Königsmarck really spent most of his time at various battle fronts where he participated with distinction in the operations of the French armies. Diplomatic affairs were handled by a Swedish secretary with commission who resided in Paris. Königsmarck's actions were reciprocated by a French ambassador in Sweden who accompanied the king of Sweden in his battles against Denmark and, according to a French memoirist, enabled the Swedes to win three battles because of his valor and his advice.[20] In the mid-1670's Béthune, the French ambassador to King John Sobieski of Poland, ran many dangers in order to join the king who was with his army surrounded by the Turks. While doing so, the ambassador rendered a great service to the Poles. Through negligence and bad faith six thousand Polish troops had been prevented from joining the king by some nobles who refused to advance with them. Béthune was able to persuade the nobles to bring up the troops to reinforce Sobieski who was then able to rout the Turks from their camp. Béthune received the public thanks of the king, senators and the whole army.[21] As one might expect, these kinds of military activities were most likely to be undertaken by ambassadors accredited to a prince who was allied to his master. In any case, diplomats engaging in such activities were unlikely to be the subject of any complaints by their hosts.

Protection of Countrymen Abroad

So far in this chapter the discussion has focused on diplomatic duties which were somehow connected with negotiations, in other words with the political interests of the sovereign. But a seventeenth century diplomat was also charged with protecting the interests of his master's subjects abroad. The variety of these activities is astonishing! It is less surprising when one considers the variety of reasons for which a subject might be abroad. These included commerce, shipping, military service, tourism, education, and missionary work.

All diplomats, even those representing princes who were fundamentally uninterested in trade, spent a large portion of their time dealing with commercial matters. This occurred despite the fact that many states also had a rudimentary consular service whose specific function it was to deal with such matters. One of the formal clauses normally included in British diplomatic instructions stated:

> You shall protect and countenance on all occasions Our subjects trading to any of the dominions of that crown or who may have any suits or pretensions depending there, procuring for them good and speedy justice and all the favour you are able.[22]

Not all rulers included such orders in their instructions, but giving aid to merchants was generally assumed to be part of a diplomat's functions, even to the point where it was difficult to separate the diplomatic and commercial functions of some diplomats.

The ministers of all early modern states having so much as a single port under their control were bombarded with memoirs, memorials, notes, and petitions filed by diplomats on behalf of ship owners, captains, and seamen. In one typical week, Matthew Prior presented no less than nine memoirs dealing with English ships to the French secretary of state for foreign affairs. The notes were on varied subjects: complaints about coast guard ships interfering with fishing boats, requests that merchandise saved from a wrecked ship be returned, and many others. One of the main purposes of Lord Manchester's embassy to Venice in 1697 was to persuade the Venetians to free English seamen who had been pressed into service in the Venetian fleet and were kept past their enlistment period or were thrown into the galleys when they tried to escape. Even the envoys of German princes whose lands did not touch the sea occasionally sent requests on behalf of their masters' subjects who did own ships or cargo. Diplomats regularly tried to help their merchant countrymen by asking another country to lower tariffs, lift quotas on imports or exports, and provide honest treatment in dealings between the merchants and natives. Some diplomats even helped at the risk of their own safety. One Swedish resident in Portugal suspected that the methods the Portuguese used to weigh salt being bought by Swedish captains were disadvantageous to the Swedes. He succeeded in proving that in fact fifty measures were missing from each two hundred measures supposedly weighed. He demanded that a remedy for the fraud be found. The Portuguese government agreed that in the future salt would be weighed on board ship, thereby allowing the captain to be sure that he got his full weight and also avoiding loss due to spillage during loading. The new procedures so angered the Portuguese salt sellers that the Swedish resident had to have an armed escort to protect him against the hostile crowd. But the resident estimated that Swedish captains gained about twenty per cent by the change.[23] Other diplomats intervened to assure that their merchant countrymen were given fair exchange rates for their money and were treated honestly in court cases.

Seventeenth century diplomats helped their countrymen in a number of non-commercial ways. For instance, an ambassador usually felt a special responsibility for a queen who had been born in his master's dominions. Thus, Louis XIV's ambassador tried to protect the wife of Carlos II, his niece, against her uncongenial Spanish environment, sometimes successfully and sometimes not. After her death the French ambassador insisted on being present at the autopsy, that her goods be sealed, and that her will be opened before him. Diplomats often took charge of the wills and goods of their lower ranking countrymen who died abroad. They also tried to help their countrymen get inheritances abroad, acted as a sort of notary public by taking oaths, guaranteed the identity and peaceful intentions of their countrymen, tried to help get their debts from foreign governments paid, conveyed messages for them, distributed alms to sick and wounded soldiers, and provided food and lodgings to visitors. The list of "good works" which diplomats performed for their countrymen seems almost endless.

Yet the concern of diplomats for their countrymen was scarcely altruistic. It was often just the opposite. At least one theoretician claimed that a diplomat had "no right of constraint or coercion on his fellow countrymen,"[24] but practice did not bear him out. Diplomats coerced their countrymen in many ways. If a person did something like taking a manufacturing secret abroad or fleeing to escape a trial, the diplomat might try to persuade him to return home. If persuasion failed, threats were made to harm his family back home. If the individual were accused of a crime, the diplomat could try to have the host government arrest him and send him back home, a primitive form of extradition.

If all these methods failed, diplomats were not above using chicanery. A French exile named Brécourt, for instance, hoped to regain Louis XIV's favor by kidnapping another French subject who was working against French interests in Holland and returning him to France. Brécourt communicated his plan to Jean-Antoine d'Avaux, the French ambassador, who thought it might work, and Louis gave d'Avaux permission to conduct the affair. However, the plan was betrayed and failed. D'Avaux, of course, pled innocence to the Dutch authorities.[25] Personal plans of individuals were not exempt from a diplomat's interference. An ambassador in Denmark disapproved of one of his countryman's plans to wed a young girl because she had little wealth and that little was not easily convertible into cash. The young man met the girl during the ambassador's absence, but he stopped visiting her after the ambassador's return and promised not to get married before he returned home. A French ambassador in London was less successful. In 1663 Philibert de Gramont was in exile in England. He seduced a young noblewoman and then left. When her brothers caught up with him on his way to Dover, they asked him if he had forgotten something. "Of course," he replied, "I have forgotten to marry your sister. Let us return." The ambassador tried unsuccessfully to persuade Gramont not to follow through on the marriage. These stories show how far diplomats were willing to go in order to exercise the rights of coercion they felt they had over their fellow subjects if it were in their masters' interest.[26]

Early modern diplomats also took responsibility for people who were not even their countrymen. For instance, the envoys of the Holy Roman Emperor felt they owed protection to Germans whose princes did not have diplomats abroad. A curious situation arose in 1664 when the French ambassador in the Netherlands tried to get the States General to release and reimburse a ship's captain who was a citizen of Holland but who had accepted a commission as a privateer from a French Duke. The captain had captured a ship belonging to the Dutch East India Company in the Red Sea, and the States General was unwilling to recognize the validity of his commission. Other diplomats simply seem to have forwarded letters requesting favors from the host government from a variety of his countrymen and non-countrymen alike.[27] The diplomats' feeling of obligation to help non-countrymen usually took the form of helping their coreligionists in a state in which the official religion was different. In other words, Protestant diplomats tried to help Protestants in Catholic countries and vice versa.

Such intervention was less likely to breed difficulties when the recipients of a diplomat's aid were not natives of the host country. For instance, Louis XIV, as the "first king of Christendom," had his ambassador at The Hague take up the defense of the lands and benefices in the United Provinces which belonged to the Order of Saint John of Jerusalem. Unfortunately for the placidity of relations between the principals, most of the requests for aid came from subjects of the prince to whom the diplomats were accredited. It is evidence of the sincerity of many seventeenth century rulers about their religion that they continued to order their representatives to try to help their coreligionists abroad, even when relations between the princes were made more difficult thereby. The efforts of Sweden, Prussia, the United Provinces, and England to persuade the Emperor to remedy the "great and notorious griefs" of his Protestant subjects were undoubtedly a major cause of difficulty within the alliance fighting the War of the Spanish Succession. Interestingly, Catholic ambassadors were just as active in England. A Spanish ambassador, for example, sent a number of letters to the new government of William III in 1689 in favor of priests and lay Catholics in English prisons, while two years later he addressed the king on behalf of five Irish Catholics who were currently studying law at the Inns of Court in London. He noted that William had promised on his landing in England when he was still Prince of Orange that Catholics who accepted him peacefully would not be disturbed and that they would be allowed to continue their employment. But an act currently before Parliament would prohibit these students from practicing law in Ireland unless they took an oath which was contrary to the principles of the Catholic religion. Thus the Spanish ambassador requested on behalf of the students that a clause be inserted into the act which would allow them to practice law in Ireland without taking any oath other than that of fidelity to the king.[28] Incidents involving religion like these occurred in almost every European country during the seventeenth century.

In terms of the number of people and countries involved, no religious difficulties were greater than the events leading up to and resulting from Louis XIV's revocation of the Edict of Nantes in 1685 which outlawed Protestantism in France. A quarter of a century earlier, French ambassadors had taken it upon themselves to discover as much as possible about relations between the Huguenot churches in France and Protestant churches abroad, and their interest continued. In 1668 Colbert de Croissy was instructed while in England to find out about Huguenot communications with English or Scottish Presbyterians and also whether any Frenchmen were studying in Presbyterian academies with the intention of becoming Protestant ministers in France "so that His Majesty could take whatever action was necessary." [29] At the same time, diplomats in France, especially those from Protestant countries, were besieged with appeals to aid the Dutchmen, Englishmen, Germans, and others who ran afoul of the French authorities because of their religion. After the actual revocation, the proportion of time devoted to religious questions rose drastically. From September, 1685, to December, 1686, about a third of the "political" correspondence between ambassador d'Avaux at The Hague and the French government was about problems arising from the revocation. D'Avaux's reports included examples of the stories circulating in the Netherlands about the persecution of the Huguenots, evaluations of how much the French political position was hurt by the persecution, and appeals that Dutch citizens residing in France not be forced to convert to Catholicism or that they be allowed to leave France. There were also descriptions of the losses to French industry resulting from the flight of Protestant businessmen to the Netherlands bringing their families, wealth, skills, and even their workers with them. [30] It was not just French diplomats who were occupied with affairs resulting from the revocation. The English envoy extraordinary spent most of his time trying to secure redress for English Protestants in France. The uproar dampened Louis XIV's desire to have his diplomats support Catholics abroad. In the later years of his reign, his instructions frequently said that a diplomat should try to help only if it would not give the other prince an excuse for trying to intervene in France to help the Huguenots.

There is evidence that throughout the seventeenth century at least some diplomats hesitated to carry out their orders to intervene about religion specifically because they feared reciprocal attempts by their hosts. Few early modern states allowed religious toleration and even these usually did so in reciprocal terms. For instance, in the late 1680's the elector of Brandenburg signed a treaty with the duke of Neubourg in which he gave Catholics liberty of religion and the right to worship publicly in his duchy of Cleves on condition that the duke accord the same liberties to Protestants in his duchies of Julich and Berg. In general, relations between Protestant and Catholic states gave excellent opportunities for the normal pattern of reciprocity on diplomatic questions to come into full force.

Other religious responsibilities of diplomats ranged from the official to the bizarre. Nuncios, in addition to being ambassadors to Catholic rulers, were the representatives of the pope to the people of the kingdom or principality. This was because not only the ruler but all his subjects, especially the prelates, had to maintain relations with Rome, and they were pleased to have the pope's official representative available locally. Lay diplomats were occasionally called on to acquire information about the religious beliefs of distant lands and how the beliefs were related to different forms of Christianity. Relics were still important in seventeenth century Catholicism, and Catholic ambassadors were often able to acquire them because of their important positions. But such acquisitions were not always a success. When one French ambassador returned from Rome, he brought with him the body of a saint which was to be given to a church or a convent. A writer at the French court described the result:

> Such a relic, especially a saint's entire body, is always moved with great ceremony and lifted from the casket by a bishop in full pontifical robes before being placed in the reliquary. When all the preparations had been made, the case was brought in and opened with all the usual rites, but they had made a mistake, and all the bishop found were large sausages, brains and spiced pork. Everyone laughed when the sausages were taken out so solemnly, and the bishop left in a state of embarrassment.[31]

Needless to say the ambassador was rather taken aback as well.

Seventeenth century diplomats were also called on to perform a variety of tasks which were only distantly related to what was then called "negotiations." Yet they were important for keeping the creaking wheels of diplomacy and international relations turning. For instance, the movements of travellers were nearly uncontrolled compared to today. Yet diplomats abroad were constantly besieged by people wishing to obtain "passports."[32] Depending on his sovereign's goals and the organization of the state to which he went, it was not unusual for a diplomat to be responsible for directing or coordinating the activities of some of his master's other representatives abroad. English ambassadors in the Netherlands often were also commanders of the Anglo-Dutch Brigade — troops of British origin who served and were usually paid by the Dutch. As a result of her territorial acquisitions at the Peace of Westphalia, Sweden held several provinces in the Holy Roman Empire. The Swedish governors of these provinces played important diplomatic roles in the neighboring German territories.[33] Other combinations of diplomatic and non-diplomatic functions in the same person can be found throughout the seventeenth century.

On occasions, their location allowed diplomats abroad to perform a variety of miscellaneous tasks for their masters. A French ambassador in Sweden was asked to establish a large shipyard there and have six vessels built for Louis XIV while another sent swans from Denmark to be used in the ponds and canals of French royal houses. Diplomats were targets of foreign "inventors" who wished to sell their machines and processes. Among such "inventions" were devices to obtain fresh water from salt sea water, pumps which could lift water to extraordinary heights, a secret process which tinned iron in such a way that it could be used in place of more expensive copper, telescopes, compasses, and pendulum clocks. Diplomats also visited newly appointed diplomats to their own master from the host state, gave letters of recommendation or introduction to prospective soldiers, took responsibility for enforcing frontier regulations between the host and home countries, took responsibility for recaptured criminals who had escaped from their homeland, and performed a variety of other tasks which were conceivably for the good of their own governments.

Diplomats also performed tasks for their sovereigns, ministers, and/or friends which had no connection with diplomacy or international relations. Chief among these unofficial duties was the purchase of items unobtainable at home. Books, both recent editions and "rare or curious" ones, were particularly desired. Diplomats in Italy were often requested to examine paintings which were for sale and send home information about who the painter was, the subject of the painting, how many people were in it and who they were, the background, general physical condition, price desired, etc. It is curious to think of an ambassador discussing details of color and quality of fabrics, but the Earl of Manchester devoted himself to such topics when writing to the Duchess of Marlborough from Venice: "I find the velvets are better at Genoa," wrote Manchester, "but for damasks here there will soon be a gentleman returning to England, and [I] intend to send by him to your Grace three patterns in damask of different colours, and what they will cost. . . . I have bespoke some for myself, and have so managed that the person who provides me does but get sixpence in a yard." [34] Other diplomats were called upon to obtain flowers, fruit trees, engravings, medals, and manuscripts from abroad. Besides objects, diplomats were often requested to obtain the services of skilled people such as a musician "who plays on all instruments" whom Manchester sent from Venice, a physician who was famous for curing cancer to go to Paris from Holland to treat Louis XIV's mother, and innumerable painters, decoraters, singers, artisans, and magicians. Curiously, these activities which seem superfluous compared to important political developments are now among the most long lasting achievements of early modern diplomats. The great museums and libraries of northern Europe, for example, would have much poorer collections (and thus fewer tourists visiting them) if it had not been for the collecting activities of early modern diplomats.

Ceremonial Affairs

The third main area of early modern diplomatic activity was performing ceremonial functions.[35] At first glance these time-consuming activities seem almost as unimportant as the miscellaneous duties just discussed. But, early modern societies considered ceremonial a very important and necessary part of diplomatic contacts between states. According to popular opinion, no period or ruler was ever more concerned about such matters than the late seventeenth century and Louis XIV. But, like so many generalizations which are put forth in textbooks and "popular" histories, this one does not square with the facts. Great concern for matters of ceremony was characteristic of the whole period from the end of the Middle Ages until the French Revolution ushered in the age of the common man with its deemphasis of diplomatic punctilio. Even a cursory study of international relations in the sixteenth or eighteenth centuries will bring out numerous cases of conflicts, disagreements, and quarrels over ceremonial matters. Just one incident which occurred as late as 1768 will serve as an illustration. A Russian ambassador arrived early at a formal ball given by the English court and sat down next to the imperial ambassador on the first row of diplomatic benches. The French ambassador, arriving late, took in the situation at a glance and realized that his country's honor was at stake. Being athletically inclined, he climbed over the bench and slid himself forcefully between the other two ambassadors. In the duel which followed this rather forceful insistence on ceremonial rights, the Russian was wounded.[36] Even for the seventeenth century, it is inappropriate to suggest that Louis XIV was the only ruler who was concerned about diplomatic ceremonial. One of the key functions assigned the Swedish chancellery in 1661 was responsibility for ensuring that the despatches arriving from foreign sovereigns observed the respect due to the royal government. Even republican ambassadors like those from the Netherlands were very concerned about ceremonial when they insisted on being treated the same way as were the representatives of crowned heads.[37] Ceremonial matters were weighty in the opinion of almost everyone of significance in the seventeenth century.

The word "ceremonial" was used in the seventeenth century both as an adjective and a noun. As an adjective attached to embassy or visit, it usually referred to a case where the personal relationships of sovereigns were concerned. In a sense one can compare a ceremonial mission to sending a birth announcement or a graduation present today. In the seventeenth century, sovereigns congratulated each other on births, marriages, accessions to thrones, and sympathized on deaths. Such ceremonial functions could be performed by a resident diplomat on behalf of his sovereign. These were done so commonly that a resident might simply perform them without any special orders and just notify his master later. If there were close geographical, political or personal relations between the sovereigns, a special ceremonial embassy might be sent. For such missions high personal status of the diplomat and very elaborate accoutrements were the prime necessities. They were usually short and had few complications.

Used as a noun the word ceremonial referred to the mass of interrelated procedures, traditions, rights, and hopes which governed the forms of how diplomats behaved when they were with one another performing official or even unofficial acts, how the host governments treated them at entries and audiences, the wording used when one sovereign wrote to another, and a mass of related behavioral matters. Fundamentally they all boiled down to questions of precedence. "International" society in the seventeenth century was still hierarchical just as most societies within states were. Thus it was universally accepted that an ambassador would claim precedence over all other ambassadors representing rulers of lower rank than his own while ceding precedence to those ambassadors whose rulers were of a higher rank. Furthermore, diplomats whose titles were of a lower dignity [38] were expected to cede to diplomats bearing more prestigious titles no matter what the hierarchical relationship of their master was. Unfortunately for diplomatic peace, there was often disagreement on what the relationships of rulers were as well as lack of certainty as to which titles were more prestigious than others.

Where any given ruler could claim to stand in the international hierarchy depended on a number of factors including historical precedent (not to be confused with precedence) and current practice in seventeenth century states. There were numerous conflicting claims to precedence in the seventeenth century including those beween the Scandinavian crowns and another in which Poland claimed to be the equal of Spain.

By far the most famous conflict over precedence and perhaps the most significant was between France and Spain. The conflict did not originate in the seventeenth century. It dated back at least to 1564 when the pope declared that France had precedence over Spain at Rome. During the next century first one king and then the other was successful in his claims depending on the chance of the moment — whether the incident in question took place at the court of an ally, friend or relative of one or the other. One incident among many occurred in Denmark in 1633 when the king's son was to be wed. The French and Spanish ambassadors each claimed the place of honor at the wedding. The Danish ministers, hoping to settle the question peacefully, suggested one compromise after another to the French ambassador, for instance, that he could choose whether to sit next to the king or next to the imperial ambassador. But the French ambassador simply responded, "I will let the Spanish ambassador choose the place which he considers to be the most honorable and when he has chosen, I will turn him out and take it myself." On hearing that no compromise was possible, the Spaniard spread the word that he had been recalled on urgent business by his king and could not remain in Demark for the wedding.[39]

The Franco-Spanish conflict came to a head in London in 1661, shortly after Louis XIV assumed personal control of his government. In his instruction the French ambassador, the Count d'Estrades, was told very clearly that "His Majesty considers it superfluous to say anything . . . about the continuous diligence which he must have to avoid letting himself be outdone by the ambassador of Spain in any encounter involving the rank and preeminence which is due to the King [of France] above all other kings and consequently to his ambassadors, who have the honor of representing his person, before the ambassadors of all other Crowns." D'Estrades was told furthermore that he was not even to be content with equality with the ambassadors of other kings but that he should always insist on the superiority of his position.[40] An occasion when d'Estrades could try to carry out the order arose shortly, hen in October the entry of the Swedish ambassador was to take place in London. Both the Spanish and French ambassadors wished their carriages to have the place of honor directly behind the Swede's. They were aware of the coming clash and did their best to prepare for it by arming their retainers and strengthening the traces on their carriages. The result was a battle in which several people were killed and many wounded. The Spaniard won the place of honor because d'Estrade's traces were cut (the Spaniard had used chains instead of rope and leather for his) and three of the French carriage horses were killed. Apparently the soldiers sent by Charles II did nothing when a mob of the English citizenry intervened to help the Spaniards. Colbert claimed that the Spanish ambassador had hired more that two thousand English "rabble," but still the Spanish ambassador lost twenty men while d'Estrades was supposed to have had but one killed and five or six wounded. Louis XIV immediately threatened war if Philip IV of Spain did not back down and recognize that the French king, and therefore all his ambassadors, had precedence over the Spanish in all foreign courts at all times. In March, 1662, the Spanish ambassador to France publicly expressed the regrets of his master, admitted that the Spanish ambassador in London had been in error, and furthermore stated that Spanish ambassadors would no longer try to receive equal treatment with French ambassadors in the future. Unfortunatley for the diplomatic peace of Europe, even this clear-cut French victory did not settle the matter of Franco-Spanish precedence. D'Estrades was moved to the position of ambassador at The Hague where he successfully maintained French superiority in another conflict with Spain. But elsewhere French preeminence was not publicized as well as Louis would have liked because in many cases the Spanish ambassadors simply stayed away from public affairs where a French ambassador was present. In Vienna Emperor Leopold refused to allow the French to take precedence over his Spanish relatives. Even after Louis XIV's own grandson ascended the Spanish throne, there were still difficulties which were not settled until the famous Family Compact of 1761 was signed.[41]

Other conflicts over precedence, insults alleged and real, seating arrangements, giving the hand,[42] and the like were widespread through the rest of the seventeenth century. An English ambassador considered himself insulted when a Portuguese ran into a room for an audience with a governmental minister ahead of the English ambassador instead of waiting his turn. A Spanish ambassador was pushed aside by two of Emperor Leopold's bodyguards, a most grievous complaint. The youthful Prince of Orange blocked an ambassador's carriage and claimed precedence because he was a king's grandson.[43] The list could go on almost forever.

Despite their everpresent willingness to dispute, discuss, and write ad nauseam about ceremonial conflicts, there is evidence that many diplomats in fact took ceremonial less seriously than their formal statements would indicate. After describing in detail the negotiations about whether his wife would be given a straight-backed chair or a chair with arms for her public reception by the Duke of Savoy at Turin, Ambassador Villars ended his letter to Secretary of State Pomponne by saying: "And there, Monsieur, are our important affairs during this time when all of Europe is at war!" [44] The sarcasm could scarcely be heavier. Matthew Prior referred to "the old road of ceremony and nonsense." [45] A number of rulers were equally casual about ceremonial matters. Charles II of England and Charles XII of Sweden were both notorious for their unwillingness to do more than the bare minimum in ceremonies. Even Louis XIV, who has been widely described as the ruler most interested in ceremonial and etiquette in the last half of the seventeenth century, was not really as inflexible as he is usually portrayed.

There is evidence of a widespread desire to avoid conflicts over ceremonial when possible or desirable. Diplomatic fictions were undertaken to maintain the formalities while still permitting the basic work of diplomacy to continue. For instance, when the Peace of Oliva between Sweden and Poland was being negotiated in 1660, there were debates over whether the Poles or Swedes should pay the first visit for the exchange of ratifications. The mediator solved the problem by having the plenipotentiaries meet, as if by chance, outside the town. Louis XIV's ambassadors participated in the same sort of sophistry. The Sun King wanted his ambassadors to receive the first visit from German princes, even reigning ones, so there was the possibility of difficulty when the Prince and Princess of Wolfembutel arrived for a visit in Copenhagen. The

French ambassador arranged to visit the individual with whom they were staying, meet the princess as if by accident, and invite them for a visit. Thus appearances were preserved, and relations between Wolfembutel and France were not hurt.[46]

Perhaps the most important device for easing ceremonial conflicts was the distinction which was drawn between occasions when a diplomat was formally acting as the representative of his master and those when he was paying friendly, informal visits. Sometimes there was still some formality in informality as when the imperial ambassador visited the son of the king of Poland. The ceremony for official visits was almost the same as for visiting the king. Both the ambassador and the prince had armchairs and went through a ceremony of covering and uncovering their heads. When the visit was unofficial the two armchairs were still necessary but the covering-uncovering ceremony did not take place — this showed that the visit was not official.[47] On other occasions there was almost no formality at all as when a French envoy stayed several times while the Elector of Brandenburg was eating, although such had never been the practice of envoys from crowned heads. When questioned about it, the French secretary of state replied that the act was of no consequence since it was done at one of the elector's country houses and that the French envoy was acting *en cavalier,* out of gallantry, rather than as a diplomat. Matthew Prior commented about this that it was rather extraordinary how the French government let its representatives abroad do anything *en cavalier* whenever it was to their advantage, although the French on other occasions were always trying to gain a point or two in ceremonial.[48] In any case, pretending that a visit was informal and unofficial was an excellent way to expedite diplomatic business.

A question might be raised at this point: of what significance was all this folderol; what was the point of diplomatic ceremonial? Twentieth century scholars have often dismissed it as insignificant and not worth any attention. However, ceremonial was significant then, and thus we must know something about it in order to understand how diplomacy operated in early modern times. At the same time recognizing the importance of early modern ceremonial can reinforce the truism that people of all ages are fundamentally the same. Men have always used rituals to emphasize and reinforce the significance of events which they think are important — rituals which often appear foolish or incomprehensible to others. Imagine how strange graduation ceremonies from high schools and universities must appear to an outsider. Young people dress in costumes unlike anything they have ever worn or will wear again, march to music usually written in the distant past with little connection to the music they usually listen to, and are given an imitation leather cover which tells them they will receive their real diploma (supposedly the purpose of the whole ritual) after they have returned their caps and gowns. The whole ceremony will probably be incomprehensible to people living several centuries in the future. Yet, we know that the ceremonial involved in graduations does have an intrinsic meaning for many of the participants and their relatives. In the same way, early modern diplomatic ceremonial had an intrinsic meaning. Like all human rituals it helped reassure participants and observers alike that all was right with the world.

At the same time an understanding of diplomatic ceremonial can help us to understand the self-images of the participants, particularly the rulers. Ceremonial can give hints about the effectiveness of a ruler's power within the state he governed. It can serve as a sort of barometer for relationships between states. Those which improved their ceremonial position vis-à-vis other countries were probably becoming more important in the international system of early modern Europe. States which did not try to improve their position and merely retained what they had might well have been on the decline. In sum, early modern diplomatic ceremonial served many and varied purposes. It was a worthy object of a diplomat's attention.

FOOTNOTES

1 A. Pecquet. *Discours sur l'art de negocier*, Paris, 1737, pp. xxx-xxxij; F. de Callières. *On the Manner of Negotiating with Princes*, Trans. by A. F. Whyte, Notre Dame, Indiana, 1963, p. 109; A. van Wicquefort. *L'Ambassadeur et ses fonctions*, Vol. II, The Hague, 1681, pp. 9-10.

2 Callières. *Negotiating with Princes*, see note 1, p. vii.

3 The Sound is the body of water now between Denmark and Sweden. See above, Chap. II, pp.   for discussion of diplomats who were policy makers at home. H. Walpole. *An Honest Diplomat at The Hague, The Private Letters of Horatio Walpole, 1715-1716*, ed. and intro. by J. J. Murray, Freeport, New York, 1971, originally published 1955, p. 9 & *passim;* C. Lindenov. *The First Triple Alliance: The Letters of Christopher Lindenov, Danish Envoy to London, 1668-1672*, Trans., ed and introduction by W. Westergaard, New Haven, 1947, *passim.*

4 W. J. Roosen. "The Functioning of Ambassadors under Louis XIV," *French Historical Studies*, Vol. VI, 1970, pp. 313-14.

5 See above, Chap. VI, pp.   for discussion of the use of bribery to acquire information. Callières. *Negotiating with Princes*, see note 1 pp. 24-25.

6 [W. Keith]. "Observations on the Office of an Ambassador," in *An Essay on the Education of a Young British Nobleman*, London, 1730, p. 53.

[7] J. W. Thompson and S. K. Padover. *Secret Diplomacy: A Record of Espionage and Double-Dealing: 1500-1815*, London, 1937, p. 90.

[8] W. E. Brown. *The First Bourbon Century in France*, London, 1971, p. 164.

[9] Public Record Office. London. SP 104/153, Foreign Entry Book, Sweden, Secretary's Letter Book, 6/16 June 1691; J. F. Chance, ed. *British Diplomatic Instructions 1689-1789; Sweden, 1689-1727*, London, 1922, p. 9.

[10] Callières. *Negotiating with Princes*, see note 1, pp. 24-25.

[11] E. Michaud. *Louis XIV et Innocent XI d'après les correspondances diplomatiques*, Vol. I, Paris, 1882, pp. 478-79.

[12] F. Krämer, ed. *Lettres de Pierre de Groot*, The Hague, 1894, p. 10, 19/29 May 1669.

[13] There were as yet few newspapers in most parts of Europe, and, with the exception of the Netherlands, newspapers were mostly government oriented and supported. Even in England newspapers did not yet play an important role in communicating political news and opinion.

[14] Brown. *First Bourbon Century*, see note 8, p. 162, is simply wrong when he says that unlike William of Orange, Louis XIV "made no use of propaganda in foreign countries. . . ."

[15] Chance, ed. *British Diplomatic Instructions Sweden*, see note 9, pp. 56-57, 23 September 1712.

[16] *Calendar of State Papers . . . Venice*, Vol. 37, London, 1939, p. 211, 19 May 1672.

[17] G. L. Belcher. "Anglo-Spanish Diplomatic Relations, 1660-1667," Ph.D. dissertation, University of North Carolina at Chapel Hill, 1971, pp. 64-67.

[18] Wicquefort. *Ambassadeur et ses fonctions*, see note 1, Vol. II, p. 75.

[19] Roosen. "Functioning of Ambassadors," see note 4, pp. 325-26; R. A. Stradling. "Spanish Conspiracy in England, 1661-1663," *English Historical Review*, Vol. LXXXVII, 1972, *passim;* A. Baudrillart. *Philippe V et la cour de France*, Vol. I, Paris, 1890, p. 230.

[20] *Mémoires du marquis de Sourches sur le règne de Louis XIV*, ed. by G.-J. Cosnac and others, Vol. I, Paris, 1882, p. 175.

[21] M. Rémusat. "Un Ambassadeur de France en Pologne (1674-1680)," *Revue de Paris*, Vol. 26, 1919, p. 573.

[22] Chance, ed. *British Diplomatic Instructions Sweden*, see note 9, pp. vi-vii.

[23] K. Mellander and E. Prestage. *The Diplomatic and Commerical Relations of Sweden and Portugal from 1641 to 1670*, Watford, 1930, p. 78.

[24] Pecquet. *Art de negocier*, see note 1, pp. 127-29.

[25] *Mémoires de Sourches*, see note 20, Vol. I, pp. 59-60.

[26] C. E. Engel. *Le Chevalier de Gramont*, N.P., [1963], p. 145; Archives des Affaires Etrangères. Paris. Correspondance Politique, Danemark, Vol. 58, 16 June 1697.

[27] G. L. d'Estrades. *Lettres, mémoires et négociations de monsieur le comte d'Estrades*, new edition, ed. by [P. Marchand], Vol. II, London [actually The Hague], 1743, pp. 360-74; for samples of the letters forwarded by diplomats see Public Record Office. London, SP 100/55.

[28] Public Record Office. London, SP 100/55.

[29] J.-J. Jusserand, ed. *Recueil des instructions données aux ambassadeurs et ministres de France . . . Angleterre*, Vol. II, Paris, 1929, p. 81, 2 August 1668.

[30] E. Mallet, ed. *Négociations de Monsieur le comte d'Avaux en Hollande*, Vol. V, Paris, 1754, *passim*.

[31] *Letters from Liselotte; Elisabeth Charlotte, Princess Palatine and Duchess of Orléans, 'Madame' 1652-1722*, Trans. and ed. by Maria Kroll, New York, 1971, p. 112, 4 January 1703.

[32] See below, Appendix, for a sample passport.

[33] A. Munthe. "L'Administration des affaires étrangères de 1648 à 1720," in S. Tunberg, et al. *Histoire de l'administration des affaires étrangères de Suède*, Trans. from Swedish by A. Mohn, Uppsala, 1940, p. 148; J. Carswell. *The Descent on England. A Study of the English Revolution of 1688 and its European Background*, New York, 1969, pp. 22 and 52.

[34] Duke of Manchester. *Court and Society from Elizabeth to Anne*, Vol. II, London, 1864, p. 323.

[35] The first two areas were information gathering and negotiating. See Chaps. VI and VII above.

[36] J. B. Scott. *Le Français, langue diplomatique moderne*, Paris, 1924, p. 18.

[37] Munthe. "L'Administration des affaires étrangères," see note 33, p. 132; for the Netherlands see, for example, Public Record Office, London. SP 101/23, June 1698.

[38] See above, Chap. III, pp.

[39] Flassan. *Histoire générale et raisonnée de la diplomatie française*, Vol. III, Paris, 1809, pp. 13-14.

[40] Jusserand. *Recueil des instructions Angleterre*, see note 29, Vol. I, p. 273; L. André. *Louis XIV et l'Europe*, Paris, 1950, p. 55.

[41] Most of the relevant documents about this incident can be found in "Le Conflit Estrades-Watteville et la préséance de la France," *Mémoriaux du conseil de 1661*, ed. by J. de Boislisle, Vol. III, Paris, 1907, pp. 140-76. A

good brief discussion is given in E. Satow. *A Guide to Diplomatic Practice*, 2nd edition, Vol. I, London, 1922, p. 27. There is a combination of narrative and documents in Jusserand. *Recueil des instructions Angleterre*, see note 29, Vol. I, pp. 286-303. For a general discussion of Louis XIV's relations with other rulers see R. M. Hatton. "Louis XIV and His Fellow Monarchs," in J. C. Rule, ed. *Louis XIV and the Craft of Kingship*, [Columbus, Ohio], 1969, pp. 155-95.

[42] "Giving the hand" meant to give a visitor the place of honor at the right hand of the host. Satow. *Guide to Diplomatic Practice*, see note 41, Vol. I, p. 179. Ceremonial problems between European diplomats and Turks were eased by the fact that they could walk and sit easily together because the left hand was the place of honor in Turkey. Each, the European and the Turk, could take what he considered the place of honor without losing face. W. H. Lewis. *Levantine Adventurer, The Travels and Missions of the Chevalier d'Arvieux, 1653-1697*, London, 1962, p. 26.

[43] C. Cole, ed. *Memoirs of Affairs of State*, Trans. by C. Cole, London, 1733, pp. 63-71; F. de Bojani. *Innocent XI, sa correspondence avec ses nonces*, Vol. I, Rome, 1910, pp. 74-75; S. B. Baxter. *William III and the Defense of European Liberty, 1650-1702*, New York, 1966, pp. 37-38.

[44] P. Villars. *Mémoires de la cour d'Espagne de 1679 à 1681*, ed. by A. Morel-Fatio, Paris, 1893, pp. xxxij-xxxiij.

[45] L. G. W. Legg. *Matthew Prior: A Study of his Public Career and Correspondence*, Cambridge, 1921, p. 55

[46] R. Przezdziecki. *Diplomatie et protocole à la cour de Pologne*, Vol. I, Paris, 1934, p. 150; Archives des Affaires Etrangères. Paris. Correspondance Politique, Danemark, Vol. 61, fols. 84-85, Chamilly to Louis XIV, 19 May 1697.

[47] Przezdziecki. *Diplomatie et protocole*, see note 46, Vol. II, pp. 175-76.

[48] Great Britain. Historical Manuscripts Commission. *Calendar of the Manuscripts of the Marquis of Bath Preserved at Longleat*. Vol. III, *Prior Papers*, London, 1908, p. 246, Prior to Portland, 1698.

Conclusion

Many exciting and important events occurred during the Age of Louis XIV —
the Austrians created a giant new state in central Europe which was to dominate
the region until the present century; a Bourbon king replaced the centuries old
Hapsburg dynasty on the throne of the Spanish Empire; and the possibility that
the Kingdom of France would dominate western Europe was ended. Yet, in
terms of practice and institutions, diplomacy was carried on in essentially the
same way in 1715 as it had been in 1648. The last half of the seventeenth
century seems to have been a period in the evolution of diplomatic method
when change and development were momentarily absent. As happened in early
modern government and society in general — change, when it came at all,
occurred slowly and often imperceptibly. Apparently the diplomatic procedures already developed were ordinarily satisfactory in serving the needs of the
"international system." It might even be appropriate to say that diplomatic
methods had become mature in terms of the early modern era.

Two apparently contradictory impressions emerge from this study of diplomatic practice in the Age of Louis XIV. On the one hand, individual people
from kings to lowly secretaries seem to have been extremely important in both
making and carrying out foreign policy. On the other hand, the diplomatic
institutions and practices can often be shown to have determined the framework
within which these decisions could be made. In this way the experience of the
seventeenth century is timeless. In the debate over which is more important in
human affairs — men or vast impersonal forces — it supplies evidence for both
sides. Perhaps this duality is significant for showing that neither extreme is a
sufficient explanation in itself. In an age like today when there is a tendency to
insist that only those things which can be measured or counted are worthy of
serious study, a study of the seventeenth century reminds us that in such areas as
diplomacy the individual personality is still often the key to success or failure.
The counting and computers are valuable for showing the framework, the
institutions, and general practices of human affairs. But it is still people who
change and adapt the generalities to the specific needs of the moment.

Chronological List
of Important Diplomatic Events
1648 to 1721

Time keeping and date recording were handled by a variety of methods in the seventeenth century. In Italy for instance, the hours of the day were numbered from zero to twenty-four. The first hour varied slightly each day as it began exactly at sunset. But today the exact hour at which an event took place is no longer significant. We usually are satisfied simply to know the year. Only occasionally are the day and month significant. In this list only the year of events is listed, and within each year the events are arranged chronologically with the earliest given first.

Chronology

1648   Peace of Westphalia. Fronde begins in France.

1649   Charles I beheaded.

1650   William II of Orange dies.

1651   Formation of Catholic and Protestant Leagues in Germany to carry out the Peace of Westphalia.

1652   England declares war on the Netherlands beginning the First Anglo-Dutch War. Fronde ends.

1653

1654   Peace of Westminster between England and the Netherlands. Abdication of Queen Christina of Sweden. Charles X (1654-1660) accedes.

1655   Defensive treaty between Brandenburg and the Netherlands.

1656   Spain declares war on England. Treaty between Philip IV and the exiled Charles II. Treaty between England and France.

1657

1658   Oliver Cromwell dies. Treaty of Roskild between Denmark and Sweden. Leopold I (1658-1705) becomes Holy Roman Emperor. League of the Rhine.

1659   Peace of the Pyrenees between France and Spain.

1660   Restoration of King Charles II of England. Charles XI (1660-1697) becomes king of Sweden. Peace of Oliva ends the First Northern War.

1661   Louis XIV (1643-1715) takes personal control of the government after Mazarin's death. D'Estrades-Watteville affair in London.

1662   England sells Dunkirk to France.

1663   Ottoman Turks declare war on Austria. Diet of the Holy Roman Empire becomes permanent at Regensburg.

1664   20 year truce signed between Austria (the Holy Roman Emperor) and the Turks.

1665   Second Anglo-Dutch War begins. Death of Philip IV of Spain and accession of Carlos II (1665-1700).

1666   Quadruple alliance of the Netherlands, Brandenburg, Brunswick and Denmark.

1667   Peace of Breda between England and the Netherlands. Treaty between Charles II of England and Louis XIV of France. War of Devolution between France and Spain in the Spanish Netherlands.

1668   Triple Alliance of England, the Netherlands, and Sweden. Spain recognizes the independence of Portugal. Peace of Aix-La-Chapelle between France and Spain. Partition Treaty between Louis XIV and Leopold I.

1669

1670   Secret treaty of Dover between Charles II of England and Louis XIV of France.

1671   Secret neutrality treaty between France and the Emperor.

1672   England and France declare war on the Netherlands (Third Anglo-Dutch War). Alliance between France and Sweden. William III becomes Stadtholder. Alliance of the Holy Roman Emperor and the Netherlands. John de Witt murdered.

1673   Emperor declares war on France. Abortive peace attempts at Congress of Cologne.

1674   England withdraws from the war against the Netherlands. John III Sobieski (1674-1696) elected king of Poland.

1675   Victor Amadeus II (1675-1730) becomes Duke of Savoy.

1676

1677

1678   Peace of Nijmegen (France and the Netherlands, France and Spain).

1679   Peace of Nijmegen. (France and the Empire). Peace of Saint Germain (Brandenburg and Sweden). Peace of Fontainebleau (Denmark and Sweden). Maximilian II Emanuel (1679-1726) becomes Elector of Bavaria. French "Chambers of Reunion" established.

1680

1681   France occupies Strasbourg and Casale. Publication of Abraham van Wicquefort, *The Ambassador and His Functions* (in French).

1682   Brief war between France and Spain.

1683   Turks besiege Vienna.

1684   Holy League of the Emperor, Poland and Venice under the presidency of the pope against Turkey. 20 year Truce of Regensburg between France and the Emperor. Carlos II declares war on France.

1685   Charles II dies. James II (1685-1688, dies 1701) accedes. Revocation of the Edict of Nantes.

1686   League of Augsburg formed (the Emperor, Spain, Sweden, Saxony, the Netherlands, and others).

1687

1688   War of the League of Augsburg begins. William III of Orange lands in England. James II flees to France. Frederick William, Great Elector of Brandenburg dies. Frederick III (1688-1713) accedes.

1689   Mary II (1689-1694) and William III (1689-1702) become queen and king of England. England and the Netherlands join the League of Augsburg and the war against France.

1690   Spain and Savoy join the Allies in the war against France.

1691

1692

1693

1694   Augustus the Strong (1694-1733) becomes Elector of Saxony.

1695

1696   Savoy withdraws from the alliance and makes peace with France (Treaty of Turin).

1697   Augustus of Saxony elected king of Poland. Peace of Ryswick (France and England, the Netherlands, Spain, and the Emperor). William III sends Portland to France as ambassador. Charles XII (1697-1718) accedes to the Swedish throne.

1698   First Partition Treaty of the Spanish Empire between France, England, and the Netherlands makes the Electoral Prince of Bavaria the main heir.

1699   Peace of Karlowitz (Turks with the Emperor, Poland, and Venice). Electoral Prince dies.

1700   Second ("Great") Northern War begins. Second Partition Treaty. Carlos II dies. Louis XIV accepts testament of Carlos II and accepts the Spanish thrones for his grandson, now Philip V (1700-1724, 1724-1746) of Spain.

1701   "Grand Alliance" against Louis XIV is renewed. War of the Spanish Succession begins. Frederick of Brandenburg is crowned king in Prussia. Louis XIV recognizes the son of James II as king of England.

1702   William III dies. Anne (1702-1714) accedes as queen of England. England, the Netherlands and the Emperor declare war on France.

1703   Portugal and Savoy join the Grand Alliance. Methuen treaties (England and Portugal).

1704   Stanislas Leszczinski is elected king of Poland at the instigation of Charles XII. England captures Gibraltar. France and Bavaria are defeated at Blenheim.

1705   Emperor Leopold I dies. Joseph I (1705-1711) accedes.

1706   Peace of Altranstadt (Sweden and Saxony). Augustus of Saxony renounces his claim to be king of Poland.

1707

1708

1709   Allies offer harsh peace terms to Louis XIV. Louis refuses and continues the War of the Spanish Succession.

1710   Whig Ministry in England falls. Harley and St. John form Tory Ministry.

1711   Emperor Joseph I dies. Charles VI (1711-1740) accedes. Marlborough dismissed. "Matt's Peace" between England and France (preliminary to the Peace of Utrecht).

1712   Peace Conference opens at Utrecht. Truces (France with England and the Netherlands). Torcy founds the French Political Academy.

1713   Peace of Utrecht (France with Britain, the Netherlands, Savoy, Prussia, Portugal; Spain and Britain).

1714   Peace of Utrecht (Spain with the Netherlands). Peace of Rastatt-Baden (France with the Emperor and the Empire). Queen Anne dies. George I (1714-1727) accedes. Philip V marries Elizabeth Farnese.

1715   Louis XIV dies. Louis XV (1715-1774) accedes. Barrier Treaty between the Emperor and the Netherlands.

1716   France and Britain sign defensive alliance. Publication of François de Callières, *On the Manner of Negotiating with Princes* (in French).

1717   Triple Alliance (Britain, France, and the Netherlands). Spain attacks Sardinia.

1718   Quadruple Alliance (the Emperor, Britain, France and the Netherlands against Spain). Peace of Passarowitz between the Emperor and Turkey. Charles XII of Sweden is killed.

1719   France declares war on Spain.

1720   Peace between the Quadruple Alliance and Spain.

1721   Treaty of Nystad ends the Great Northern War.

1722

APPENDIX

Letters of Credence

From James II of England to Louis XIV of France accrediting Sir William Trumbull as Envoy Extraordinary. Translated from French:

> Very High, Very Excellent and Very Powerful Prince, Our Very dear and Very loved Good Brother, Cousin and Ancient Ally. As we strongly desire to carefully maintain the good relations established between Our Crowns, We have found it appropriate to this end to send you the Chevalier Trumbull bearing the quality of Our Envoy Extraordinary. We request that from time to time you give him favorable audiences and that you will have complete confidence ["credence"] in what he will say to you on Our behalf, particularly when he will assure you of the sincerity of Our friendship, of which we request that you be completely persuaded. And thus We commend you, Very High, Very Excellent and Very Powerful Prince, Our Very dear and Very loved Good Brother, Cousin and Ancient Ally, to the Holy Keeping of God. Written in Our Court at Whitehall this 20th of October 1685.
>
> Your good Brother, Cousin and Ancient Ally,
>
> James R.
>
> Sunderland [1]

From Louis XIV to William III of England accrediting Monsieur Poussin as Secretary of Embassy dated 9 June 1701 at Marly. This letter of credence is much less formal than those given ambassadors and envoys. Furthermore, France and England were on the verge of open warfare at the beginning of the War of the Spanish Succession. Translated from French:

> Very High Prince. After having granted our Ambassador Extraordinary to you, the Count de Tallard, the permission he requested to return after an embassy of three years, we would have sent another ambassador if we had not learned that before he could arrive in England you will have left to go to Holland. Therefore, suspending the choice that we will make [of an ambassador] until after you will have returned to London, we have charged the Sieur Poussin, Secretary of Embassies, with the execution of our orders. We will be very pleased if you will have complete confidence in what he will say on our behalf. And we pray to God that he will keep you etc. [2]

Instructions

The goals of a sovereign were usually set forth in conversations and in written instructions given an ambassador before his departure. The content of most of the conversations has now been lost while the instructions have been described as sources whose virtues "are exceeded only by their short-comings."[3] Nevertheless, attempts to understand any diplomat's role must begin with his instructions.

The length, topics included, and format of seventeenth century diplomatic instructions varied from country to country and time to time. In their most developed form they included a variety of materials. First the reasons why the prince had chosen the diplomat were enumerated. Then followed a long and complete historical resumé of relations between the two countries and the international situation as a whole. Next the diplomat was told about the goals (especially political) toward which he was supposed to work. Some very specific notes were given on etiquette and ceremonial. It was also thought useful to include a gallery of psychological portraits of kings and queens, ministers and favorites, with particular attention to their political sympathies and bribability. Paragraphs on ciphers, correspondence, preparing a "rela-tion" about his tour of duty abroad for submission on his return, and miscel-laneous matters completed the contents of the instructions. None of these topics was found in every instruction, and almost no instructions covered all the topics. Since complete copies of instructions are widely and easily available,[4] only outlines of a few typical examples will be given here.

The instruction given to the Sieur de Thou, Count de Meslay, ambassador from Louis XIV to the States General of the Netherlands dated 9 March 1657: De Thou is told that, in addition to these general instructions, he will receive specific orders about the negotiation of affairs during the course of his embassy. If a situation arises about which de Thou sees no problem, he is to act on it with measured zeal for the best interests of the king. He is to report accurately and diligently about his actions. As for doubtful questions which are not pressing, the ambassador is to ask for orders from home after describing the situation as accurately as possible. Finally, for problems which cannot be delayed, he is to take as much time as possible to think them over; then he is told to execute his decision without vacillating, trusting in divine providence to bless his actions and give him success.[5]

The instruction given to the Duke of Jovenazo, Spanish ambassador from Carlos II to Louis XIV on 15 September 1679, tells the ambassador how important the Paris embassy is and how much anxiety the Spanish government feels about their relations with France. Jovenazo is reminded of the "need for good correspondence between the two crowns" and the importance of persuad-ing the French to observe the peace. The ambassador is told that it is most important that he be prudent and "observe the most minute courtesies and be careful of proper protocol because these things are very important at the French court." Furthermore, Jovenazo is cautioned to watch his expenses and to take no short cuts in attempting to do business. "Always go through the proper channels in gaining audiences, obtaining credentials and licenses." The ambassador is informed that "France has no prime minister, but the most important figures in the government are Colbert, Louvois, Le Tellier and Pomponne. It is your duty to find out all you can from them about the king's plans." Moreover, he is instructed to keep in contact with Spanish agents in Brussels in order to learn everything possible about French plans in Flanders, secret negotiations, and other intelligence. In the matter of reciprocal commerce with France, he is to "transmit all information and requests without making any commitments. Be careful of their obvious pretexts and do not fall into any traps. It is of great importance to get all details of information and special secrets to Spain immediately. Above all, be careful and prudent." [6]

Letters of Recall

From the Elector of Saxony to Queen Anne of England dated 23 January 1710 at Dresden. Translated from Latin into an attached English copy in 1710:

> Whereas Our Trusty and Wellbeloved Charles Christian Kirchner has for these several years discharged the office of Our Resident in Your Majesty's Court with singular fidelity and diligence, We have at length thought fit to recall him from thence. And that We might not seem wanting in the respect due to Your Majesty, whom We have always so great an esteem for, We have given Our said Resident orders to communicate this resolution to Your Majesty, at his departure to give you fresh assurances of Our friendship. As to what remains, We heartily commit Your Majesty to the Protection of Almighty God. [7]

From Queen Anne of England to Louis XIV recalling Matthew Prior from France dated 23 April 1714 at St. James. Translated from French:

> Very High, Very Excellent and Very Powerful Prince, Our Very Dear and Very loved Good Brother, Cousin and Ancient Ally. Whereas Mister Prior has served for nearly two years as Our Minister Plenipotentiary in Your Majesty's Court in a manner which has made Us completely satisfied with his conduct, We have thought fit to recall him to serve Us in some important affairs within Our Kingdom. Since we have always had complete confidence in him and since he has therefore had occasion to know our sentiments about you and your affairs, there is no one who is more capable of telling you of the perfect esteem and the sincere friendship that we have and that we will always have for You. Thus we request that you have complete faith in what he will have the honor to say to you on this subject as well as on the other

points about which he is instructed to speak to you on our behalf. Thus we pray to God that He will keep you, Very High, Very Excellent and Very Powerful Prince, Our Very Dear and Very Loved Good Brother, Cousin and Ancient Ally, in his Holy and Worthy Keeping. Written at St. James this 23rd day of April, one thousand seven hundred and fourteen.

Your good Sister, Cousin and Ancient Ally.
Anne R.[8]

Passports

In the seventeenth century a passport was not issued by a government to its subjects who were going abroad; rather it was a letter which a diplomat gave to someone who wished to visit his country. The passport was analogous to a visa today although the processes and regulations were not as formalized as now. The terms of the passport were usually left to the diplomat or, more often, to his secretary. Since the other calls on a secretary's time were great and the number of requests was large, effective supervision was impossible. The original of the following passport was in English:

Matthew Prior Esq. Her Majesty's
Plenipotentiary to the Court of France

Whereas His Excellence Thomas Earl of Strafford has thought fit to grant his passport unto Monsieur Bianchini, a Roman Gentleman, in order to his going into England, and that the time allowed for such his voyage is elapsed, I have thought fit to grant the said Bianchini this my passport for himself and two servants provided he do imbark within fourteen days after the date hereof; and do hereby accordingly desire all Her Majesty's officers, military and civil, and all others whom these presents may concern to let and permit the said person and his said servants to pass free and unmolested, and to show him all civility in this his voyage.

Paris the 9th of January 1713.

Mat Prior.[9]

Autopsy Reports

Report on the opening of the cadaver of Queen Marie Thérèse of France on Saturday, 31 July 1683 at five o'clock in the evening. Sent to Pope Innocent XI by his nuncio or auditor. Translated from French:

At the opening of the abdomen we found the bowels, the epiploon, and both the interior of the stomach and its exterior membrane entirely sound.

About a half a pint of reddish watery liquid came out of the abdomen.

The liver was pale and the exterior part a little tainted. The gallbladder was very large and full exceeding the length of the liver. The spleen and the kidneys were natural.

We discovered upon exposing the muscles of the chest on the left side directly under the tumor that all the glands and the whole cavity were filled with a purulent and fetid stuff. All the muscles in the area of the tumor were rotten.

After having opened the chest, we found both the inside and outside of the left lung (the same side as the tumor) completely black and gangrenous. There was nearly a half pint of the same purulent stuff which filled the gland cavity. It had penetrated the chest along the muscles and the rotten flesh.

The heart was completely withered up and filled with a stinking liquid. Its vessels were filled with a hard black material like ground cannon powder. The vessels of the lungs were also filled with the same material.

After opening the head we found that the brain was quite normal without any liquidness.

Signed by the physicians and surgeons of the king.[10]

Ciphers

The keys of ciphers often do not include any indication of who owned and/or used them. This in itself was a technique used to increase their security. Two types of seventeenth century ciphers are illustrated here. The first was completely handwriten: I & J were written the same. U & V were also.

A	B	C	D	E	F	G	H	I	K	L	M
10	11	12	13	14	15	16	17	18	19	20	21
34	35	36	37	38	39	40	41	42	43	44	45

N	O	P	Q	R	S	T	V	W	X	Y	Z
22	23	24	25	26	27	28	29	30	31	32	33
46	47	48	49	50	51	52	53	54	55	56	57

Rules for using this cipher.
1. There are two numbers for each letter. Either can be used whenever you choose.
2. The numbers from 1 to 10 are meaningless.
3. You can write your first letter wherever you wish, provided that you write the number 60 above or below it; the number 61 above or below the second; the number 62 above or below the third; and so on consecutively. Thus you will know which letter you must read first, which the second, etc.
4. You can mix in meaningless numbers among the significant ones as you wish.
Example: Monsieur

67	64	61	22	60	51	65	53	9
50	42	23	62	21	63	38	66	68

This cipher is more complicated than those commonly used in the seventeenth

century because of the need to rearrange the pairs with numbers 60, 61, 62, etc. before deciphering the words. More often, the numbers were simply written in the correct order so that the decipherer could simply fill in the correct letter above the number and then read the message. The same key might be used but the word Monsieur would simply be written in Cipher:
21   47   46   27   42   14   50

Another common cipher used printed forms. Each individual could make his own by using whatever numbers he wished. Some numbers were blanks (or nulls) while others were handwritten to refer to specific individuals, places, events, etc. For example, in the following cipher the left hand column was preprinted, while the middle and right hand columns were filled in by the user:

A	542				729	null
ab	543				730	null
an	544			F	731	
at	555			fa	732	
B	556				733	France
be	557				734	king of France
ble	558				735	null
but	559			G	736	
C	560				737	Great Britain
cl	561			H	738	
	562	Charles II		ha	739	
		Continues				Continues

Philip of Anjou Becomes King of Spain

Louis XIV to William III of England announcing Louis's acceptance of the late king of Spain's will. Translated from French:

Very high, very excellent and very powerful Prince, Our very dear and very loved good brother, cousin and ancient Ally. We are sending to you the Count de Tallard, Lieutenant General of our armies and in our province of Dauphiné, with the same quality of our extraordinary ambassador that he has had for almost three years. He will particularly explain to you the just reasons which have obliged us to prefer the public tranquility rather than our personal interests in accepting as we have the testament of the late Catholic King in favor of the King our grandson. We have no doubt that you . . . [unclear] to his assumption of the Crown of Spain; we are also persuaded that after being informed about our desires you will agree that nothing will be capable in the future of troubling the general tranquility of Europe. Thus we pray to God that he will keep you, Very high, very excellent and very powerful Prince,

our very dear and very loved good brother, Cousin and ancient ally, in his
holy keeping. Written at Versailles, the 7th December 1700.

Your good brother, Cousin and ancient ally
Louis
Colbert [11]

Mutual Expulsion of English and Spanish Ambassadors in 1699

Letter of 27 August 1699 translated from Spanish by C. Cole:

> Don Antonio de Ubilla kisses the hands of Don Alexander Stanhope, Envoy
> Extraordinary of his Britannic Majesty, and lets him know, that the King his
> master having been frequently informed by his ministers [diplomats] in the
> North, of the strong informations, and even evident proofs, which they have
> had by different advices and accidents, that the English, Hollanders, and the
> French, in consequence of what was last year concluded and stipulated at
> Loo, are now again forming new treaties for the succession to his Crown, and
> for the dividing of it; which notices have been corroborated by other ways, so
> that they are public over all Europe: it would be against his dignity to
> dissemble and take no notice of them. The King his [Ubilla's] Master thinks it
> inexcusable not to oppose what might produce such irreparable inconveni-
> ences, if it came to be put in execution; and has ordered his ministers in the
> Courts of France, England, and Holland, to make known to those princes and
> overnments, the just sentiments His Majesty has of those advices, never
> heard of before in the life of any king, and more improper in that of His
> Majesty, which consisting at present (by the Divine Mercy, and for our
> happiness) is only thirty eight years of age, we may naturally promise
> ourselves, and especially from His most high Providence, that He may give
> His Majesty the important succession which we hope for from him, by the
> affectionate prayers and votes of his vassals; . . . [if God takes away Carlos's
> life] without granting him the benefit of a succession, his affairs will not be
> left without a due reflection on what is most just and most important for the
> public tranquility, and so that nobody shall be able to find fault with his
> justice nor his foresight. For which reasons, His Majesty has ordered his
> aforesaid ministers to make instances and use their diligence to cut off those
> negociations; weighing the ill effects which they now produce, and what
> their continuance may produce. And that the complaint of His Majesty and
> the orders he gives to his ministers abroad to notify to the princes at whose
> courts they reside be at the same time made public, he has lately ordered that
> it be made known to the ministers here. For this reason does Don Antonio de

Ubilla communicate it to Don Alexander Stanhope, by order of his master, that he may also give notice to His Britannic Majesty, assisting with his prudent representations this just and honest purpose; that so the universal quiet may be maintained and that he may quit the scandal of this negociation which is feared will be an unhappy motive of kindling a voracious flame of a new war, which being once lighted, will be difficult to extinguish either by the greatest force or the most dextrous and most powerful mediation; and he remains obedient to Don Alexander Stanhope with all affection. . . .

Letter presented by the Marquis of Canales, Spanish ambassador in England, to the English government in September, 1699, protesting against the Partition Treaty. Translated from French by C. Cole:

First, that His Catholic Majesty having been informed by evident proofs that His Majesty King William, the Hollanders, and other powers (in consequence of what they have treated and stipulated last year at Loo) are now at this time actually hatching new treaties for the succession to the Crown of Spain, and (what is most detestable) contriving its division and partition: His Majesty [Carlos II] orders his Extraordinary Ambassador residing in this Kingdom to make known to the first Lords and Ministers of England, the just resentment which His Majesty has against these operations and proceedings, never before seen, nor even attempted to be treated of by any nations in regard to the interests of another; and still less during the life of a monarch who is of so fit an age to have reasons to hope (for many years) a succession so much wished for by all nations; who, without a detestable avarice, could not be provoked to usurp and overturn another prince's country.

That if this was permitted and was not contrary to the Law of Nature, no nation nor dominion could be safe against the machinations and deceits of the strongest and most malicious; whereas reason, and not force, confines nations.

That if it was permitted to strangers to take notice and to put their hands into the lines of succession of kings and sovereigns, there would be no statutes nor municipal laws to be observed in the one nor in the other; nor could any be free from the attempts of others, and the Crown of England less than any.

If we lie watching the indispositions of sovereigns, no health would be constant and no life safe because the two depend on the hand of the Almighty, Who regulates life, death, and empires.

That the impressions which one kingdom makes upon the other, to tempt the faith of the subjects, and to excite their minds to a rising, are an offence and but a degree less than the betraying the good faith which ought to be observed among Christians, particularly among allies and friends.

That we ought not to presume that any prince or nation, and still less the king of the Spanish nation, is so negligent as not to take just measures against accidents that may happen when least thought of to secure the public peace and the repose of Europe, which has been the aim of the king and the nation [of Spain] for so many ages, as it is now and will always be.

That if these proceedings, these machinations and projects are not quickly stopped, we shall without doubt see a dire and universal war all over Europe which will be difficult to stop even when we are willing and which will be most sensible and prejudicial to the English nation which has newly tried and felt what novelties and the last war have cost them. This matter is so worthy of reflection and consideration, that it is not doubted but it will be admitted as such by the Parliament, the nobility, and all the English nation which has always been so full of foresight into the present and future times.

The same nation must consider its particular interests, the trade and the treaties which she principally has with the king and the Spanish nation; the alteration, the division, and separation of which, would of necessity draw after it considerable prejudices and damages; and all this is prevented by cutting short the project that is begun, and not to help on novelties that have from all times been hurtful to empires and sovereignties.

That the Extraordinary Ambassador of Spain will manifest to the Parliament, when it shall be assembled, the just resentment which he now expresses as his master has caused it to be notified to all the public ministers of the kings, princes, and republics that reside at the court of Madrid.

Paper sent by the English Secretary of State, Mr. Vernon, to the Marquis of Canales, Spanish Ambassador in England, 30 September 1699. Translated from French by C. Cole:

His Majesty [William III] has seen the paper which the secretary of the Embassy of Spain has recently delivered, by order of Your Excellency, to several of the Lords Justices of the Kingdom; His Majesty has found the contents so insolent and seditious that, in resentment of so extraordinary a proceeding which can by no means be justified by the Law of Nations, he orders that you go out of his dominions precisely in eighteen days, to be counted from this notification, and that you keep in your house, without going outside its walls until your departure. I am also ordered to let you know that His Majesty orders that no writing be any more received from you nor any of your domestics.[12]

FOOTNOTES

1 *Quoted from R. Clark. Sir William Trumbull in Paris, 1685-1686,* Cambridge, 1938, p. 172.

2 Archives des Affaires Etrangères. Paris. Correspondance Politique, Angleterre, Vol. 210, fol. 154.

3 C. H. Carter. *The Western European Powers, 1500-1700,* Ithaca, 1971, p. 46. For a valuable discussion of instructions and related documents, see pp. 45-63 & 276-77.

4 See references in bibliography.

5 France. Commission des Archives Diplomatiques. *Recueil des instructions données aux ambassadeurs et ministres de France . . . Hollande,* ed. by L. André and E. Bourgeois, Paris, 1922, Vol. XXI, pp. 131-55.

6 Royal Instruction, Madrid, 15 September 1679, 28 pp., Archivo General de Simancas. I wish to thank Guy Bensusan for summarizing and translating this document from Spanish.

7 Public Record Office. London. SP 100/14, Foreign Ministers in England, Germany (States) 1689-1722.

8 Public Record Office. London SP 105/27, Matthew Prior's Letter Book, fols. 193-94.

9 Public Record Office. London SP 105/27, Matthew Prior's Letter Book, fol. 498.

10 F. de Bojani. *Innocent XI, sa correspondance avec ses nonces,* Vol. III, Rome, 1912, p. 148.

11 Public Record Office. London. SP 102/7, Royal Letters, France, fol. 1.

12 C. Cole, ed. *Memoirs of Affairs of State,* Trans. by C. Cole, London, 1733, pp. 37-38 & 58-59.

BIBLIOGRAPHY OF SOURCES AND READINGS

In order to make this bibliography more valuable to English speaking readers, English translations rather than foreign language originals are listed whenever possible. There are excellent studies of diplomacy in the Age of Louis XIV available in many languages, but, with the exception of some unique or unusually important books and articles in other languages, the selection here is limited to works in English. Students interested in particular topics are encouraged to use the titles listed in the footnotes or to examine some of the numerous general bibliographies of the seventeenth century including A. L. Moote. *The Seventeenth Century*, Lexington, Mass., 1970, pp. 435-54, and J. C. Rule. *Louis XIV and the Craft of Kingship*, [Columbus, Ohio], 1969, pp. 407-62.

General Studies

Older works which are still valuable as narratives of events include D. J. Hill. *A History of Diplomacy in the International Development of Europe*, New York, 1921-25, 3 vols.; R. B. Mowat. *A History of European Diplomacy, 1451-1789*, N.P., 1928 [reprinted 1971]; C. A. Petrie. *Earlier Diplomatic History, 1492 to 1713*, London, 1949; these must all be used with care as they swarm with minor inaccuracies. The relevant chapters in vols. IV, V, and VI of *The New Cambridge Modern History*, Cambridge, 1961-70, are valuable as are L. André. *Louis XIV et l' Europe*, Paris, 1950, and G. Zeller. "Les Temps modernes, II, de Louis XIV à 1789," Vol. III of *Histoire des relations internationales*, Paris, 1955. Information about early modern diplomatic practice in general can be found in the first two editions of E. Satow. *A Guide to Diplomatic Practice*, London, 1917 [first] and 1922 [second], 2 vols. Two guides designed primarily for researchers also are extremely valuable for their information about practice: C. H. Carter. *The Western European Powers, 1500-1700*, Ithaca, 1971; D. H. Thomas and L. M. Case, eds. *Guide to the Diplomatic Archives of Western Europe*, Philadelphia, 1959. No student of diplomacy in the Age of Louis XIV can do without the lists of diplomats given in L. Bittner and L. Gross. *Repertorium der Diplomatischen Vertreter aller Länder seit dem Westfälischen Frieden (1648)*, Berlin, 1936.

The diplomatic service of England in the seventeenth century has received more attention than that of any other country: P. S. Lachs. *The Diplomatic Corps under Charles II & James II*, New Brunswick, N. J., 1965; D. B. Horn. *The British Diplomatic Service, 1689-1789*, Oxford, 1961; M. Lane. "The Diplomatic Service under William III," *Transactions of the Royal Historical Society*, 4th ser., Vol. X, 1927; H. L. Snyder. "The British Diplomatic Service during the Godolphin Ministry," in R. Hatton and M. S. Anderson, eds. *Studies in Diplomatic History*, London, 1970. C.-G. Picavet. *La Diplomatie française au temps de Louis XIV (1661-1715): institutions, moeurs et coutumes*, Paris, 1930, is still important for France despite its shortcomings of organization, lack of an index, and age. Certain aspects of the Swedish diplomatic service are discussed in A. Munthe. "L'Administration des affaires étrangères de 1648 à 1720," in S. Tunberg, et al. *Histoire de l'administration des affaires étrargères de Suède*, Trans. from Swedish by A. Mohn, Uppsala, 1940.

Early Modern Theoretical Works

Studies written by contemporary theoreticians can be very helpful as aids to understanding diplomacy as long as one remembers that these works were often descriptions of an "ideal diplomacy" rather than of "real diplomacy." In many cases the ideal and the real coincided, but the authors often did not make the distinction clear. J.A. de Vera's *El Embajador* was best known in the French edition of 1642 entitled *Le Parfait ambassadeur*, Paris. A. van Wicquefort. *L'Ambassadeur et ses fonctions*, The Hague, 1681, 2 vols. includes many specific examples of practice. Two studies which were not published until the twentieth century are. H. J. Chaytor, ed. and trans. *Embajada Española: An Anonymous Contemporary Spanish Guide to Diplomatic Procedure in the Last Quarter of the Seventeenth Century*, Spanish and English texts, Camden Miscellany, Vol. XIV, London, 1926; L. Rousseau de Chamoy. *L'Idée du parfait ambassadeur*, ed. by L. Delavaud, Paris, 1912. F. de Callières. *De la maniere de negocier avec les souverains*, Paris, 1716, is available in an English translation of questionable value as *On the Manner of Negotiating with Princes*, Trans. by A. F. Whyte, Notre Dame, Indiana, 1963. A new edition of another translation is in press, edited by H. M. A. Keens-Soper. See also [W. Keith]. "Observations on the Office of an Ambassador," in *An Essay on the Education of a Young British Nobleman*, London, 1730; A. Pecquet. *Discours sur l'art de negocier*, Paris, 1737.

Primary Sources

So many examples of different kinds of primary sources have been published that only a bare sample of those which are most easily accessible can be given here.

Collections of treaties: F. G. Davenport, ed. *European Treaties bearing on the History of the United States and its Dependencies*, Washington, 1917-37 [reprinted Gloucester, Mass., 1967], 4 vols. focuses primarily on the early modern period; each treaty is placed in its historic setting and translated into English unless the original is in French. The seventeenth and eighteenth centuries are dealt with in vol. I of F. L. Israel, ed. *Major Peace Treaties of Modern History, 1648-1967*, New York, 1967; all treaties are in English. The most complete modern collection is C. Parry, ed. *The Consolidated Treaty Series*, Dobbs Ferry, New York, 1969—; treaties are photographically reproduced from earlier publications in many different languages; each volume includes treaties for a period of two or three years, starting in 1648.

No country has done a better job for publishing the official instructions given its diplomats at the beginning of their embassies than France has. Beginning with the first volume in 1884 for Austria, the *Recueil des instructions données aux ambassadeurs et ministres de France depuis les traités de Westphalie jusqu'à la Revolution française* has appeared for every major power and is still in progress. The English instructions were nowhere nearly as elaborate as the French but three volumes of *British Diplomatic Instructions, 1689-1789* have appeared: Vol. I, *Sweden*, 1922, ed. by J. F. Chance; Vol. II, *France*, 1925, ed. by L. G. W. Legg; Vol. III, *Denmark*, 1926, ed. by J. F. Chance. See also B. C. Brown, ed. *The Letters and Diplomatic Instructions of Queen Anne*, New York, 1935 [republished 1968].

Among the published collections of letters it is worthwhile to look at *The Letterbook of Sir George Etherege*, ed. by S. Rosenfeld, London, 1928; *The Dispatches of Thomas Plott (1681-1682) and Thomas Chudleigh (1682-1685), English Envoys at The Hague*, University of Michigan, no date [1928?]; *The First Triple Alliance; The Letters of*

Christopher Lindenov, Danish Envoy to London, 1668-1672, Trans. and ed. by W. Westergaard, New Haven, 1947; Letters of William III, and Louis XIV, and of the Their Ministers, ed. by P. Grimblot, London, 1848, 2 vols.; F. de Bojani. Innocent XI, sa correspondance avec ses nonces, Rome, 1910-12, 3 vols.; J. De Boislisle. Les Suisses et le marquis de Puyzieulx, ambassadeur de Louis XIV (1698-1708), Paris, 1906. In a class by itself is the Calendar of State Papers and Manuscripts Relating to English Affairs Existing in the Archives and Collections of Venice and in Other Libraries of Northern Italy, ed. by H. F. Brown and A. B. Hinds, London, 1864-1940, 38 vols. This is often referred to as Venetian State Papers. The material has been translated into English. Before using these papers it is worthwhile to read E. R. Adair. "The Venetian Despatches," History, new series, Vol. 20, 1935. The reports published by the British Historical Manuscripts Commission often contain information about diplomats and diplomacy.

Journals, Diaries and Memoirs

Relatively few diplomats kept diaries during the times when they were serving abroad in the early modern period. One of the most interesting because of its innumerable details is B. Whitelocke. A Journal of the Swedish Embassy in the Years 1653 and 1654, new edition, ed. by H. Reeve, London, 1855, 2 vols. See also H. Sidney (later Earl of Romney). Diary of the Times of Charles the Second, ed. by R. W. Blencowe, London, 1843, 2 vols. which deals with the period from 1679 to 1682 when he was English representative at The Hague. An unusual journal kept by an important French decision-maker, Louis XIV's last secretary of state for foreign affairs, is J.-B. Colbert de Torcy. Journal inédit de Jean-Baptiste Colbert, Marquis de Torcy, ministre et secrétaire d'état des affaires étrangères, pendant les années 1709, 1710 et 1711, ed. by F. Masson, Paris, 1884.

Diaries and memoirs written by people who accompanied diplomats abroad give information about daily life and activities but little about negotiations. A French émigré who accompanied English diplomats to Switzerland and to Savoy left a diary which has been excerpted in E. Johnston. "The Diary of Elie Bouhéreau," The Proceedings of the Huguenot Society of London, Vol. 15, 1934. Memoirs of Lady Fanshawe, Wife of Sir Richard Fanshawe, BT. Ambassador from Charles II to the Courts of Portugal & Madrid Written by Herself Containing Extracts from the Correspondence of Sir Richard Fanshawe, ed. by B. Marshal, London, 1905, were partially intended as a defense of her husband who died in Madrid. [La Combe de Vrigny]. Travels through Denmark and some Parts of Germany: By way of Journal in the Retinue of the English Envoy in 1702, Trans. from French, London, 1707, includes details on topics like the laws of Denmark, the cost of carts and horses, churches, and the inscriptions on tombstones.

Modern Studies

E. R. Adair. The Exterritoriality of Ambassadors in the Sixteenth and Seventeenth Centuries, New York, 1929, is an old but reliable work which examines such topics as diplomatic immunity and freedom of worship both in theory and in practice. J. W. Thompson and S. K. Padover. Secret Diplomacy: A Record of Espionage and Double-Dealing: 1500-1815, London, 1937, republished as Secret Diplomacy: Espionage and Cryptography: 1500-1815, New York, 1963, is a simplistic view of international relations which interprets events in terms of small personal relations of diplomats, rulers, mistresses, etc. E. Vaillé. *Le Cabinet noir*, Paris, 1950, deals with the secret organizations which intercepted correspondence in the early modern period. N. Girard d'Albissin. *Genese de la frontière franco-belge: les variations des limites septentrionales de la France de 1659 à 1789*, Paris, 1970, is a study in "legal" history which is very illuminating about the long term techniques and problems of diplomacy concerned with an important border.

Among the numerous studies of negotiations or specific problems between countries are several works of particular interest: K. Mellander and E. Prestage. *The Diplomatic and Commerical Relations of Sweden and Portugal from 1641 to 1670*, Watford, 1930; G. Pagès. *Le Grand Electeur et Louis XIV, 1660-1688*, Paris, 1905; G. Quazza, "Italy's Role in the European Problems of the First Half of the Eighteenth Century," in R. Hatton and M. S. Anderson, eds. *Studies in Diplomatic History*, London, 1970; R. A. Stradling. "Spanish Conspiracy in England, 1661-1663," *English Historical Review*, Vol. LXXXVII, 1972; A. Lossky. "La Piquetière's Projected Mission to Moscow in 1682 and the Swedish Policy of Louis XIV," in A. P. Ferguson and A. Levin, eds. *Essays in Russian History*, Hamden, Conn., 1964. M. A. M. Franken. *Coenraad van Beuningen's Politieke en Diplomatieke Aktiviteiten in de Jaren 1667-1684*, Groningen, 1966, has an English language summary on pp. 257-73.

French diplomats and institutions have been the object of much interest in recent years. W. J. Roosen, "The True Ambassador: Occupational and Personal Characteristics of French Ambassadors under Louis XIV," *European Studies Review*, Vol. 3, 1973, and his "The Functioning of Ambassadors under Louis XIV," *French Historical Studies*, Vol. VI, 1970, can be called collective biography. Two recent articles deal with an abortive attempt to formalize the training of French diplomats: J. Klaits. "Men of Letters and Political Reform in France at the End of the Reign of Louis XIV: The Founding of the Académie Politique," *Journal of Modern History*, Vol. 43, 1971; H. M. A. Keens-Soper. "The French Political Academy, 1712: A School for Ambassadors," *European Studies Review*, Vol. II, 1972.

Biographical studies of decision-makers often include much valuable material for the study of diplomatic history. S. B. Baxter. *William III and the Defense of European Liberty, 1650-1702*, New York, 1966, is a "life and times" biography which is worthwhile if one overlooks the author's extreme anti-French and anti-Louis XIV bias which make the Sun King appear to have acted like a fanatic in international relations. J. B. Wolf. *Louis XIV*, New York, 1968 is marred by some curious errors but is invaluable for the diplomacy of the seventeenth century. R. M. Hatton. *Charles XII of Sweden*, New York, 1968, draws on the author's wide knowledge of diplomatic history. Recent studies of ministers include H. Rowen. "Arnauld de Pomponne," *American Historical Review*, Vol. LXI, 1956; J. C. Rule. "King and Minister: Louis XIV and Colbert de Torcy," in R. Hatton and J. S. Bromley, eds., *William III and Louis XIV*, Toronto, 1968.

Among the biographical sketches of diplomats we can note the old but still interesting J.-J. Jusserand. *A French Ambassador at the Court of Charles the Second*, New York, 1892. H. Rowen. *The Ambassador Prepares for War: The Dutch Embassy of Arnauld de Pomponne, 1669-1671*, The Hague, 1957, deals with the crucial period before Louis XIV began his Dutch War. J. T. O'Connor. "William Egon von Fürstenberg, German Agent in the Service of Louis XIV," *French Historical Studies*, Vol. V, 1967, deals with a man who never achieved the rank of diplomat but played a key role in seventeenth century diplomacy.